2 KULTIVATE A NON-KONFORMIST KULTURE

The Manchild Manisfesto

By: Danyil Hettainz

ISBN: 9798746566072

We Help You Self-Publish Your Book
Crystell Publications
PO BOX 8044 / Edmond – OK 73083
www.crystellpublications.com
(405) 414-3991

Printed in the USA

DEDICATION

To whom do I dedicated this book?

That question I cannot answer, yet those who remain loyal 2 war's true alliance, know that it is always deception and skill that keeps the real revolution advancing.

Who will read this manuscript?

Many will stare at these pages and paragraphs but, only a handful will truly interpret the map which gives them light on such a dark road.

So, from this point on, I'll give you a history lesson, and a definition, then a mission 2 carry out. But it will be totally up 2 you 2 understand how 2 keep the construction and continue the legacy of our politikil line. On the evening of December 16, 1773, 50 men, masquerading as Native Americans, the true natives of this kountry, went abroad 3 ships and broke open the tea chests, and heaved, 9,659 lbs. worth of tea into the harbor. Those imposters posing as Native Terrorist, better known as Indians, were never caught by the authorities, or punished, but eventually these imposters were the ones who would help in the rebuild of this kountry entitled Amerikkka, under their oppressors' very noses. Only later 2 become the very tyrants that oppress us 2day.

I know my rights, as did so many other politikil radicals, revolutionaries, and militant organizations. There would be no uprisings if koverments, and futile leaders, and members of society didn't fail 2 uphold their Treatise, Promises, Contracts, and Konstitutions.
It is by this that life stop being life 2 the youth, underprivileged, and respected pupils of the world. Therefore the masses of the world are taking on a far more hostile, disrespectful, brutal, and volatile role. The people stop wanting 2 be heard.

The people wanted revenge, and now have begun 2 demonstrate it. The people no longer fear their rulers, political policies, laws, and koverments. The people no longer care for voting rights, and lopsided legislation. Therefore We, the people have killed off that old imagery, 2 secure a more authentic Identity. A terroristic aura that will one day give face 2 the various people struggling throughout the globe, now and 4ever more.

'post hoc, ergo propter hoc'
(After this, therefore Because of this)

KONTENTZ

BOOK: I

Chapter 1 Bastard Bloodline........................ pg. 3
Chapter 2 New Integration ....pg. 19

Chapter 3 Draft A Scarecrow..........................pg. 64
Chapter 4 Extending...................................pg. 86

BOOK: II

Chapter 5 Adjusting ....pg. 97
Chapter 6 Silence ....pg. 112
Chapter 7 Equalz ....pg. 137
Chapter 8 Masquerading: The Perfect Form ....pg. 155

BOOK: III

Chapter 9 Impoverish Armz ....pg. 184
Chapter 10 3rd World Propaganda......................pg. 201
Chapter 11 True Martyrdom.......................... pg. 231
Chapter 12 Penetrating................................ pg. 243

BOOK: IV

Chapter 13 Strong Unionz........................... pg. 264
Chapter 14 Caches.......................................pg.273
Chapter 15 Paying Our Respects......................pg. 281
Chapter 16 High Praizes.............................. pg. 285

Disclaimer

Warning

This book was designed 2 provide information on how 2 keep history, history, and not have people try 2 change it 4 their personal beliefs. It was written 2 show the masses how 2 assess the history they read, and how 2 study it's viewpoints, and how 2 avoid all the contradictions blatantly written and written between the lines.

This book is a foundation of recollection of all the hard work, faith in the higher power, 2 endure the constant toil and abuse, that came with one's moral standard. This book is from those who dedicated their lives as well as from those who helped them create what has come 2 be.

This manuscript is being sold with the over standing that the publisher, and author are not engaged in rendering ignorant services 2 the public within this kountry, and the people who dwell beyond its perimeters.
If additional assistance is needed, consult the services of a competent professional. For You Are Urged, 2 read all available material outside of this text, and learn 4 yourself as much as possible from those other sources 2 compare against this text, but in no way shape or form should the reader attempt 2 rearrange the original ideas, that the author has put forth.

This book is for anyone who is interested in history, activeness, in the future, as well as in the present. For every effort has been made 2 make this manual rewarding. However, there may be mistakes in the typo, and uncertain clarification due 2 boundaries that have been set by the powers that be. This text should be understood that it is the fundamental principles, not the prime source of information. For obvious reasons the info., in this book came from many viewpoints, and opinions, 2 personal experiences of the author, and other people in this kountry that had 2 learn these intimate details under extreme duress. Should the reader happen 2 disagree, it is highly suggested that you do not detract from the real nature of the text itself. This manual contains information only up 2 the printing date, or after, depending on the signs of the times. The purpose of this text is 2 educate, and promote artistry, for the author, and or the publisher shall have neither liability, nor responsibility 2 any person or entity with respect 2 any loss or damages caused or alleged 2 have been caused directly or indirectly, by the content contained in this book. IF YOU DO NOT WISH 2 BE BOUND, BY WHAT HAS BEEN WRITTEN, AS A FULL WARNING, AND DISCLAIMER, PLEASE TAKE TIME 2 UNDERSTAND THAT THERE IS ABSOLUTELY NO REFUND, THE AUTHOR ADVISES STRONGLY THAT THE READER PASS ALONG THE BOOK OR SIMPLY DESTROY IT!

CHAPTER 1

BASTARD BLOODLINE

A bastard bloodline is a bloodline which is distinguished in insignias. Rather tattoos or kolors, the bastard bloodline owes its existence to recognition. To be seen is the bastard bloodline's way to show off its strengths as well as weaknesses.

It is impossible for the bloodline of a bastard to stay an enigma, because it's neither formed nor structured on the principles of discipline entitled shadow warfare. In organizations, especially on the adversaries' turf one should never place oneself or one's resources in the cross hairs of the enemy.

To understand in full, the nature and scope of a bastard bloodline analyze these examples.

A). The Black Panther Party
B). Any prison or street gang
C). And The National Sozialistische Deutsche, better known as the Nazi Party

There are many more, but there's too many to name yet these examples should serve sufficiently. All these examples prove one thing, and they all have one thing in common.

This was extremely detrimental to their livelihood, all these organizations shared the spotlight and politikil platform, and all were easy to pick off by any analytikil opponent.

Many great bodies of armed men and women such as these and cults/ kultures, count on their strength to adjust their war footing, yet in battle it is always (how), we are to look at war.

Although there is strength in numbers, conventional warfare tactics will never suffice in an era where technology "seems" invincible, and the mind seems minute, to be able to qualify as the first stage of being individual tacticians.

In other words, the mind was given to these kinds of people to be able to operate in great depths so that generals of real caliber could be found succumbing to extensive study in order to understand at great lengths **THE ART OF WAR**.................

The Black Panther Party was a highly unique vanguard of the late 1960's and 70's, but they lacked the understanding of shadow warfare. Not only did they lack the understanding of shadow warfare, but conventional warfare as well.

This organization really lacked depth of the revolutionist criteria. They failed 2 grasp the universal tongue of the guerrilla, in which they studied. They chose a flag and a uniform that kept a well-trained eye on them from such tactioneers as J. Edgar Hoover, and his team of F.B.I., agents. They were easy enough 2 track down with their large afros, or naturals, leather jackets, with blue shirts. Oh, and please let us not 4 get their famous BPP., insignia the extremely large picture of a black leopard, called the Black Panther, fist salute, and dark sunshades.

Come on people let us ask ourselves who wears dark sunglasses in Kombat?

Although their logic or philosophy was very uplifting, their war methods were quite deficient 4 being alleged **"FREEDOM-FIGHTERS,"** of oppression. They had no true knowledge of authentic militancy.

For example:
one of their main guidelines was 2 patrol the police...which the BPP., established as **Ride Or Die**, in which they followed/ countered the establishment's enforcer's movements (**ARMED**), yet the BPP., never made an official attempt 2 set these pigs up legally, and when they did ambush these overseers, they weren't able 2 successfully get away clean. There were instances when some of the members were armed with small arms, (pistols), which they kept inside of shoulder holsters, 2 some, who carried shotguns, instructed by their leader Huey P. Newton, 2 keep these arms pointed downward or angled. These Panthers would be seen riding around their cities and neighborhoods, four, and five at a time in a car in racist Kalifornia/Amerikkka and expected not 2 be pulled over and spotted by the landlords of this kountry. Every one of the Panthers were black and expected not 2 get harassed especially with guns in hand riding in a moving vehicle. Even I know that that shit is suspect.

They thought that the United Stakes Of Amerikkka, was going to continue 2 allow these black nigger's antics 2 go on throughout its grounds without some form of surprise attacks, yeah right. Yet that is precisely what happened. These crooked white superior ideology having muthafuckas would catch this party preoccupied with guns in hand stop their cars, surround their vehicles, and some kops were even bold enough 2 just walk up 2 these so called trained militant prospects and literally take the gun out of their holsters and hands. Therefore, again we must ask ourselves, if supposedly well-trained freedom fighters can be so loosely relaxed when on duty or in war, how could they possibly save our lives? And how can this be considered, fighting oppression.

We all know how Amerikkklans think…they are highly crafty the reason why people like the Nation of Islam, called them devils. They are well organized, somewhat sophisticated, many taught the black man how 2 become soldiers…there was much studying 2 do on the BPP's part. Their actions were fruitless on these killing fields, but their intentions were phenomenal.

These were easy assassinations...and such easy simple assassinations have taken place due to unlearned men and women in grass root revolutionary organizations, not knowing themselves or their enemies to ever be able to battle and win the kind of war that overthrows, undermine, and undercut these cynical coverments.

There could be no POWER TO THE PEOPLE, when the leaders never expected the courses of action that our foes are willing to take. By this and many other issues the BPP, dealt with internally caused their adversaries ranks to close in on them and eliminate them before an actual war could commence.

Even today in the year 2015, the BPP, still make sure that they are seen making their presence known with media footage kapturing them arguing with other bastard bloodlines such as the Ku Klux Klan. So again, the story/history repeats itself after decades of trying to strengthen, and reorganize the BPP, the faults of this fractured group still lie in the leadership, as well as their teachings.

Robert F. Williams, expounded on these various ways of our foes, and the establishment that they protect. Mr. Williams, in his book Negros With Guns, whom the BPP, took various portions from this man's thoughts. A veteran of the Amerikkklan armed forces, warned and showed the many outcomes that could happen if not careful when orchestrating revolts. But again, the BPP, failed 2 study, internalize, and listen 2 an original politikil philosophy.

Let us now turn our attention to the notorious street and prison gangs. Rather Black Mafia Family, The Crips, Bloods, MS 13, Black Guerrilla Family, Gangsta Disciples, etc., strength these groups or organizations do have with the many members in each set to the collective whole but, how many have actual minds 2 be able 2 dominate and hold the cities and prisons in which they reside?

The artillery in their possession is alarming, yet their downfall konstitutes no understanding of true warfare, therefore they fight amongst themselves to get nowhere or anything other than a name, death toll, or an ass hole full of time in prison, and if not that than possibly a few frivolous luxurious items.

These gangs (families), are known by their affiliated/initiated kolors, or branded badge of honor. A series of fruitless riots may have arisen from out their ranks, but a full-scale assault by the koverment (G-Men), would crush these baby brigades because their structure like I've previously said is not founded upon strategies of discipline and tactikil revolutionary thinking, nor is it upon shadow warfare.

Their education consists of a diluted form of economics, the wealth of materialism, and their blind lead blind methods considered strategy is a helpless effort. By this objective it exterminates them rather than have them realize their flaws 2 regroup.

A drive by, and a couple of hand signals does not konstitutes a body of uniformity. Not just uniformity but trained uniformity consisting of both women and men that suppose 2 be able of holding impoverished ghetto hoods and middle klass neighborhoods down outflanking the flat-footed police and agile light equipped forces, such as the green berets, seal team six, or other koverment security enforcers, that swore 2 take bullets, die, etc., all 2 protect the United Stakes Of Amerikkka.

The only thing good that these gang/families, have going 4 themselves is that they face danger on a regular basis starting out young. This is what leaves them battle hardened in poverty before they actually pick up their first gun. Unlike many of those recruited by the police and military, they have actually seen more death or some form of violent action very early in their lives.

Then it's their hatred of the police and the system. This is one of their greatest assets in this war of kaos, because they identify with prosecutorial abuse, politikil set ups, as well as kovermental extermination policies, that are designed esp., 4 them. But what hinders them are their mentalities of not giving a fuck about what happens 2 themselves and those of the same condition. They have surrendered themselves, so now their sense of survival and staying healthy is diffused due 2 their lack of interest in living and establishing themselves in something that contributes 2 their rise rather than their demise.

Making oaths 2 govern themselves rather than anyone else who sees and wants to oblige in a new method of change so that all can obtain, rather than the few whose luck can't last forever.

Their blinded by the materialistic state of attraction which kontrols their roles that they play in society and in each other's lives, **which inkludes** the large amounts of currency which runs through their hands on a regular basis...from drug transactions, robberies etc. They believe in their souls that red, must lead the day, or blue, guarantees that they will be strong enough 2 last to alleviate the minute competition in their suburbs, and inner cities. They are plastered in corners, and on corners. Hundreds of them city and statewide, in prisons, and night clubs. Many professions and neighborhoods have deprived them of their youth, limbs, housing, friends, families, kountry, structure and spirit.

Some but not all rise 2 fame or super stardom, yet they are unable to see their power. The koverment allow them 2 see their position, only in the goal that's killing them by the hundreds, thousands, and millions each second, minute, day, and month, 2 each year of their pathetic lives.

Their ranks grow thinner and feeble, while their true enemies continue 2 strengthen their numbers deceiving them, causing them 2 think that they are in kontrol, or have power 2 kontrol, but they are in no position to kontrol anything, and they have not the knowledge 2 accept that essential logic. Yet it is black this, and guerrilla that. Dog this, or sanger that. Non has ever explained 2 them, neither has anyone stopped 2 even think about this one thing.

When were these organizations, families, and gangs first assembled?

The 60's, 70's, 80's, etc. This is however the twenty first century, and what has been done over that time period besides kriminal participation, jail house politiks, talk, and **manipulation?** They have all gotten high and died!

The alpha males of these groups have had children by broken females who have become tormented trophies, too pretty or unreceptive 2 be any kind of real war bride. Many are welfare recipients, full or half legal bi-sexual or lesbians of the state. Few have achieved trades, college, and high school certificates...yet the majority have track records a mile long. Others have lost their lives, minds, and children behind drug abuse, child molestation and families that never cared 2 see them in the world. A lot of these have fallen in love with people who have nothing 2 offer them except a cycle of confusion, and poverty. Some of these men and women of these families/gangs, are honestly too good 2 be true, but by being weak minded and spirited, they fall 2 a false or bogus cause following behind **frivolous**, victims who can never be more in life except a joke.

Bullets have snatched the very nature of their wills, so they continue 2 ache and suffer behind these tides of actual trauma. Their prison sentences have grown larger than the actual states in which they reside in. The dropout rate has become an epidemic, so much so that it makes the first slaves that came 2 Amerikkka, 2 those who were continuously enslaved here with no knowledge of how to read and write seem smarter. The koverment, watches their every move. They have been secretly sending in covert operatives of military grade 2 neutralize and kill them.

And how can these operatives miss their target, when these gangsters, komrades, thugs, are crowds, and in crowds unable 2 comprehend the attitudes of the adversaries. They don't believe that their kountry, **this kountry**, will bomb them and their neck of the woods. The koverment has already bombed its own citizens multiple times already. 911-World Trade Center., the four little Birmingham girls in the church, and the Boston marathon bros. Yeah that was **YOUR KOUNTRY...PIG AMERIKKKA**.

So fellow Amerikkkins, which one of you think that you are not the next one 2 get your ass handed to you?

Do you not remember that teenage black girl that was in school and was dramatically penalized? Sure, you remember, the little black skinny teenage girl who was in class and was allegedly disrupting it and the teacher got tired of it and called in a white security enforcer, 2 deal with her the (**problem**).

That white enforcer came into that classroom 2 where the girl was stationed meaning sitting in her seat, and he snatched her out of that seat and slammed her on the floor like Dwayne Johnson, or the Undertaker, would do a professional wrestler. This wasn't a training session 4 the

enforcer, the girl wasn't a tactikil training dummy the girl weighed 115 lbs., does this story ring a bell now?
All the young black males in the girl's classroom stayed seated as they watched this minor, a female get **physically fucked up by** this white enforcer and they did absolutely nothing. These are your children your passive ass pacifist. That is what you are and have become over the years…pussy ass passive aggressive weak muthafuckas.

You teach your children 2 throw up their hands, say yes sir, no mam, smile when they get pulled over just like you all's fearful asses. Next these pigs are going 2 do the unthinkable. They are Literally going 2 do something none of us are expecting them 2 do. At first glance, in the blink of an eye, no matter what we tell ourselves, or what gang affiliation/krime family you belong to. It's not as if you are making it hard for them, or difficult 4 them 2 spot you. You gangs have been in the same ghettos, suburbs, and prisons 4 how long now? The coverment has tutored you...they have literally trained and indoctrinated this way of life for and to you and your siblings, and don't 4get the rest of the world population of oppressed people.

Look at them. Look at the strings around their wrist, it tells who they are. Look at their shoestrings, listen 2 their slang. In all their songs they explain their "**CULTURE**," 2 you, it is separate from us as a whole. Their tattoos, the paint on their vehicles, the kolor on their hats and head wear, clothes etc., all of it tell who and what they are a counterculture and a target 4 white Amerikkklans.

Their actions testify against them even if they don't say a word. They walk 2gether, and stay huddled 2gether, you can't be fooled by anything that they do. Those beads around their necks, prove who they are. The books that they keep in their circles, and in circulation, or have in their possession, expose who and what they are TARGETS!

If you can recollect in school rather you've already graduated or still attending, people use to place kick me signs on a person's back. Whether they were popular or not, it was all done out of fun or spite.

This is what they have done, meaning these gangs, krime families, etc. They have placed signs on their person while the coverment has revolutionized the game, by placing **SHOOT ME SIGNS**, on these defective participants...who basically say 2 Amerikkka, "**Kapture Me, Kill Me, Here I Am Amerikkka, Your Target!**"

These silly groups fit Amerikkka's profile, because they are **AMERIKKKLAN MADE**, and Amerikkka's proverb: **Easy Pickings, Spics, Dumb Ass Blacks, Porch Monkies, And Poor White Trash!!!!!!!!**

Now let us turn our attention 2 a battle in history, on a more grander scale, Nazi Germany. Oh yes, I said this korrectly, I am **politikally korrect**, history. To form such a movement so quickly is still a baffling mind fuck. It's complex examination is of a past that constantly remains a shock, yet insightful 4 any generation who truly wants 2 learn swift mobility, patience, absolute discipline, disorder, common belief, impatience, and an exquisite style that robbed a entire kountry of itself, its own success, beauty, and glory.

It wasn't just the leadership. It was also those that supported the ideal of superiority, before contemplating the masses and growth of a nation that wasn't taught such a way their koverment had prepared them. Rising from the ashes and needing anything rather than anyone 2 bring back those essential qualities of spirit, and heart 2 it's **fatherland**, as well as people that would one day serve this ideal for that chance to be free again and regain that once great independence as a nation.

But here is that ol cliché' in regards 2 structure, patience, non kompromise, and study. There should never be a leader or leadership, that rushes or allow others 2 pull their strings. Impatience kills, and develops these undesirable disturbances in the people, as well as in the mind of the **Thinker**. This is where that ancient proverb comes into remembrance that:

"**ROME WAS NOT BUILT IN A DAY.**"

The Nazi soldiers were trained 2 march ferociously, with power and force in their footsteps, along with saluting with a salute of the hand that was soo sharp that it could literally chop a man's head clean off his shoulders. And it was all done 4 their beloved Fuhrer, or was it?

The Nazi's made parades with unified esteem, they even had a glorious array of flags 4 their display. These were specifically hand crafted by professional propagandist, and simple home bodies.

These people were selected so that the kolor scheme and decor could fit the likings of champions. Their women made actual blood oaths to never marry anyone that did not have blonde hair and blue eyes, or with whites who were not fit for racial breeding.

This indoctrination was instilled in the people's minds so that they could understand the strength and power of a superior race, versus inferior races that other nations surrendered-to. Yet building the white race up in courage and commitment caused the people of Nazi Germany, to kill their foes whoever that might be, not just physically, but also psychologikally. The Nazi doctrine propagandized those that genetically carried within them the passion 2 raise such a nation that would carry on the world.

A half assed plan was laid out, but the most perfect photo arrays was photoshopped to be personally used, so that the propaganda of the Aryan, could reach deep within the hearts of every man, woman, and child 2 brain wash those who wasn't sure what it all meant.

UTOPIA...,
that's what was being conveyed 2 the German and Austrian people... in the-agenda entitled "HITLERIZM." 2 them it became a dream-world and the masses of the people served tirelessly 2 get the task at hand done. The speeches Adolf, and his chiefs of staff drafted were debated over and redrafted until every paragraph was laid down geniusously.

Hitler loved to tap into the psyche as well as the emotions of the people. The pictures in which he posed in, the electrifying words of hate, the marches, salutes, etc., were all done for dramatic effect. Hitler was prepped 4 the stage...his larger than life words stirred the hatred. His stare gave every Caucasian of his time the drive that they needed. The Hitler, regime needed the people 2 have (purpose), to increase the new war climate 2 fight for this UTOPIA, and the savior who came for them and stood in front of them 2 dictate not behind them like a coward.

The people in return provided Hitler, with the pride that he always wanted, but never got. Here was the demi-god...here was the people's power, as if it was the Jews messiah. Everyone great and small was forced 2 submit 2 this new era of sophisticated triumph, and its remarkable leader. Millions fell in love or in line, with these teachings...they became (absolute), the trademark, of Nazi Germany. Yet even with all of this, the kountry was not yet ready 4 war, esp., with Russia, Amerikkka, and England, the three most feared war kountries.

Germany, and it's leadership. went to war tooo sooon with nations that were and weren't greater in military strength. All the marching and photos in the world, and all the words in the galaxy, don't win wars. Impatience, and improper planning helped 2 destroy the Nazi nation. No matter how beautiful the flags etc., men's hearts, must win them over 2 want to fight, and the strategy must never be illogikil. Not knowing your enemy, or yourself, your people, or the terrain, is a foolish mistake and it cost Germany, their lives. Not listening 2 your generals, or those that are more knowledgeable than yourself in certain things is even foolisher.

Hoping rather than believing in reality is a dumb move. The S.S., and the S.A., were distinguished groups, along with the Luffwaffe the aerial division or war pilots, yet all were too easy 2 identify.

In the name of ideal, not common sense caused brave women and men of Germany, to perish, some by committing acts of suicide. Before Hitler, ever thought about becoming Supreme Ruler, of Germany, he too was once a war veteran, a corporal, in the first world war. Known or at least decorated for his solo attempts of bravery, but even then, not fit 4 command, he understood what war could do to a kountry and its citizens.

Hitler, was indeed keen, he knew what the then leadership of Germany, should've and could've done 2 win the cold war, but like them, they allowed 25 million to die in WWI, Hitler, and his Third Reich, as they were called, caused the depletion of 60 million lives 2 be wasted under "<u>DECORATED LEADERSHIP</u>."

Decorated leadership, yeah, I said that right. It was under the decorated leadership of Adolf Hitler, that cost sixty million people their lives. All the insignias were discredited, and desecrated. It all burned to the ground with all of Nazi arrogance, and foolish pride. All the Nazi's accomplishments, at least that which has been told throughout hisstory has been destroyed.

With all their propaganda displayed, the German, people failed 2 comprehend conventional as well as guerrilla warfare. It takes true structure and discipline including other necessary methods of strategikil tactiks 2-win battles and fight real wars.

By knowing the millions that fell in the great war.... Hitler, himself should have understood better than anyone how high kommand should be conducted. Hitler grew a deep-seated hatred for the leaders of his time in that great war, which gave him much grief as he mourned and regretted their field operations which massacred the lives of platoon members.

Yet,
those leaders didn't display a quarter of the decorations of the Third Reich, used during and before their war efforts, and parades. This was a man who like many was talented, but he Hitler, like many never had a position/power, in his life and once obtained it went to his head. The cosmetics weren't warranted, this is where the Third Reich, lost the war. There was no real foundation, that the German nation could build upon.

There were a great number of rituals, and grand standing illusions, but Hitler's mind moved faster than his council, troops, and the German people. Yet non realized this until it was too late, the UTOPIAN, theory could not have been reached and the damage was too great to recuperate from it.

Sometimes when great thinkers or unique thinkers are before their time, they end up lost in time, and it may take millennials to uncover the genius of their ideas, but fruitless in their ideals. Hitler sent his entire kountry and other kountries such as Italy, and Japan, on suicide missions. They were all disillusioned by those mock wars of Poland, as well as Spain. And by this, those useless decorations and decorated ideals caused Germany, and the Third Reich, to become BASTARDS OF THEIR BLOODLINE.

"THE STRUGGLE OF MEN AGAINST POWER, IS THE

STRUGGLE OF MEMORY AGAINST FORGETTING."

quote of:
Milan Kudera, in her
Book….
The book of Laughter,
and Forgetting…

CHAPTER 2

THE NEW INTEGRATION

Webster's dictionary defines the term integration as follows:

> "TO UNITE OR TO UNITE WITH SOMETHING ELSE. TO INCORPORATE AS EQUALS INTO SOCIETY, OR AS AN ORGANIZATION OF INDIVIDUALS OF DIFFERENT GROUPS AS (races).
> TO END SEGREGATION AND TO BRING INTO EQUAL MEMBERSHIP A SOCIETY OR AN ORGANIZATION."

Before I get into depth of this chapter let me clarify this title. By no means have I written this section of the book to take away the platform of the forefathers, and foremothers, of the peaceful Civil Rights Movement, or their fight 4 black integration of white Amerikkka. I personally wish to thank Mrs. Rosa Parks, and Dr. King, for their kontribution of trying to forward black achievement in this segregated "FREE WORLD."

It shall always be counted and konsidered as the people's foundation, or steppingstone. But for that reason, which was the right reason for that era and time, was exactly that, their reasons then, all 2 say that this is our reason and time now.

This is why I entitled this chapter the new integration.

However,
this time it is not to incorporate us into them, meaning their society, world, or race but 2 combine the people in its entirety in to a war body, no longer separated klasses in an of the world.

That definition of Webster is indeed one-sided. We've understood that particular phrase/phase which has been uniquely done as the curation of Whites, Blacks, Latinos, etc., causing the climate 2 become again

segregated into individual groups with whites at the 4front, without "co-parenting."
This prevents us as a whole to be considered equals because the portion of white Amerikkka, is still segregated from the whole of society.

It is by this that we thwart protection or service from these coverment sources, those who choose to understand under G-d's, watchful eye....the people's conditions in society rather than those who only see the condition of (1), race as the whole and director of all politikil movements and civilizations.

This integration of which I speak is of cell form.

A cell, not of prison, red, or white blood, stem, or otherwise, the cell that I'm referring to is underground, revolutionary, clandestine, militant. Some say that the term (cell), generated from a communist philosophy...but trust me when I say that I BY NO MEANS HAVE AFFILIATIONS, OR ANY DEALINGS WITH COMMUNIST OR COMMUNISM, CHRISTIAN EXTREMIST GROUPS, NIHILIST, NOR ANY ISLAMIC EXTREMIST FACTIONS.

I am simply a man who has been studying extensively and have analyzed my surroundings. In his book of War, it states:

> "Terrorism is not war, it is only an important tactik of war."

The late undisputed guerrilla of Argentine(a), Guevara, was said to have opposed terrorism. Che, expounded in his writings on Warfare, that terrorism is not for true revolutionaries.

I beg the differ,
here I will partially explain. Martin Luther King Jr. had a tactik/strategy in the civil rights war. King used a shrewd way to formulate his position which unified this kountry's population as well as divide it.

Tzu, also stated in his book The Art Of War, that:

> "Wars are politikil…it is the people against the other, from sovereignty over lands, beliefs, territory, and ideology. But war either way requires a definite enemy, or object."

The conduct of war consists in the planning and conduct of fighting/rebelling. Fighting consists of a greater or lesser number of single acts each complete in it 'self-called engagements.

This would be close in definition with the term Guerrilla Warfare. This gives rise 2 the completely different activity of conventional warfare, due 2 it's shrewd planning, as well as executing engagements themselves by single acts, coordinated by strategist like King, in order to further the rebellion strategically in the civil rights war, a politikil war I might add. This would make King, a mastermind therefore we must redefine King's actions and this so-called theory of (NON-VIOLENCE)!

This would adequately define Dr. King, not as a peaceful man, but a indescribable Terrorist. Let me break down the term terrorism by Webster's standard.

Terrorism: the systematic use of terror esp., as a means of "COERCION."

Terrorize: 2 fill with terror or anxiety (scare), to coerce by threats, and violence.

Terror: To frighten, a state of immense fear, one that (inspires fear), and worry. An appalling person or thing. REIGN OF TERROR.
Violence as bombing, committed by groups in order 2 "INTIMIDATE" a POPULATION, "GOVERMENT," into GRANTING THEIR DEMANDS. (insurrection, and revolution)

Tzu,
clarifies this more by saying that:

> "Mass murder is not necessarily terrorism, and mass murder and terrorism, are not necessarily war. War, is not beer-hall brawls, and war is not blind struggle between mobs of people, but rather engagements or a series of them between (well organized masses), coverment or klasses of race...moving as a team, acting under a single overarching will and directed against a definite objective."

War,
is not defined by damage however great, but an intent 2 konquer.

So this King, an appalling person classified by white Amerikkka, as a thing...intimidated his coverment, and the whites of his era labeled Amerikkka. Not only did he just intimidate them, he caused them 2 give into his demands which is why Amerikkka, is integrated today. King, and his kourt the Civil Rights Movement, started 2 place fear in AMERIKKKLANS, by threatening the establishment's economik growth and kontinuance, by boycotting stores, buses, etc.

King got into the minds of the white children, and by formulating national/international appeal and attention, coerced the masses to fight against a well-organized white civilization.

The single acts done by Rosa Parks, the sit ins in restaurants etc., where all to engage the enemy knowing that this tactik would enrage white Amerikkka, but also benefit those who fought through the politiks, which again under-minded the adversary.

These small groups/bands operated under the banner of freedom of speech, and peaceful assembly which is kritikally considered as protest. The protest was against inhumane standards, and equality for all as the Amerikkklan bill of rights, established for the real CITIZENS of its kountry.

With this noted this should also be inserted to clarify the strategy/tactik, of James Meredith....which he used on and against the college campus of

Ole Miss.

The objective was the integration of this white's only college and also the United Stakes konstitution, and like King, this also fell under the guise of the 14th amendment, which regarded all CITIZENS, of Amerikkka, **equal rights**, and **equal protection**.

The college Ole Miss, we must remember at the time was southernly segregated by the ideology of white racist, and equally supported by its governor Ross Barnett, back in 1962, but rather than fight these southerners physically Mr. Meredith, let the United Stake's coverment do the fighting 4 him single handedly.

James Meredith, a former armed forces veteran and a Afrikkkin Amerikkkin, wanted 2 be the first negro to attend this college. By trying to enroll as a student, a major riot was started between federal enforcers, and state enforcers.

This war of hatred was waged between thousands of angry whites from all over the south and former president John F. Kennedy, 2 which I must add that some of these whites were sworn under an oath 2 the state in which they held, and the United Stake's Konstitution, who were in fact state troopers, police (local) enforcers, and the Amerikkklan armed forces.

As we know or should know, these are only milestones of the previous battles against this warped system's dogma which prevents people of any kolor, from eating, drinking, shopping, educating, and securing themselves etc., as a collective body or united kountry.

Yet,
here is where things also gets tricky, our enemies have also studied and formulated the possibility of **strength in numbers**, 2 kreate a continuous mentality that outflanks the Amerikkklan, population's mind by using the Civil Rights Movement, strategy and James Meredith's tactik 2 hold us

back from further achievement of that "**Dream**," that White Amerikkka, alone konsidered equality 4 themselves, not those who have pigmentation which 4 us kreate the more darker undertone of help and aide.

So, who is this "**One Nation**," that these politicians, masons, and international bankers, keep referring to? By their propaganda and orchestration, it is they who are the **Nation**, and **Face**, not us the mere peasant klass or alleged citizen.

It is their principles which they instill in us 2 kontrol us, not govern our determination. It is their ambitions and agenda now that we are carrying out as alwayz. But now, it's under the banner of integration. Many Afrikkkin Amerikkklans, that we've come to know such as Malcom X, and the Jamaican born Marcus Garvey, was against integration as we should've studied, and in that essential sense, they were in fact **Anti-Amerikkkin**.

These two men's logic also was that the negro needed 2 come 2 terms on their own alone without interference, in this race and war of klassism. And yes, I am all 4 that concept, but there is also a method and evolution 2 that frame of mind.

2 increase the agenda on what many consider **Black Amerikkka**, they had to destroy the brainz of the operation. 4 this is what defines a terrorist it is by the way that he or she thinks. **Terrorism is psychologikil**, therefore reverse the psychology, the people will revert back 2 the slave way of advancement being men and women **boxed in**, **trapped, and in doctrinized**, rather than being mantalities that revolutionize the masses.

Martin Luther King Jr., kreated a platform which transformed the psychology of the masses versus the **Black Amerikkkin's Militant Stance and Non-Versatility**. He over stood the way 2 embody the people which caused them 2 become much stronger than if separated as a **black foundation**. We have never heard Dr. King, say that when negros become integrated we should lose who we are, and become lazy in the process of forwarding our progress, because that wasn't what integration was about.

The structure of Amerikkka, is the people it 'self, not the few but the majority who educates those who are uneducated which causes the feuds within families, kommunities, inner circles, as well as the economical elite. Therefore, the new integration isn't as vocal as the previous generations of the Civil Rights Movement, or as approachable, never 2 be seen in a systematic sense of formation. We are more sub-ground, raw, and unpolished, the not so experienced the grassrootz. We the revolutionist will not publikly display terrorism, and we the terrorist revolutionary, will not be publicated by a surfaced way of klassifying this celled population, or newer klass of amassed people seeing that unity can be utilized far greater on our terms than how it was 4 those back in the Civil Rights, and pro black Nationalist era, as well as the establishments.

Denmark Vesey understood this form of integration to a degree, although he was a freed slave in his time, he refused 2 be ruled and regulated by **Pig Amerikkka**, neither was he going to continue 2 stand by and watch his race stay subjugated in such an inferior state. Mr. Vesey utilized these teachings unlike the rebel Nat Turner, who sped before truly comprehending freedom, and what a body of **armed souljahs** could do **if**, they became a revolutionary movement.

This would have given Nat' Turner, a structure 2 continue 2 build not a rebellion that only spooked the enemy in which he tried 2 terrorize by murdering those, white plantation owners.

Although Nat Turner, and his group of angry armed slaves stormed those plantations in the middle of the night, killing the white overseers, and owners that oppressed them, he did not see the **Science Within The Art Of War**. Vesey, however walked amongst all, free....in which he encountered daily.... the slave and master both. He went about his affairs as if he wasn't noticing the problems going on around him.

Assuming him 2 be a common citizen upon Amerikkka's soil, he played his role well, when it came **2 Shadow Warfare**. Vesey was fortunate in life little is known how he was able 2 buy a lottery ticket to obtain his freedom out of the depths of slavery, yet he did hit the lottery and had his shackles removed. But that did not stop Denmark Vesey, with a **Military Mind**, he began to study, and he used his earnings 2 travel.

When he began traveling, he started talking to the local slaves building a line of communication. He studied the terrains and took all that was left of his money to educate the learned as well as semi-learned slaves. Not one dime was spent on fancy attire, Vesey, was not to lose focus like the many who left the slaves in their ruined shacks, instead he invested in himself and those who would become that integrated body of terrorist.

Denmark viewed like we all view the cowards of his time/our time as worthless failures of our race, and society. He could not feel free until they the people was able 2 be free. And like us in the **21st century**, the oppression still lurks, never taking a back seat. Vesey, saw then what we see now he needed 2 do something about their situation and he did. He initiated a rag tag bunch of nobodies and trained them to become a manifestation of **resistance**. He stressed the importance of **Cell Life**, for he expounded that it was the very essence of **Terrorist Thinking, and GrassRoot Embodiment**. Denmark showed these slaves structure, he didn't want them to become just another organized body, and it was by this that made these nobodies stronger until they became the concept of revolution!

Unlike Nat Turner, Denmark Vesey, was a lot more hands on with his training of his cadres. The slave was now the **Sub-Ground**, not the **Underground**. His orchestration blended the terrorist revolutionary into society. Vesey, made it necessary 4 his cadres to realize how imperative it was not 2 stick out like a sore thumb. Out in the open where their mobility was better utilized it started a formation that worked 4 them on their own terms rather than that of the slave masters. It transformed in 2 a faction styled formation. Although there were no other races in his integrated movement his **1821-22 machination**, had other religious backgrounds involved, as with Dr. King, but it was that **Pig Philosophy**, of Willie Lynch, that **commercializing slave breaker**, which contaminated the mental capability of the still trapped slaves. This was why Denmark's revolt didn't reach its goal. The slaves became what Willie Lynch said they would eventually become over time...submissive, labor, forced 2 voluntary. Mr. Lynch's **psychological animalization** created the slave and continues 2 keep them **transparent and sub-human**. There were no have and have nots, because the house negro and the field negro both **feared and cringed at the crackin of the whip, and the weilder of that whip, which was and still is the Cracker**.

Those negros were the **plantation**. They were planted here by the white human and mechanical vessels. They were picked here, and they planted their seeds here on the Amerikkklan plantation where they grew up. This doesn't register with the revolutionary terrorist. The divide and conquer ideology are endorsed by the slaves so that the **slave system** can function the way it always has, yet in the **21st century it's even worse than before**. Rather it's by klass, color, or just identity, it's oppressive meanz continues to destroy the people who want to carry on to' out slavery. Those of you who are reading this book (if), you can seriously analyze the methodology of terrorism, and it's essentials, than you can honestly embrace how shrewd and calculating Vesey, actually had 2 be 2 be able 2 organize such a lay body of men. Scrutinize every possibility and you will find that Denmark Vesey, was the **Brainchild,** of **Terrorism**, and by integrating other religious groups in his cell like King, did much later made **him phenomenal,** and **supreme** 4 his day; even if his plan did not come 2 fruition.

In my opinion, it was 4 Dr. King, 2 capitalize 2 achieve his moment of greatness, but without these fundamentals the Civil Rights Movement would've not made the impact that it did. It was never about revolt…it was the pondering of how 2 effect change which allowed King and his kourt, 2 become immortalized throughout history. Tzu, stated in his book: **'The Art Of War '**

> **"The only way 2 prevent war, is 2 know how to wage war and win it better than your enemy."**

Yet let us back up 4 a moment so that we can develop a clearer understanding of spearheading integration as James Meredith, had done. Meredith knew the strong holds that Amerikkka built 4 their people, they made contracts and promises that it never intended 2 use in the uplifting of the **Slave Nation**. Therefore Meredith, produced a revolutionary tactic that caused the south 2 take up arms again against the north's former president John F. Kennedy, in a treasonable manner. Blatant disrespect to the **Commander-in-chief**, 4 the south told him 2 go fuck himself, because they were never going 2 let a nigger in their University Ole Miss, which Meredith, went 2 enroll in as the first Afrikkkin Amerikkkin.

The war that he formulated wasn't by marching, boycott, neither was it by speech. Meredith, waged war on this kountry through his kountry s enforcers and it's founder's konstitutions.

James Meredith, integrated with Amerikkka's former president John F. Kennedy, and his northern army. Meredith knew the politiks that regulated in those times, along with the men and women that learned those politiks and used them 2 their advantage.

James Meredith,
almost brought this kountry into another Civil War, in that great politikil sense. Meredith, as with Martin Luther King Jr., introduced us to that inner spectrum of **Terrorist Engagement.**

(A) . James Meredith, without raising as a defense a finger or a gun, caused the north and the south 2 collide with one another. Meredith, caused inner strife between these two konstitutions (**Federal and State**), and the **White Supremacist Ideology**, that ruled the **U.S.A.**

It took alarming efforts not 2 have **White Amerikkka**, go to war against their own kind again esp., over a negro. Meredith, and his methodology of psychologikil warfare, ultimately became an ongoing attack on Ross Barnett, the then governor of the slave state of Mississippi, and this kountry's konstitutions, in regards 2 its obligation 2 desegregate not only the south but the entire **United States** as a whole.

(B). The politiks that James Meredith, learned subtlety…he used to counter the racist hatred on both sides of the Mason Dixon Line. Meredith made it become a situation where the nation it 'self, would have to think about its future, and it's welfare, 2 the key politikil figures who would have to choose a side no matter the outcome, one way or another. This,

is what protected James Meredith, his assessment of **White determination to secure their wealth, status, and security** here in dear old Amerikkka. Therefore Mr. Meredith had the better seat to watch the festivities unfold before his eyes, in comfort behind fortified walls of the University. Meredith,

watched as his enemies fought over him and 4 him, all to be the first negro to enroll in the university of Ole Miss. He utilized Uncle **Sam's training**, and transformed himself into that needed revolutionary terrorist for the people, and his foes never understood what was being done.

It was Meredith's adversaries that classified him, as a **thing**, and that **negro** of inferior meanz, as well as the disruptor of their establishment, and ideology. Yet it was Meredith, who out thought and outflanked this so called "**White Nation and Their Strong Hold**."

Dr. King, and his kourt on the other hand, closed ranks on good old Amerikkka, by taking this kountry 2 war head on. King placed himself and the Civil Rights Movement in harm's way. Even while confined to a prison cell Dr. King, infuriated his coverment, and the status quo, here in Amerikkka, by writing his most controversial critically acclaimed speech: "**I HAVE A DREAM**."

This speech was highly diabolical, and it was truly a subliminal militant message. The speech was extreme on a level that changed the dynamics of this racially charged kountry. The way Dr. King, inserted **psychologikil warfare** on the people of Amerikkka, it gave the people something to fight 4 and it organized (**that**), strategy which made negros no longer **Fear Their Rulers, Their Power, and their Power Structure Of Oppression**.

King, made negros **confront their kountry**, better known as **White Amerikkka**. King, made **White Amerikkka, Fear for the 1st time since Nat Turner, "The Strength of Negro Intellectualism**,"

It caused the people of the world to come together at least for that one moment in time regardless of religion, klass, or color. King, embodied this new mass movement of resistance, he became the face of an international, national mass movement.

Dr. King,

pushed to get the people to look at themselves and dig deep down in themselves and to forget about their differences, setting them aside for the sake of humanity, so that the masses could see that if they came 2gether and worked with one another, they could overthrow their oppressors, and their oppression. Saul Alinsky, a Jew by the way, evaluate things a tad differently than I convey in a book that was written about him, by his dear friend Von Hoffman, entitled "RADICAL," A Portrait he states:

"King's strategy and the civil rights movement was doomed for failure." (chapter 5 pgs. 70-77)

Alinsky continues:

"King, had many people none of whom demonstrated an ability 2 convert the enthusiasm and potential of the civil rights movement into a stable ongoing kind of organization which gets things done, inch by inch, and year by year. In an interview in 1965 Alinsky told an interviewer that the Achilles heel of the (CRM), is the fact that it has not developed into a stable, disciplined, mass-based power organization. Many of the significant victories that have been won in the in Civil Rights, were not the result of mass power strategy.... they were unfortunately assisted by helpful aid or the impact of world politikil pressures. The incredibly stupid blunders of the status quo (whites), of the south....and elsewhere, along with the supporting klimate kreated particularly by the "churches"....
WITHOUT THE MINISTERS, PRIEST, RABBIS, AND THE NUNS, Alinsky says: I wonder who would have been in, the Selma march?!"

Alinsky also stated about King, and the CRM., that:

"By analyzing Dr. King, and the operation he used keenly, it foretold it's failure outside of the south and after his assassination. It's disappearance from the scene etc. The tragedy is that the gains that have been made, have given many CRM., spokesman the illusion that they have the kind of organization and power they need. Self-deception like this is easy 2 understand, but the truth is that the CRM., and its organization has always been minute in actual size and power. Periodically or periodic mass euphoria around a charismatic leader is not an organization, it's just the initial stage of agitation.

Belatedly-many civil rights leaders have been rudely awakened to this situation. When King, went 2 Chicago, the gang bangers who

dominated the area whose name on the map **Lawndale**, but was called Slumdale, had a different take on King's presence.
In other words, the civil rights organizations that came into Chicago, were not working with (HARDCORE), people.
They were supposed to have been 4 the grassrootz, but the middle klass, was running them.

King's group didn't know the people. The people who wouldn't mind being in a riot were never touched. They were still out on the corners, laying in the alleys, and in the summertime sleeping in the park at night. The Nobel Peace Prize winner had his outside volunteers pounding on the doors were HARDCORE, people lived.
"They,"
wanted to recruit them but 4 what purpose other than the grand generalities, was ill defined. Explaining 2 the people exactly why he and his outside friends had come among them was a recurring obstacle during Dr. King's Chicago sojourn. King, and his outside friends were cut from a different cloth. Those outsiders from Alinsky's perspective were a hodge/podge of young white idealist! Kollege kids, and summertime soldiers, most who had no knowledge of the people that they were suppose 2 recruit. In the south, youthful (idealist), (white), were used as civil rights cannon fodder...but in Chicago they were dead weight! Instead of pestering lower income black people, with their good intentions, they might have made a kontribution if they had stayed home and organized (white people), in Chicago, and the environ who were 9/10's of the problem. IT WAS ANTI-THESIS OF AN ALINSKY OPERATION, WHERE OUTSIDE VOLUNTEERS WERE GENERALLY SHOOED AWAY NOT ONLY BECAUSE THEY GOT IN THE WAY, BUT ALSO BECAUSE THEY DIDN'T HAVE ANY SKIN IN THE GAME.

Laudable, as it is 2 volunteer 2 help other people wrestle with their problems, effective organizations are built with people who have a direct and personal interest in their success. With no change in the kampaign for justice in Chicago, both blacks, and whites kontinued 2 view King, as the outsider... hated by some, heroic to others, but non-the-less still an outsider.

The local people were not shut out, but as in the King kampaign, in the south their role was more to be led than 2 lead. King, didn't know the terrain, which he should've studied as Nicolo Machiavelli, states in his book the "Prince"...and he didn't know how 2 approach the situation which differed from the south.

Alinsky continues:

"You must know where you are b4 you try 2 go someplace else! The outsider is the catalyst...the invisible element who also starts the process and then departs.
The lumpen proletariat or the poorest of the poor are worthless, 4 founding a functioning organization.
Once a powerful an effective organization is up and running, the membership may want 2 try to help the very poor but, you cannot start with them because they suffer from what some call Social Pathologies, meaning their lives are a chaotic sequence of emergencies, terrible coincidences and unforeseen **disasters**.
The lumpens, are accident prone and emotionally unstable. Their lives are a chain of bad news. Gas is cut off, electrical service cut off, or terminated. The landlord is evicting them, a cousin in jail, the baby has to be rushed 2 the E.R., one of the kids sassed the social worker and the family is being cut off social welfare.
The alpha male came home and beat the hell out of the mother. In Alinsky's view the very poor are unreliable, not of the stuff of organizations, which are composed of people bound 2gether by keeping their kommunities, and kommittments.

Even the late James Baldwin, once said on a similar topic that the problem with kulture as with politiks is that it isn't and almost never produces the sort of action that only challenges but changes politikil structures.

"It can change minds, and it can remind people of the fact of human commonality-this is no small achievement, but kulture shifts very swiftly. It promotes, confuses, and destroys ideologikil arguments; but its materials are too easily transported, bought and sold. It can help us name ourselves, it can remind us how 2 grow but, it is slippery and hard to pin down. It is an honorable shelter 4 the wary, but it also is a HIDING PLACE FOR THE WEAK OF HEART, AND THE POSERS. KULTURE IS OUR LIVES: KULTURE IS THE WAY WE ARE, BUT OUR KULTURE SYSTEM IS MORE INCONSISTANT AND. DIRECTIONLESS THAN IT'S POLITIKIL KOUNTER-PART.

In a kounter-analysis 2 both of these theories, we must see the truth and falsehood in them. Dr. Martin Luther King Jr., although an outsider was not a militant kombatant, or military strategist, yet he utilized a tactic of philanthropy. Dr. King understood the human capability, and his sole purpose was not 2 string along the people or carry on a mass organization or series of organizations.

Dr. King had one goal in mind, 2 carry out a **humanitarian agenda and** that's all he needed to carry out. The charismatic influence, or immortal influence was divinely inspired therefore King, as a man as well as reverend, **embraced** his characteristic of being the, personification of a leader. Adolf Hitler was this way as well, but King, konducted a war in the position of a warrior rather than a general. He was with the people not just with them but one with them. He became them not just a part of them through a movement. He didn't just lead the people he gave the people direction. Dr. King, caused the politikil field 2 transition at that time. The negro of middle klass, and the negro of impoverished meanz was unaccomplished in the shrewd thinking of this Southern Baptist preacher.

Dr. King, knew that dismembering white society could not be done with nonwhites, therefore he used the college white middle klassed youth which by the way had 2 be the cannon fodder and the spark, 2 be the body while he remained the face.

The white educated young and curious were the fundraisers and Molotov's, that helped to set ablaze a movement for Civil Rights which was not a Pro Black movement, but a movement of equality. An All People's Movement, which is a true revolutionary movement.

The reciprocation holds true to the view today. King's comprehension went beyond black and white hatred, it caused the people who were local, 2 those around the world, 2 be able 2 study, own nondiscriminatory businesses, etc, in a nation that wasn't big on Chinamen, Arabs, Blacks, and Latinos, because it was a strong hold 4 **White Amerikkklans**. King, if we actually rationalize, started modern day **Civil War**.

This kountry wasn't thinking about change until King, intervened. And although rivals when Malcom X, voiced his opinion both gave the inferior slave nation an opportunity that none of us could resist. This is where your Black Panther Party, ascended the stage, but get this **Not With Guns Alone, but also with Books**.

Secondly-
is it really culture that we're solely trying 2 pin down, or understand?

Some may say yes, while others may say no. The BPP, were **Black Nationalist**, and it consisted of its party being of the majority if not the entire Afrikkkin Amerikkkins. It wasn't that the party was racist, Huey P. Newton, one of the party's founders was a minister of defense-4 the people in general with pro black dominant themes. It consisted of what communist label the lumpen poor, who with proper education could've been more than what they became. But let's just focus on what they became "**POWER 2 THE PEOPLE**,"!
These militant poor activists were a organized splinter group like many

that came to the forefront, with or after the Civil Rights Movement. But if we study many key figures started under Dr. King, and his campaign. Especially members such as **Stokely Carmicheal**.

Mr. Carmichael,
no longer wanted to be church orientated so he channeled all his energies 2 help kreate something more aggressive, with possible influence by another ousted member of the (CRM), Robert F. Williams, who was said 2 have made the NAACP, uncomfortable with his militant statements, and book "(**NEGROS WITH GUNS**)," so he split.

The poor which we can see 4 ourselves had just as much dedication than everyone else who konsidered themselves politikil activist in the sixties and seventies, but their mentality was too extreme 2 really turn things around as Dr. King, predicted in regards to mob style organizations or movements that are illogikil, wild, and miseducated to the social standing, the very thing he knew that would jeopardize the hard work put into his founding cause. The whites in which he tried 2 show restrained konduct, began 2 fear negros with guns and intelligence, although at that time Huey Newton, was not telling black people 2 start shooting their weapons he wanted them to learn politiks or laws that governed the land.

King, made white Amerikkka, fear white Amerikkka, because it was headed by a black man. The Panthers, made white Amerikkka, fear the hatred and anger that Huey Newton, was not trying to unleash but was willing 2 show white Amerikkka, that blacks were prepared 2 save themselves "**BY ANY MEANS NECESSARY**"!

The slogan of black nationalist minister Malcom X, which caused the separate not integrated voice of Carmichael's stance of "**BLACK POWER**"!

The same people who were gang members in California, and places like San Francisco, these low income hard core social degenerates and outcasts of society along with those of Chicago, as described by Mr. Alinsky, were drop outs, and those beating on their spouses, prostitutes, girlfriends, etc., where the same ones that rose out of a sane desperation yet their ingenuity kreated one of the most militant third world styled sophisticated all black guerrilla organizations this nation has ever laid eyes on.

Yet they were incoherent 2 King's warning about moving too fast, gradualism and patience history shows as I've previously expounded on with Hitler, and his Third Reich. Without deep critique and a vast analysis, the leadership of the BPP faltered.

There became more than one leader…sexizm, drug addiction/ dealing, arrogance, paranoia, and extortion started curtailing its full potential and direction.

They were trying 2 keep up their kommunitis, and its programs, along with the people, but they couldn't keep up the party's appearance. **THEY COULD NOT TRANSITION**, the way that King, did when he at one point was a southern preacher who became the politikil leader of humanity. King, a kollege graduate had those of like mindedness in his movement. This is the politikil shift, to have those equipped like one's self with education, restraint, articulation, and discipline under one head not several individuals trying 2 lead one movement.

Huey Newton didn't educate his movement properly he feared the educated man/woman, although he became one himself. Rather than wanting 2 establish a regime of totalitarianism, oppression, and subordinates. He Newton, became a walking kontradiction.

He undermined his own cause, and kept his army/underlings in the dark, and his very own hench men he kept at odds with the very Souljah's he had marching with him 2 support the (People's Cause), and Black Armed Self-Defense. Since he didn't understand how 2 utilize both the book and the gun as well as his own abilities he cost the people whom he loved dearly their lives along with the Black Panther Party.

King,
brought 2gether the people, rich, middleklass, mostly but also a couple of the straggling poor, the true poor he allowed to enter into the fold not his fold but the people's fold, and this is who became history not what became history. The charisma of King is the catalyst that brings the movement together.
The people who are dedicated are the real skin because they all were educated, and they saw an opportunity to seize their time as Bobby Seale, and Huey Newton, would later say and write about.

The organization was different races who integrated amongst themselves first. King removed kulture from the equation all together. He conjured up the human Psyche, which allowed the (**rank and file**), 2 question themselves and the future of the kountry in which they all were deemed citizens of including the president.

He King, is the new civil war.... a history by old recording removed the shackles from the slaves a second time. If Abraham Lincoln, wrote the Emancipation Proclamation, to forward this kountries plight both the educated black, and white and the non-educated than King, gave it a newer vision as a kountry in its entirety and a newer and greater step 4 us 2 achieve it. The modern-day **NIGGA, versus the Mis-educated NEGRO**.

Just as James Meredith, did except ON A FAR LESSOR SCALE, and King, initiated the exclusion of white society and ideology 2 bring forth the bigger role or picture of Amerikkka.

King placed Amerikkka's future (it's white children), in the cross hairs, to be fired upon and brutalized...this halted white Amerikkka, their own sons and daughters were in the crossfire fighting with their black adversaries.

Again, as with Hitler, King, marched at the frontline not the rear of the movement accepting the beatings and brutality like those with him, unlike the nation of Islam, and its controversial minister Malcom X, who by the way had a gun and never fired at the cops or the establishment that he always spoke against.

Dr. King, on the other hand was nonviolent he was never supposed to kreate black intolerance, yet Malcom X, labeled him a coward when minister X, never ever himself threw a punch, or cocktail (Molotov), at the politicians, etc.

This Malcom X, is now immortalized by all black people of the militant klass...he's not seen as a coward although he's seen in posters and pictures in the ghetto and suburbs of black "U.S.A," standing peering out the window not aiming at anything with his rifle like he suggested. Therefore, the integration theory inducted many into its war which the people themselves fought not just the charismatic leader. Leaders if we truly study the (**ART OF WAR**), are not the fire, only the spark.
The civil rights war was not, but was psychologikil war, it threw off the enemy and those who were on the side lines spectating. It is said that:

> "A wise general's troops feed on the enemy."

Mehmet Ali Agca, a lone terrorist like James Meredith, is said to have tried to assassinate Pope John Paul II, once said during his trial that he was an international terrorist…, like King, determined 2 help, terrorist of every kolor, and 2 no longer make any distinction between the left and right wingers. This new integration is not blended in society, it is camouflaged in or as the background and back drop of society, it's societies within society. It acts like Mehmet Ali Agca, would later say independently in the name of truth above ideologikil dogmas, in this case it would be Amerikkklanizm or Amerikkkin Kon-institutionalizm.

The new integration doesn't belong to any organization it is not concerned with ideology, and it no longer needs an idea! It needs a gun, or like former president Bush, said, (**weapons of mass destruction**).

Karl Marx once wrote there is only one way 2 shorten the murderous deaths agonies of the old society only one way 2 shorten the bloody birth pangs of new society............

"REVOLUTIONARY TERRORISM."

Which 2 us only means one thing **FUCK REVOLUTIONARY TRADITION**!

Upon more study we learn that Lenin, enhanced or heightened Karl Marx's theory of this when he states:

> "Terror is one of those military meanz that can come in handy and be even necessary ata certain shape and under certain circumstances."

Here the new integration disregards this way of utilization and concept. "**Certain Circumstances**," means 2 us that we must constantly outsmart the opposition. 2 us, **War is life long**, this is why we've coined the phrase **LIFERZ**.

To us terror is not violence, it is our main method of structure. It isn't barbaric, or savagery when one is running kounter 2 what the truth actually is.

It meaning the **truth** is intensity. It is not klass wars, the operative action is war, against whomever due 2 falsehood, and oppressive directives. There is never a liking or want of being **liberal** solely. The understanding is 2 be structuralized and organized by its application, which we now call **WOLF WARFARE**.

This is a non-systematic directive of cause and effect. In the cases of **conventional warfare** and **guerrilla warfare**, there are set and semi-set

patterns.
Wolf Warfare, also regarded as **Terrorist Revolution**, has no shape or body 2 be able 2 identify it. It is abstract and no longer an **Art**, it is by nature sporadic and its ability can be made to fit any if not all climates, terrains, and circumstances. This **science** is stingless, yet it can be coordinated 2 inter link.

This inter linking can be complicated due to international alliances versus pure cadre hood. Bonds are not necessarily an embodiment of a said structure, recollection proves this. Look at past revolutionary groups, terrorist etc., and their individuals who was on one page while there were other figures who were behind the scenes puppetizing the whole entire movement. **Wolf Warfare** is a different form of power politiks, that restricts kovert operatives, but convert operations of diversed meanz.

Not bloodline, religion, etc., The new cell is total trans formation. The belief is in who we are as a people, this is what formulates a better **Bible, Torah, and Qur'an**. It is not theorized; therefore, it cannot be learned through a book or books. It is set in a mantality of alleged inferior people under a **Third World Scientific Politikil Revolutionary Terrorist Movement**. In other words, pure underestimation on our enemies' part.

This under privileged paradigm utilizes currency, but not kapitalism...which overthrows dogma 2 gain komplete kontrol over self and the people, rather than kountry or empire. The people are not programmed. We are followers or separate leaders of a grander scaled belief of unification although individuals.
It is like cells in the body, one portion dies off when we fail 2 use those things learned in the brain. Yet once these cells break down other cells form and become stronger. Ideas needs 2 regenerates. They make abstract strategies, 2 empower the other members of the body.

In 1982 a president then of Italy, who studied terrorist and mentalities, Sandro Pertini, said when he spoke at John Hopkins University, which confirms our outlook that:

> "Terrorists are now talking which means that they are not guided by any true politikil belief. It means that they are feeling the ground erode out from under their feet. They are not fighting for some higher or noble cause. If they are talking, it is because they are, **all Puppets,** and they are in the hands of some puppeteer!

Dr. King, mind you was a preacher evidently who became a revolutionary by giving blacks an outlook that would transform their mentalities, almost like Malcom X, who said:

> "To those of us whose philosophy is **Black Nationalism**, the only way you can get involved in the Civil Rights struggle is 2 give it a new interpretation. That old interpretation excluded us, now you're facing a situation where the young negro is coming up...and they don't want 2 hear that turn the other cheek stuff. No, in Jacksonville, those were teenagers that were throwing **molotov cocktails**. Negros have never done that before, but it shows you that there is a new deal coming in. There is new thinking coming in, and a newer strategy coming in. It'll be **molotov**, this month, hand grenades next month, and something else the month after that.
>
> **IT WILL BE BALLOTS OR BULLETS...IT WILL BE LIBERTY, OR IT WILL BE DEATH. THE ONLY DIFFERENCE ABOUT THIS KIND OF DEATH, IS THAT IT'LL BE RECIPROCAL."**

And this by 1965, Malcom X, attempted 2 organize an ecumenical politikil organization of black people, and he called it The Organization Of Afro-Amerikkkin Unity. Malcom X, attempts 2 convey his message by saying:

> "And I dedicate myself to the organizing of black people, into a group that are interested in doing things **konstructive**, not just 4 one religious' community, but for the entire black community. This is what the purpose of the organizing of Afro-Amerikkkin Unity is, 2 have an action program that's 4 the good of the entire black community...**BY ANY MEANZ NECESSARY**!"

Yet the majority who listened 2 Malcom X, were black Muslims, gangs, and the very poor. 2 view this more strongly or analytically, Malcom, was **calling to armz a bomb, not an organization**. Excluding **whites** who were willing 2 assist in the black struggle was absolutely **bananas**. Malcom X wanted 2 use **White Monetary**, but not white people which is again Malcom X, being a walking contradiction. Angry oppressed blacks, **ARMED, and SEMI-CONSCIOUS**, many misguided...and you want them 2 run loose in communities around Amerikkka? That would have been our end, as Dr. King, analyzed and made this statement that:

> "Black rage, was so destructive and self-destructive that without a **moral theology**, and **political organization**, it would wreak havoc on BLACK **AMERIKKKA**!"

But I say not just black Amerikkka, but Amerikkka, as a whole. Business could flourish a whole lot more, the nation of Amerikkka could now become that super power, if the policy makers as well as people would broaden their minds 2 the koncept of Dr. King's view, but like King, assessed, the dogmatik antiks of ALL **BLACKISM**, proved 2 be a fatal mistake when organizations like the black liberation army and the SNCC, came into the picture.

There were robberies, and extortions, murders, and rapes, by these organizations not 4 the kommunities' welfare, but 4 their own selfish gain. This gave the coverment an opportunity 2 disband and destroy as a ploy all **Black militant Organizations**, when it assembled in 1980, a terrorist task force back then konsisting of **NYPD** officers and **F.B.I.**, agents....the first of its kind which konsisted of twenty investigators, ten agents, and ten **NYPD** detectives, working with minimal supervision, but giving these politikil enforcers the sole authority 2 kill and set up **BLACK ORGANIZATIONS AND IT'S LEADERS**.

These organizations of pure black aggression and anger were more explosive than secretive and strategik. It is said that their first big cases came out of the year 1981, for a Botch Armored car robbery that left two kops and one guard dead in Nyack New York, the suspects were said 2 have got away with 1.6 million dollars. The alleged suspects were from the Black Liberation Army, The Black Panther Party, The New Afrika Republik, and the notorious white group The Weather Underground, which was thought 2 be disbanded.

This terrorist unit also linked those organizations 2 numerous other armor truck and bank robberies, as well as the prison break of still at large with a bounty now of two million dollars, the legendary Assata Shakur, who still to this day is konsidered a female pig killer.

This terrorist task force kaptured, and killed many falsely.....but they were semi-international radikils, by a who's who network, **most** domestik terrorist, so it was far more easier 2 find them and put an end 2 leaders such as Cathy Boudin, Marilyn Jean, and others from the Weather Underground. Mutulu Shakur, Eddie Josephs, were those from the Black Liberation Army.

In a **1963**, speech sponsored and addressed 2 Afrikkin **Students Association** and the Campus of the **NAACP** at Michigan State Univ., later published under the title: **20 Million Black People, In A Politikil, Economik, and Mental Prison**, Malcom X, was recorded saying:

> "The organization stopped being 4 the people, it started 2 become self-initiating factions. It became groups organizing 4 riots rather than for overthrowing the coverment. As it is spear headed by black on black crime, as 2day it continues 2 be. The structure became dogmatic.

> Integration, was side stepped 2 produce what Dr. King, said it would become. It brung blacks further down than what we had previously started out."

Proving what James Baldwin, and Saul Alinsky, said concerning culture, and the lumpen, to a degree that:

> "The lumpens are accident prone and emotionally unstable...their lives are a chain of bad news. Gas cut off, their being evicted, they want 2 remain the kriminal element, which solidified Malcom's definition of a **NIGGER; "A VICTIM OF AMERIKKKLAN DEMOCRACY**!"

The Italian political analysis and writer Nicolo Machiavelli, once wrote in his book **"THE DISCOURSES OF LIVY,"**
that:

> "A crowd is too neutral, although a mob is 2 pejoratives. The masses can never become a people while they act like a mob."

The Move Organization, also had this 2 say about political functionaries like Jessie Jackson, and other fearful blacks, that:
"THESE ARE THE SAME DUMB ASS NIGGERS THAT ARE BEGGING FOR FAVORS FROM THE SAME SYSTEM THAT OPPRESS THEM!"

I say this to say these favors were in instances, such as these examples. The legendary Mutulu Shakur, and the famous political prisoner Geronimo Pratt. Both of these men sought justice and relief from Amerikkka's **kangaroo kourtz**, and a konstitution that has no empathy or respect 4 **NIGGERS**.

Thee exception was not by militancy, even though that was their perspective and still is but by book as Huey Newton, preached 2 his

Panther Party in which these two men were members of once upon a time, and also by Dr. King, and his court's sacrifice 4 Civil Rights.

One cannot seek peace, justice, or anything else when one calls the system cynical, diabolical, oppressive, a Fascist state etc. If one decides 2 defend the kountry, then one should be able 2 utilize their kountry's benefits, but if one is compelled to go against its coverment and leadership than one should not request from its enemy happiness, sympathy, and love. A revolutionary terrorist must accept fate, 4 it was he/she who voiced and acted in opposition.

It allowed Geronimo Pratt, 2 be released from prison as well as Mutulu Shakur, 2 finally get to see the light of day by this integration which many blacks are still against or fools to the fact.

Assata Shakur, escaped because she knew that the system wanted 2 kill her or to possibly have her grow old inside the walls of prison, and like a militant she used another method 2 aid her in her freedom, not by kourt house remedy, but by holding kourt by the streets yet even though she did things this way, she still uses integration by way of selling her novel 2 the publik, and using the kracker kreated internet.

Afeni Shakur, studied while in prison the law to be able to get nutritious food and exoneration, although an ex-gang member, turned activist, made into a **politikil prisoner**, she realized that everything can't be won by a gun but also with the pen.
This,
she learned was the white man's rule of politikil process utilized by a black woman who would one day birth a son Tupac Amaru Shakur, in the world of not just to a black kommuniti, but a world at large rather than a jail cell.

By the integrated system her son became a multi-millionaire, by Dr. King's kombatancy. And although 2pac, valued black people he rapped and voiced 2 all not just his race but all who are oppressed.

The origin is konsidered single kombat not mass, because the war is both within and without. Politikil asylum has no junction with what is taking place in the midst of revolutionary warfare. Politikil Asylum is an exile not a konfrontation or forefront fight....so those like Assata Shakur, can only give an indication of the war though she still has earned her ashes that immortalize the martyrz of all kolors who've read about her rather from a feminist, point of view or a revolutionary acceptance.

This is what makes the new integration crucial in this day and age, because like in Saul Alinsky's prediction, the war doesn't come with the lime light like King allegedly came to Chicago, but unlike Saul Alinsky's analysis that the outsider should come than should disappear, is a rookies mistake, because 4 one thing, revolution is not a business that people can just build up and then sale then it's on 2 the next project those are merchant koncepts and Arnerikkklan's ideology, of lets help others in their kountry then evacuate when they use our doctrine at a said price. This is what keeps kountries economikally crushed because we'd rather integrate armies 2 remodel citizens here and elsewhere and build infrastructures rather than the people of these kountries unity on their terms.

Now we kontinue to have haters of politicians and business which hate 2 face its populo with the real truth...only with the **hidden agenda**, which alwayz comes with the heroik speech and sinister smile. Therefore, the wargame is centered around universal appeal and socialism, which they propagandize as a kommuniti based Democracy. This is a polity rather than a politik, by separating the masses we have endorsed socio-politikil tactiks, in other words again we have been divided and konquered. Which means that it's relating 2 or involving a kombination of social and politikil factors. It's also socio-psychologikil, which is a kombination of social and psychologikil factors which brings us back 2 our exploitation, as they experiment and revert our way of thinking back to their science and scientifik ways of psychologikil warfare.

This framework was kreated by sociologist for those of you who don't understand or don't know what sociology is. It is a scientifik study of social institutions and social relationships and its developmental structures, interactions, kollective, and systematik study of behavior of organized groups.

To summarize it, it is an analysis of human beings, as a functioning whole and how its institutions relate 2 or with the **rest of society**. So by comprehending the new system of "**ORDER,**" INTEGRATION'S GAME OF WAR YOU MUST SCRUTINIZE THE DAILY T.V. INFORMERCIALS, LIKE CHRISTIAN ONLY.COM, FARMERS ONLY.COM, BLACKS ONLY.COM...CoverGirl, Kemi, cosmetics for blacks etc. Again separatism...**DIVIDE AND KONQUER**, but all the while re-konstructing the ideology of integration, 2 reorder races, kulture, and klassizm.

Face book, Instagram, My Space, etc., is a social media assault to distract young and old minds. The war allows commentary to view and show whose listening and watching our daily interactions.

This registers in the system and the koverment keeps a klose watch on those who are most popular and able to influence. And these application designers kreate audio, visual effects so they can use slogans and new double speak street terms, etc., all 2 produce a different form of world domination. This way there can be no more Assata Shakurs, in politikil exile because of tags left behind...and this way no one can stay off the grid.

Keep the grid up and catch the fools which are us the world population, who are prone to accepting what's before them. Now we eat up these audio visuals who teach us these attitudes and actions of separatism and unification through gang life, because the thoughts are sent directly 2 us by our new world leaders.

These are the mentors of both the old and young. They kontrol the movements of their followers, and they connect us 2 what has now been dubbed the **World Wide Web**: Surplus these clothing lines and shoe lines. Steal, murder, rob, sell narcotics, and kreate your street cred off of them.

It is a reinventing of the masses, a video game with more (GB). It's a phychologikil warfare that keeps the world's attention and its mobility and immobility stationary or functioning like robots rather than like human beings. So now China, can instantly influence multitudes, unlike when Dr. King, and Malcom X, was in position of influence. The new challenge is how 2 set the stage?

What the masses fail to adhere 2 is that, when books like these are published and the people have understood the universal language of terrorist revolution, and how it's politics work, once these workings start 2 intertwine its way into the very fabrics of our lives and social networks, the businessmen and koverments begin to shut it down and start setting restrictions on the social network. Look at what Google is trying 2 do in China right now. It is readying its people 4 a **censored version of its model**. These people's form of integration has come to function like H.I.V. AND AIDS. What was once free or free accessibility, now is prohibited. Now we are limited and have to pay. What was once a great advertising tool and a marketing strategy 2 be seen, sold, and heard 2 promote one's goods all of a sudden there are laws being put into motion 2 screen all who come or choose 2 visit and be a part of our lifestyles the establishment don't want that, they want us 2 rely on their system's version of societal support.

Has no one sat down 2 ponder the specifics of such terms as **Web Site, or Web Page**? Spiders spin webs 2 catch and kill their prey. Our koverment has concocted a web, a world wide web of artificial lines and fiberoptic linkages 2 kapture, spin, and kill us. But it spins it's concepts and teach us that Bill Gates, and Steve Jobs, were multi-million and billionaires so that we can't comprehend their social agenda of our eradication. They found these scientists, and fund these scientists, so they can be the builders of our mental mazes....and then once the web is up an running, they dispose of the minions. **Paid Programming**, is it all starting 2 make sense now? Hasn't anyone noticed the titles of our t.v., programs?

Power, How 2-Get Away With Murder, Blacklist, Blackish, Lucifer, Satisfaction, Quantico, Blindspot, etc., Modern Family, Meet The Browns, Queen Sugar, And If Loving U Is Wrong. How is it that no one seems to have caught on to this, or these rapper's album titles? Church In The Streets, Jesus Piece/peace, Yesus, Watch The Throne etc.

They are virtually endless with satanic rituals, yet it is sold 2 both the old as well as the young, and no one is telling anybody to turn that stuff off. The older generation is worse than the youth, **everybody seems to be lost**!

The people young and old are dancing to it, exchanging sexual favors 4 it, and 2 it. They made musik 2 mock **Holy** terms such as **As-Salamu-Alaykum** homie. Black Muslims endorse this.... they encourage it, yet not one **AL-QADEA terrorist killed French Montana, Wale, Ricky Rosae, or Di Khaled**, 4 using it as a joke, and defaming **Allah's Noble words**.

Music is unlawful or **Haram**, in **Islam**, yet Muslims that are born Muslim, and in Muslim kountries, help finance many of these record companies. Whites are entertained by it, the Latin community, is utilizing it, and are captivated by it as well. **But it is the blacks who are killed behind it for both positive, and negative reasons**. Yet the Asians, are engrossed in it because it is **Big Business 4 everybody except NIGGERS**!

This creates the politikil poles. This is the ambition which manipulates and monopolizes the koverment's Civil Rights Movement not ours. Our integration is moving at a much slower pace than theirs is. Fans are impressed with Selena Gomez. The world is about who you are, or who you are, seen as versus like in James Meredith's day, and 2pac's era, of:

"**<u>This Is Who We Are, and this is who we got to be, and this is what we got to do</u>**."

Who are women like Susan Rosenburg, or Sojourner Truth? No one that the masses know especially in the younger generations. The new game is **<u>fuck them</u>**, and once that remark was introduced, it became the inner circle's mantra that our youth strongly allows to be their all-in hope and decision making, versus the old order of choose your friends wisely, and don't follow the crowd.

It used to be **<u>Be Your Own Woman Or Man</u>**, therefore these newer guidelines are formulated 4 these young generations, where it is now instant gratification, while the drug era, use 2 have a fast but slower impact on the masses esp., the black people of this nation. It destroyed communities by layers, but now the computer era, destroys households by plaguing everyone for the technological age has infiltrated us worldwide. These drugs have become commercialized, but they are no longer narcotics.... they are chemicals which are now seeming better than the natural drug it 'self. Therefore, drugs are only a fraction of what use 2 be a big fuss. A kilo of cocaine is no longer in its pure form from Columbia, or Mexico, it goes thru labs 2 be cut and redesigned 2 appear as, but it is not what it appears to be. The low budget drug dealer has no clue, neither can the trained eye of the **<u>Baller, or Boss</u>** detect the product because it is able to withstand the average drug purity tests.

The simple reason why this has come about is because your coverment has created a market and a mass generation of fiends who now support **synthetiks**! The design of the war has transformed itself into a science not the art we all once knew. The psychologikil game is now who, and what is popular 4 that moment without anyone realizing that the initial drugs are no more.

The sweep can change dramatically currently without having to struggle or wait for certain periods. The revolution is a diversified machine. It is a thing to say, no longer a cause 2 uphold.

It is similar 2 the old record players, versus a cd player, or a cassette player, versus a MP3 player. Technology can now multitask, like the revolutions in the past use 2 be able 2 do yet the difference between revolution and technology is the fact that technology has evolved, and revolutions have failed to advance.

2day the revolution is fun and games, no longer life and death in the eyes and, minds of the., people esp., the youth. There is no more discrepancy/privacy, the entire foundation has been modified into a Marxist State. There are no more real people in real positions watching over our children, whose world has been opened to much more than just violence, sex, and drugs.

The slogans of the protesters have been severely altered. What use to be: **<u>NO JUSTICE, NO PEACE,</u> has regressed into a more inferior message that doesn't have the same effect <u>as RESISTANCE AND WAR</u>**, 4 the black race has favored: "**<u>NO PEACE, NO PUSSY</u>**!"

The revolution is no longer about **<u>LOVE</u>**, it's about comparing the **<u>New World, 2 The Old One</u>**. At one time in the ghetto and suburb communities, the neighbors, and street urchins, protected our children, not the state. Now these states are refusing to look after our lost kids, because the kountry and world opinion, are starting 2 kontrol every fiber of our lives, thinking, etc., through politiks, and propaganda.

These politicians have taken these welfare programs and drastically changed them. They have entered our homes and have taken hostage our household by dismantling the principles of it so that they can make laws **especially** 4 our kids 2 be able to fight against their parents. In the 1960's and 70's, the gangs wanted better than what they had in the slums, and this is why they listened and gravitated 2 Malcom X.

The middle klass elite, wanted better education, better jobs, land, affordable housing of adequate definition, and equal rights so **blacks** joined both the Nation Of Islam, and the Civil Rights Movement under King.

In this era of popularity, the people listen 2 Barak Obama, and Weezy F. Baby, not because they can relate to going to college like these two individuals have, graduating and majoring in yeah you guessed it **Propaganda, and Politiks**, and what I mean by propaganda is they majored in **PSYCHOLOGY**.

The youth relate to Lil Wayne, due to his drug addiction, and his initiation into the blood gang, and let's not 4get him shooting himself. In the younger generation's eyes these two individuals are considered cool and one of them.

Our kids and the masses of people no longer assess their leadership. Their leaders are assessing them. These 2 favorites of Amerikkka, and abroad, are our leaders and the so-called **faces of our unity, and kulture**.

They can say to the public: "let's all purchase strawberry filled chocolate cupcakes, post it online, and within ten minutes 50,000 to 1 million or more people would all agree to buy strawberry filled chocolate cupcakes. Yet who listens to **John Afrika**, when he made the statement:

"**THE TRUTH IS FREE, IT AINT 2 BE SOLD!**"

But our koverment used people like 2pac, Master p, and Snoop Dogg along with countless others to reverse John Afrika's words to fit their propaganda on the masses by exploiting shit like this:

"**THE GAME IS TO BE SOLD. NOT TO BE TOLD!**"

Yes, the famous 2pac Shakur, the son of Black Panthers who orientated Shakur, with all his real nigga magnetized glory utilized this slogan. Kaptivated by the fast cars, women, and jewelry, yet screwing around with the establishment the reality came to bite him in his ass. He too chose **the** wrong friends which landed his black ass in prison. He too like Huey Newton, forgot the revolutionary way until it had to break him in, which in return led him back to that conscious terrorist.

It's no more "ALL EYES ON ME," he leaves that party and bullshit mentality and dies to give us a 12-track masterpiece......
MAKAVELI DA DON KILLUMINATI 7th DAY THEORY.

Again, it's no more Christopher Wallace's, Party and Bullshit, it's Makaveli, the new reinvented and reincarnated. It's back 2 **Strictly For My N.I.G.G.A.2** it's **Me Against The World**, **it's POLITIKIS** it's back to 1831 and the Exodus....meaning Nat Turner the terrorist and killing off the establishment!

It's the thinker, the revolutionary terrorist, it's no longer the young black male of THUG LIFE, it's the **manchild**, it's the death of 2pac. It's what was explained in a book written about Malcom X entitled: **In Our Own Image**, edited by Joe Hood, in chapter one it states:

> "There were two mask of Malcom X,".......

The first one simply needs to be changed.
The second one is the mask, Malcom is X'd out.......

Malik will speak for our new kommuniti, the one without the Honorable Elijah Muhammad's teachings.

The second mask EL' Shabazz, has something to say. The old prisoner and Nation Of Islam convert which is the first mask it's movement has passed. We are in transition alwayz...black people still provide the example today only because so many of us still die younger than we should and live far more difficult than we should just because of who we are.

Our talk will lead us to no valuable solution if the politiks involved is directly changing our characters 2 keep us komfortable in stagnated positions. It is not clearing away the obstacles for the people in general; These unprofessional profiteers are our problems we are paying for our own downfalls as a integrated society, and beware this new politikil thinking might-will-result in a complete reworking of the very idea of black people and will put it to rest, such as we might like any people evolve and die...evolve and die evolve and die.

Chevron said:

> **"We must not allow routine 2 set in, terror is a form of militant kombat...a form of war...whoever military methods are outdated, exposes themselves 2 defeat, so in internal warfare we must master modern techniques if terror is 2 remain TERROR, in it's true sense."**

Or like Johannes Most reverberated:

> **"MURDER THE MURDERERS!"**

Trevon Martin isn't a martyr, neither is Freddie Gray, nor was Michael Brown. They were as Malcom X, himself said they were: **NIGGERS who are the real victims of Democracy**. There is no true fight for them, they're instant deaths, equal to fads in an economy whose short sighted on what is the real definition of society. **LAB RATS!**

They were killed because it was us who killed them. The police didn't pull the trigger, we…did. George Zimmerman did what he was supposed to do…**HE FOUND A IGNORANT TOO KOMFORTABLE IN AMERIKKKA, BLACK YOUTH AND LYNCHED HIM**.

The stores may burn, the footage may kapture the speeches, tears, trials, etc., but what it doesn't show is the educated educating the youth, and other remedies 2 kombat false integration, and 2 orchestrate the masses until we terrorize the establishment's economik development, imagery, and politikil pressures.

These organizations don't show restraint, order, or true militancy. What it does show is dumb ass blacks...northern and southern urban and suburban slaves who have paved the way 4 this kontinual outbreak, throughout this kountries inner cities, and rural areas. It is you who have paved the way for this 2 happen. It teaches the terrorist revolutionary 2 observe the kounter-kulture. It validates the deaths of dummies, rather than souljahs.

The terrorist revolutionary looks 4 weak links in the armor of the protectors of this cynikil nation. The IRB was similar the physikil force group, or Irish Republikin Brotherhood, also known as the Fenians, which started around 1858, as a klassikil insurrection group. Like them in a way, we believe in the capacity of small armed vanguards who can energize and feed people into open rebellion, but their difficulties were how 2 organize in **secret**, to avoid police surveillance, and choosing the correct moment or instance to raise the revolt.

They tried to follow free masonry 2 incorporate the sequence so that they could carefully kontrol their levels of initiation, but their biggest problem was a secret organization could do little 2 prepare the people 4 the insurrectionary moment. It had 2 hope that what it presumed to be the innate popular sense of the need for independence, would be enough 2 spread the spark of **Armed Action**, 2 send the masses up against the guns of the coverment.
Yet let's examine this logic in the new integration, our integration...the playing field has already been set into motion, by the founding mothers and fathers of the Civil Rights Movement. The C.R.M., gave us the people of all races, and religions 4 the past fifty plus years. We have already been businessmen and women, to militant organizations familiar with all kinds of small arms, shotguns, and automatic rifles.

Some of us want 2 defend the real kountry, not this fictitious one, while others contemplate true religious freedom from the oppression of other religions, koverments, and sects/people of their own kind. Some want relaxation and peace, not wanting another war, but we must face the reality that oppression though forced upon us is forcing us 2 "Know Our Neighbors." Therefore, why shouldn't we take advantage of the strategy that our coverment is using against us. By the way this is also Christian gospels/scriptures.

There's a saying that I came across by Yoritomo in a book called **Dangennes**, where he says:

> "O' divine art of subtlety and secrecy....through you we learn to be invisible; through you inaudible...and hence we hold the enemy's fate in our hands...The struggle 4 life more and more arduous, and the power of our hidden faculties should expand in accordance with every growing, necessities."

We go looking for love on internets, and all kinds of dating sites and services. We find quirky nerd functions 2 attend. We still own some farmlands, while many farmers surrendered 2 the demands of **eradication from their** koverment, 2 eat and survive in a konforming manner. Few withstood—the pressure and we thank you all 4 that, but since the koverment wishes to push you out off the land...**your land**, then why not we all pull our resources 2gether, both black, Hispanic, and white, farmers. You all can help save your lands by selling your goods to us the revolutionaries, and not only that you can rent us your land certain parts of course, so that our cells can train 4 the strike against our oppressors. War if we truly understand it also causes opportunities so that one can gain monetary due 2 supply and demand, fear of starvation and the local markets, and grocery stores will sell out, so that leaves you. **HELP TO SUPPLY THE REVOLUTION, HELP THOSE WHO ARE THINKING ABOUT YOU YOUR FARMS, AND YOUR FAMILIES, WHICH IN THE KOVERMENT'S EYES ARE NOTHING TO THEM BUT SLAVES WHO WORK THE LAND**, and this is what they don't want you to know.

Here I'm not excluding you Rastafarians either, because wasn't you allotted land in your precious Ethiopia? By non-other than King Salasie....so why are you still in Jamaica, in poverty, why aren't you. traveling 2 a place where you can build your families and resistant forces, if these are your lands, allotted to you than **Help Support Your Freedom Fighters So That We All Can Enjoy Our Time Here On Earth**. You do know that we are here for you, 2 serve you and ourselves because we are all revolutionist?

Wasn't it said that:

> "All men can see the tactics whereby I conquer, but what no one can see is the strategy out of which victory is **evolved**."

1. Rather than spying on your neighbors, invite them over as guest in your home. Open the relationship up 4 **BBQ's**, dinner, brunch, or whatever. Why be coaches 4 little league, and professional sports, when it should be more important to us rather than the kountry, school, and Uncle Sam.

Bring the unheard-of religious leaders together. Weed out the fake suppliers of salvation, and doctrinized dictatorship like Dr. King did. Why diet and exercise just to fit into a sleezy dress, or mini skirt, all to look crazy later if you get raped? Why not use these fitness trainers 2 get us healthy to fight? We don't need media coverage telling the world what we are doing to get our goals accomplished. All of you who are flipping property, invest in them, you can cause them to be safe houses for our-future fugitives.

Fuck Uber, not as a company, but using it as a cab to get from A to B, naw...let's turn Uber into a carpool. We can teach them about terrorism, and revolutionary warfare. All it takes is for one 2 create alliances to be able to spread the **Holy Language**, throughout the land that we the people alone make **Holy**. Get out the hearing range of your koverment, because it's time to talk terrorist strategies. All you drug dealers with trap houses, stop making it about money only, learn how to push things other than drugs through the community. Turn the trap house into halfway houses 4 those who we know is and will be the konvicted klass, coming home and ready to go to war with the establishment. Or start transforming the ghetto streets into militre academies, so that our youth and children can understand what 2 use our currency for, because it is not to buy diamonds, cars, and women. It's to purchase land, and artillery, in all places around the world not just here in Amerikkka.

All you grocery store cashiers, you can put leaflets in the bags, and boxes of the customers you serve. Toss in press kits, if anyone ask, you know nothing about it. This goes for your local diners, fast foods spots, to you soul food places, club owners, etc., invite guest there to sing, do **poetry**, rap, training the community how to organize so that your places of business can operate like a business is suppose 2, and not like a hole in the wall hang out spot where kriminals and violence accompany it. I'm not going to sit here and lie 2 you. This revolution is, not, about owning businesses, or continuing to build up Amerikkka. That's still aiding our oppressors and oppression in this kountry, and I can't do that. This is about us owning up 2 our responsibilities. Our residents, and residences, shouldn't be victimized and vandalized, robbed, extorted, or burned down. Those who do this to their people and their homes etc., should receive some of the worst treatment one can think of.

You gang members should be shooting where those who sleep good at night in their double king beds with no worry of death or the consequences that they should be receiving but aren't, after they have been fucking over the masses for a long time.
You
should be robbing their stores. Their Sacs, or Sack 5th Avenue, Louis Vuitton, etc., in broad day light. Our neighborhoods should be receiving lots of relief after so long of a volatile nature.

It is our obligation 2 have our neighborhoods understand what peace, and silence is, so that our children's prayers and people who have been suffering night and day due to your reverse roles, and lack of comprehension of what life and G-d, truly is. Our kids, and many people want their voices to be able to reach heaven, so that they can thank and praise G-d, 4 his assistance, and his guidance for returning us all into the human beings that he alone created us 2 be rather than the savages we have become due to self-destruction, and politikil oppression. Our people shouldn't be screaming and panicking, crying out in an outrage because we can't wrap our thoughts around the situation laid upon our shoulders that we alone have given up staying slaves, and in these master's eyes always the inferiors.

You schoolteachers, scouts, politicians, politikil priznors, of all kolors and shapes...privileged, to unprivileged, what does it mean to have an educational background, if you can't come to the realization of where we are. You have 2 see what true integration can do 4 us, not the (U.S.), that governs these policies to depopulate our lands and under populate our races. **This Is integration On A Much Deeper Level!!!**

This is 4 those police enforcers to, who see the bullshit in their precincts. Those who say that they are protecting and serving, are brutalizing and discriminating, those whom they feel don't deserve 2 be in this kountry free and wealthy. This is the time where you step outside of your comfort zones, and strike to make a difference with the people who have grown tired of the daily harassment and injustices done to them. We the people got to stop spending our money on high end cars. **WE PURCHASE ONE BRAND NEW CAR, SUV, OR TRUCK**, when we can buy two or four auctioned vehicles.

You Latin Amerikkklans, are the future mechanics of the United Stakes...volunteer to fix these vehicles up. Help contribute to the cause because your race is in question as well. **Kill Off That Old Mentality Of Pimp My Ride**, because there won't be any streets to ride on safely if we as the people don't come 2gether. This simply does not need media

coverage, and there are no need 4 placing ads in the establishment's newspapers for this what is called revolution is not entertainment, neither is it hired help.
We are not the fucking, vanguard groups of old. The time has come not to be slaughtered sheep, following after and looking 4 one leader, because those days are over.

Let us be of one mind, body, and religio-militant-politiks. The children are our next line of defense, but that's only if we place them in constructive positions. It's time to train them in survival. We must understand their views and modes of thinking so that we can value another's abilities because the people when politikly, and religiously humane, then and only then can we reach the adults and youth that we want to become in each other's eyes.

Those who refuse to change or convert with no thought must be **TRIALED**, which only means terminated. It is that simple. We cannot worry about what we don't have because trust me what I'm telling you is, **fact**, **WE HAVE PLENTY**!

Let's use their most precious holiday, which is "**Christmas**," to our advantage. Let us build a terrorist structure so vast that it puts the **ALL-SEEING EYES OUT OF THEIR SOCKETS** "

Let us start comprehending the **Order Of Operationz**, since we all have mixed bloodlines, and have been raped over the centuries, which has caused us 2 be physically integrated. That's why we can't say **all black everything**, it is now where the phrase can really resonate with the masses, when we say: **"POWER TO THE PEOPLE!"**

Your time is up prostitutes, pimps, homosexuals, male and female **molesters**, rapist, crooked kops, coverment officials, pedafouls, I know it is spelled **pedophiles**, 2 those who wish to remain kowards, and powerless criminals.

For the name of the game has always been education, 4 if you properly educate the people, **NOW THEY'LL WANT WAR**!

CHAPTER 3

2 DRAFT A SCARECROW

If we must purchase cemeteries, or have 2 go inside graveyards 2 train, then so be it. Our kountries have been building and rebuilding over our lands since they were assembled.

So, us treading over our dead to fight out of respect 4 their lives and deaths is considered admirable. This is not for the feint hearted. Maybe then by some of us understanding where we are, and all the many people that have died due to our fear of **standing** up, will instill the necessary **confidence**, some need 2 strengthen the cause.
This should show our foolish asses, that if we mess up, the next headstone will read your name and sob story revealing that you were not willing 2 see little babies grow up without having to face tyranny, and depopulation experiments like **abortion**, and **mass murder**.

We can't keep sitting around or standing around out in the cold shuffling our words through xerox machines, like in previous times, but in the words of Prince Peter Kropotkin;

> "Actions which compel general attention' led the new idea 2 seep into people's minds. A single act could in a few days make more propaganda, than thousands of pamphlets. Above all, it awakens the spirit of revolt. It breeds daring; and soon it becomes apparent that the **established order**, does not have the strength supposed, the people obscure that the monster is not so terrible as they thought."

First is the mandate for the strong and knowledgeable, 2 aid the weak on the world front or the level of the locals and individual. The issues are not with force nor armz, but it is strategy. The **conduct of war**

consist in the planning and konduct of fighting. Fighting consists of greater and lesser numbers of acts each complete in itself-entitled engagements.
Let me clarify for those of you who are afraid to **experiment** with guns and explosives. A terrorist revolutionary isn't just a person who indoctrinates, trains, educates, shoot people, or blow them—up or themselves, cars etc., a terrorist revolutionary **is a mind**! He/she thinks of ways 2 fit inside the **grand skeem of things**. Rather it's by being a liaison, secretary, nurse, doctor, driver, computer wiz- (which includes hackers), teachers, host and hostesses etc., etc.

There are all or many forms of being an active terrorist. This gives rise 2 the completely different attitude in regard to planning and executing these physikil and deadly kontacts themselves and coordinating each event with the others in order 2 further the objective of the war. (1), has been called tactiks, and the other strategy. Panic is not in the revolutionary's arsenal.

No matter the issue, the terrorist should always stay calm. The police have you cornered...the plan is going to shit, whatever the case may be, take deep breaths make no sudden moves, keep 2 the training. If by chance you cannot avoid being captured, then I advise that you martyr the situation.

Never take an innocent bi-standard hostage. Always have arms at your disposal, which may inklude floss, guitar string, knives, gun, pills that slow down the heartbeat to make it seem that you have no pulse. Never engage a full enemy team unnecessarily!

When being pursued on foot, never stay above ground. Alwayz, keep on as garments waterproof materials, meaning fabric, wind proof, water wicking/order wicking/resisting clothing no exceptions.

Odor proof clothing inkluding socks, and under wear. This keeps the hounds (dogs), from detecting your scent. A kompany called Scarpa, sells a bullet proof boot for **$250.00**, it is a hiking boot that has a soft-shell sock liner, and memory foam. It is superbly komfortable. The boot is called **SCARPA ZODIAC PLUS GTX**, go to **scarpa.com**.

Learn 2 endure heat...learn to stay cramped up in tight places for extended periods of time. Purchase watches in the likes of Casio Pathfinder, or their ProTrek time pieces. You want a low-lit compass accessorized watch with low or no alert function.

4 in war, no one needs 2 ever give themselves away, for it takes (1), glimpse from the enemy to be the kill shot. Cell phones are no good in close quarters for kommunication purposes, use Wi-Fi tech sneakers, and or satellite phones. Satellite phones are untraceable, and alwayz has service. Illegal, but who gives a fuck, we're terrorist. Yet let's make one thing clear, never put your full trust in no kind of technology, so then if you decide to not use the satellite or any other kind of phone…you have the green light.

To reduce frequency traps and signal jammers, never stay on the phone 4 more than 20 seconds. You shouldn't be on the phone any way. Throw away phones are cheap but if used right **effective**.

If need be, have three cell phones so that the lines of kommunication can stay open without interference of the enemy. (1), to make kontact, (2), to answer the awaited response, and lastly (3), for back up in case the call drops, or there's no signal, but this is for emergency only.

Wrist walkie-talkies, are good when cellphone jammers are in place, so make sure that you have them available and or on your person when in close quarters. Never purchase a new vehicle unless it's to infiltrate and carry out a mission, due to tracking, and low jack devices.

Never register anything in your own name! Credit cards, bank accounts, rental cars, homes, apartments, not even a magazine subscription. **THE TERRORIST IS A MASK, WITHOUT USING A MASK, SO ALWAYZ BLEND IN, NEVER STICK OUT**.......

Suspicious activity or Looks causes investigations and anonymous tips, so go about your day as an ordinary citizen, as if the love of life is all that pleases you. Never be seen with more than 2 or three people meaning cell members at a time not unless there's a party, function, such as a marriage, baby shower, fashion show, etc., where you can blend in and out and not draw tooo much attention to yourself.

And when around those two or three cadres, make sure that you are integrated at all times with exceptions when one is in white states where southern hospitality isn't as generous as it is in others. If pro-black, you have to bite the bullet alwayz be accompanied by fairly aged white and light skinned individuals.

If white, never be flanked by too many black people esp., stern looking black males. Try 2 use if possible, women, not just black but a diverse group of cell members. When tucked away, never get too comfortable. Wherever you are stationed at never make a lot of noise, only enough to let people know that you are alive and living there. Be courteous and semi friendly, which means in so many wordz **be neighborly**, 4 Amerikkkins, are very nosey people.

You must act like them; you must act normal by all meanz.

You must value your role, so to your theatric careerist this is where you really take your kraft to the heights that no stage or screen can ever take you. If you have an accent it is best that you not be engaged in situations that will cause people to pick up on the fact that you are a foreigner, esp., if you are an Arabian/Muslim. The mechaniks of your talents play a major part in the tactik turning out smoothly.

Chefs should utilize and get very familiar with poisonous plants, bugs/insects, fish, etc. Alwayz with the appropriate dosage, no less than what is necessary because these things do show up in autopsy reports, so be thorough as possible. To you youth rather middle schooler or what have you, get familiar but not too familiar with the siblings of the said adversary.

No matter if you are a konfidant, sweetheart, paintball buddies, roller skating friends, soccer champions, you get my point, approach all targets with mild dealings ... 4 you must kontrol without kontrolling.

One mere sweat bead can cause red flags to be raised, and aborting the mission may cause extreme difficulty, so allow yourself 2 take it easy being ordinary kidz not young assassins.

Birthday party for the toddler, Chucky Cheese, for the 9, and 7, year old’s...it's all in the pre-packaging. Presentation brings flawless victories. Home rearers, plausible poison on the gift wrap, and or on the toy. The punch can wipe out the entire party.

Alwayz remember the punch, water bottles, or wine glass and or bottle, liquor, to the self-serving of pigs in a blanket, to just basic cheese and crackers. You caterers must learn how to adapt to banquets. Bouquets, ballrooms, gyms, to the floral arrangements at weddings. "**Katering 2 Your Needs**," should alwayz be your slogan.

Use questionnaires for subtle engineering! Learning the enemy's likes and dislikes, allergies, etc., should be asked to accommodate the proper strategy. The terrorist revolutionary should take jogs through the park, and through the neighborhood, and other terrains 2 study their environment and to learn their future target's habits, checking for blind spots, or possible locations 4 safe houses or getaway routes 2 places of termination.

The terrorist revolutionary adopts society and adapts 2 society never trying to change it but to destroy it. That was and is sooo many "terrorist," mistakes.

Although antiquated maps of your areas are better than GPS, get acquainted with the old things of life. Not saying that Google Map, or Onstar, and other digitized services aren't good tools of technology it's just that a lot of times All The Roads, aren't alwayz placed in the digital version, and when the **SYSTEM SHUTS DOWN**, which it most definitely will, those of you who tried the short cut way will be **SHIT OUT OF LUCK**!

A true revolutionary terrorist takes couple's retreats, and such klasses. They allow their children 2 be boy and girl scouts. Terrorist revolutionaries, go hiking, mountain klimbing, skiing, and everything else that these so-called terrorists don't do, **WE DO**!

It's konsidered "**observation training**," there's no such thing as not a part of it. The terrorist revolutionary doesn't recruit we do not speak our minds or our ideology 2 anyone unless it is granted 2 undergo total transformation. Traveling is a must!

Mobility is the terrorist...mobility is terrorism. We must train our children from the toddler stage, that they are born and bred 2 be lifers of the revolutionary cause, not murderers. We must train our children at this tender age how they are never 2 talk about this way of life. Our cells must alwayz remind them of the consequences.

They must be trained early that they are born and bred 2 be the future, not the fabrication of genetiks. For these fictitious generations of all races are out to exterminate them and us, because we are not like them, they are the krowd, and we are the individual. They must be taught that they are our children, not our oppressors they belong to us and not these hate filled kountries in which we temporarily live.

They need 2 know that they are ours and it is us who love them. They belong to us so treat our children with respect and show them dignity and honor through action. They need to know that the war will kontinue through them and their seedz, and their seedz. We are not politicians of any kind, and we do not support the advancement of surface politiks.

But we do become their secretaries 2 know their families, files, schedules of all kinds, associates, birthdays, tag and favorite numbers. We have to know as many secrets as possible, and everything that there is to know about these korruptors of life and religion. We must get this through our heads that everything isn't about hacking information from someone's komputer...no... every cell member has to come to grips with this motto that:

MUST SITUATIONS ARE ALWAYZ HANDZ ON!

The terrorist revolutionary understands that it is best to personalize rather than trying to investigate every little thing about those that we are targeting even after we consider the option of computer and media footage. The terrorist revolutionary studies characters, as well as, characteristics. With the thought of (what makes our enemy tick?)

We study their smiles, laughter, interaction with family, friends, business partners, and associates. What kinds of clothes do they buy? What is their favorite story or joke to tell?

We're studying them now like scientist would do the human body, and as a businessman would study consumers in the economy, so that we can pre-package a product in which they can't buy or bribe themselves out of, and that product is terror.

We are not selling war...we are knowing our enemies so that we can tailor make an assault that never ends, and 4 us to never cease to amaze. These are small intricate details that these fictitious insurrectionist/ terrorist groups tend to miss.

This teaches us that they are not terrorist, they are not the trusted few.

It is not western paganizm that is robbing them/ us…it is the entire world who can't seem to follow simple basic knowledge. Throughout history we have all been internally sabotaged by our own kind, rather race, religious followers etc. It has alwayz been cowardz in our nations who allied themselves with the coverments of tyranny and oppression. Take Isis, or Al-qadea, consider their tactiks and strategies. What is their purpose, and what has it served?

What real personnel have they kidnapped or assassinated 2 prove that they are really terrorizing? Al-qadea, look at how the name is spelled…Al- Qa- D.E.A. The last three letters of their name tell us who they are Amerikkklan, made. **PUPPETS OF OUR COVERMENTS**. Need more proof? I should hope not!

If indeed their fight is against non-believing Muslims, and tyranny why are they killing innocent women and children oppose to those who are in their kountries killing them, and building tourist vacation spots 4 foreigners 2 violate their holy lands?

These Muslims extremist groups are killing their own kind, these people can't get along 2gether but can pray 2gether at certain prayer times makes no sense whatsoever. They rather kill each other than set aside their differences 2 be able 2 overthrow the enemy who keep them divided so they conquer no one but allow these same **outsiders** to spread propaganda throughout their kountries taking it over bit by bit, until there is no more Islamic unity belief in Allah, etc., only bitterness and strife 2wards each other. Shi'ite, is no better than sunni, but outsiders can see this, but not them. Yet they want people 2 convert over 2 a way of life that can't be at peace with God, or themselves.
This goes to show **us**, that they are not in charge, and that someone else is politically pulling the strings. They are created by the coverment, and the curtain behind it. For they are using these elite's political formula of **Coin-Tel Pro**, which is 2 divide and conquer **us**.
It is a farce, a mere mirage, and it is all propaganda. See it from this

view if need be, Amerikkka, has captured and figured **out** all their key targets, and either assassinated them, imprisoned them, or recruited them. The only major terrorist attack in or on Amerikkklan soil, has been the **World Trade Center. Bullshit**!

You got to be kidding me, all these threats aimed at the U.S., from Fidel Castro, to Kim Jung Un, to the very least Isis. But none of these hardcore guerrillas that came to power by overthrowing Batista, 2 they who formed Al-qadea, and took over their entire Islamic, Arabian dominated regions, couldn't place any kind of harm here?
North Korea, with all their **Nuclear Missiles**, and aggressive tone couldn't pull it off? What about Russia, non-came up with a plot of engagement to seize the times and the moment? We are talking about Communist Cuba, Russia, and the many foes of Amerikkka, no one could place a bomb here and blow up let's say a football stadium, a shopping mall, or cruise ship, come on people really?

Osama Bin Laden was a multi-millionaire, Castro, had his own kountry, along with Kim Jung Un. When England, and Amerikkka, wanted 2 put an end **2 Nazi German** and **Hitlerizm**, they put aside their differences regardless of their past history, and took them to war. And the funny thing about all this is that out of all the places I just named **Cuba**, is the only **Third World Kountry**. We can't in no way shape or form be going 4 this!!!!

Nobody has done anything other than talk, and try to demolish the World Trade Center, which has already been attacked before. Are we alleging that within a **100 years**, or since Pearl Harbor, only the **Twin Towers**, and the part of the **Pentagon**, that's not really considered the **Pentagon**, was attacked?

You do know that the actual Pentagon, is underground, don't you? In Virginia, not above but beneath ground, so how was it attacked? Yet the establishment labels this terrorism. Why does the media cover this bogus spectacle, why 2 keep you in fear? And when this book is read by enough **citizens**, the koverment will strike a devastating blow behind these writings. They say that a lone gunman killed Dr. King, Malcom Little, Lincoln, and Kennedy, and who is this they, that I keep referring 2, is it not your sweet and dearest kountry **Amerikkka, because it sure wasn't a Terrorist Revolutionary** . Not even a **cop**, or a **cabinet member**. This is truly unbelievable, and what's more interesting, is that the people can't see it or figure out 4 themselves that **A M E R I KKK A**, has been doing all the killing of its people since day one.

They don't even make it hard for the masses 2 not understand the constant cover ups put out there in front of **us**. They are the real con artist, they are your true con artist both women and men, not the revolutionary. Adolf Hitler, as was Bin Laden, were multi-millionaires. Hitler from book sells which was **Mein Kampf**, and Osama Bin Laden, from his inheriting his father's construction company. Donald Trump is what a millionaire...so didn't they have the means to bring mass destruction? Oh, and still do, in the coming years. These people have recruited real Islamic believers, the white supremacist, and so on and so forth, and they came up with these people's battle cry all 2 depopulate the kountry of men, women, and children, and to eradicate all their resources in the process. Land, money, and whatever seems of value. These things were done by placing **Democracy**, in the people's minds, and there you have it the future's new **Republic** and Totalitarian coverment. These politicians have broken the real followers of religion and made them konform. And in return allowed them 2 live as long as these broken freedom fighters, religious believers, and tarnished revolutionaries aid them in propagandizing the battle cries to gain religious, and humane, sympathizers.

Notice this in all factious groups the term **financier**, are alwayz present. Bin Laden, was a financier, but he too was being financed. Like the old saying goes "**FOLLOW THE MONEY TRAIL**." Real terrorists belong 2 a unique revolution, not the kind that they show you on television or in the movies.

We are governed by the discipline and structure of shadow warfare. This was the way of the ninja, this is the way of the illuminati, that is the way of the silent but real killers.

Batman, DC's comic hero is Amerikkka's most prized superstar. He is based on the principles of financier and shadow warfare, but his level of training and lack of understanding krime as well as politiks makes him vulnerable 2 milika. He fights villains, he fights his own city and people for respect, but he himself shares no allegiance with the story line of the poor of New York. He is well off with expensive… gadgetry he is one man versus the many. He's money versus a unique power structure which causes him exhaustion, and eventually a kreated character when he battles aliens like superman, but his aliens are a metaphor. This is also how Amerikkka, thinks, Batman, is emblematic of the bastard bloodline. Our methods of warfare cannot be used in degrees like Batman...they are designed 2 kill and destroy and to cause wars that aren't based solely on physikally fighting people.

Yet he uses our way of being two different people the masked menace Batman, and the everyday John Bruce Wayne.
Terrorist revolutionaries are not financiers and heroes, we are simply people who see the bullshit and choose 2 supplant it, exterminate it, annihilate it, or whatever one chooses 2 say about the matter. We will not konform 2 the lifestyles of those who are trying 2 push this dogma upon us.

MARTYRZ,
are of **Immortalized Influence**, which is another tool in the arsenal of the terrorist war chest. But martyrdom is a high honor the influence it's self must come with different angles 2 give the people faith in the cause not hope.

We must learn the value of the microphone, the pen, and currency. They are what go hand in hand. But money is not our financier, our modes of influence comes by way of the heart, knowing that humanity cannot function like animalz or in a unconscious state.

The kommuniti functions like a business so we must get down 2 business. We build stores but not factories. We are local and international...we don't use emblems on our quality products, which is us and we don't build 4 business, we know that business helps 2 generate people and people want kompanies and owners that they can work with, not just work under, and places of businesses that we can trust.

If this can't be done, then we kill it off and we utilize this way of engagement because it brings our foe 2 us, rather than us having 2 go to them. It allows us to see who our foes are like the proverb goes **"YOU BUILD IT, THEY WILL COME!"**

They will come 2 buy out the small kompanies and their surrounding properties. Look at the history of The United States, the cowboy era, gangster era, gang era, the klan era, the militant communist era, and now your digital era. You alwayz had big kompanies kill it's kountries' citizens.

Rather by buyouts, extortion, mergers, or just plain murder of the small businessman. The owners of the past and landowners of the past was undermined by bank debts, etc., so it made it nearly impossible 2 go 2 war with the big wigs-
but not anymore, because we have people that don't have shit, or we just don't simply give a fuck. Now we have the resources 2 do so. No one survives unless they learn to play the game, and again that game's name is politiks. But what I’m expounding 2 you is **milika**.
I,

will break down the term milika, later, but right now we need you and many others attention to stay on planting seedz. The street term would be konsidered M.O.B., rules, but the gangs and 2pac, the revolutionary rapper coined it **money over bitches**, but that makes no sense whatso ever. I'd rather say:

"**MURDER ON BUREAUKRATS**"

This shit can't be about money and who are these bitches? All the money in the world won't prevent this tyranny. It's the money that has caused all the tyranny on the streets and everywhere else. So basically, these gangstas want us to believe in getting money and let the babies die and rape etc., in the process?

Women are still with Aids, and H.I.V., while the kommunities are still unemployed and the killings of blacks hasn't ceased. Flags or rags are only another indoctrination and emulation of the k.k.k, wearing fabrics 2 strike fear in kolored sections of society. This is why terrorist revolutionary's need to be everywhere and I do mean everywhere. Back up 4 one minute, 2 answer that other question of who are konsidered the bitches?

EVERYBODY WHO IS OPPRESSED INKLUDING THE THUGS WHO ARE DOING THE OPPRESSING!

Terrorist revolutionaries alone must be the future, I'm not saying dictate 2 the world, it simply means protecting our world and our people of all races, from dictators and irresponsible world leaders. So yes, if you have 2 be a cop, FBI agent, CIA person, then you train until you fit the profile. These crooked konsultants did it 2 us, and they did it all the time in the past all the way up until now.

They infiltrate our organizations, so why are we not posing as them? We don't want to be dirty kops, we are not really kops we are simply infiltrating their way of life...not as under covers but as assassins.

Make them fear...like how they got us in fear of wondering who can we trust? This is how you kill them off.

We need 2 familiarize ourselves and families with voice disguisers, blowguns, tranquilizers, video equipment, assault rifles, cross bows, listening devices, etc. Society is a stage, it is our stage and we must perform well. There is always someone watching us but the people in the circle don't know who's who. We just know the signs of our **Character 4mation**.

When their infer red beams and lenses are trying 2 detect our body heat and temperatures, hide behind a big piece of thick mirror. And when their cameras are trying 2 spot us, shine a infer red beam directly in it's eye.

Where that jogging suit and hoodie that prevents camera phones from seeing you to identify you. The clothes that I'm referring 2 is called flashback. It's a special kind of reflective beads that washes out the smart phone's pictures.

It makes you look like a ghost, invented by the dj Chris Homes, who partnered up with Beta Brand, a San Francisco, based crowd funded company whose cost ranges from $40.00 to $1,000.00 dollars. They have these clothes not just in hoodies, and sweatpants, but also scarfs, as well as business suits.

Our vehicles should contain Bridgestone drive guard tires, only because if punctured they still travel up to 50 miles before total deflation. Kops have stinger trooper tire systems priced at $499.00. These are hand developed (spike), systems that are used 2 slow fleeing vehicles down. Made by Federal Signal, they are simply thrown across the road or pulled across by the attached (40), foot rope. It is compact, so we should also invest in them.

Rolled up it is roughly the size of a briefcase and weighs about 9lbs. It's durable, and reusable....it also has a flexible plastic modular base which holds 1101.8 inch hollow steel pikes, all which are easily replaceable. It stretches when thrown out 215.5 ft., and uses rocker arms to tilt the spikes into the tire at the correct angle ensuring maximum penetration. The spikes don't make the tire explode or burst, it just punctures and causes a kontrolled air leak, tires go flat within (20), seconds and that's with collecting **nine** spikes.

The issue or loophole is the pig or yourself can never be more than (40), feet out of harm's way. Then there's Night Hawk, priced at $2,995, this tire puncturing device takes hand deployed spikes 2 a new level with its remotely operated kreation engineered by a Arizona, based Pacific Scientific Energetic materials company.

It comes in a waterproof Pelican case which contains (15), spikes which are linked 2gether 2 extend up 2 (15), feet. From up 2 one hundred ft., away a pig can deploy the system. A replaceable tube or aluminum launch tube costs $175.00), and fires a three-pound drogue, which pulls the strips across the road and drops it in the path of the fleeing vehicle **ALL UNDER 2 SECONDS**.

Once the vehicle runs over the strip, the system's operator can remotely activate a drill motor 2 retract the strip (also under **2 seconds).** A standard (18), volt battery powers it. Both front and rear tires will fully deflate within (40), seconds and that's with suffering (9), puncture holes.

Finally, there's Arrest Net, price **is still unknown**...it is a prototype kreated by Pac Sci Emc. They call it the future of roadside vehicle immobilization. Also powered by a (18), volt battery, the development pod kontains an onboard nitrogen supply and a net rolled up in (rip stop fabric), when remotely activated. The nitrogen is stored at 2300 psi. It inflates tubes sewn into the fabric. You can roll it out and lay it flat on any surface. It holds 96 tire-deflating, barbed stainless steel spikes that are attached 2 a (16), ft., x (16), ft., net made of Dyneema, a high-strength polyethylene material. With cars like the Mitsubishi Eclipse, pushing at (50), mph, driving over it sounds like the airbags are exploding.

Full entanglement of the tires requires (0.5), seconds and (37), feet, stalling the engine, locking up the tires, and bringing the car to a stop in (207), feet. They say that there is no escaping the net, and driving backwards only makes things worse. This product came out in late 2017. It comes in a waterproof case capable being left on the roadside, near border crossings 4 example 4 extended periods of time. Look at these new designs that their using, their suiting up 4 us like we are 4 them.

Columbia, the klothing company has designed a new windbreaker (jacket), that is waterproof...it's called the **Out Dry Ex Diamond Shell**, and it is priced at $400.00. They put their waterproof membrane on the outside of the jacket. A grid pattern of abrasion resistant polymer protects it from the elements, because the membrane is heat fused, with the polymer and the inner fabric layer, it did away with sweating trappin glue.

When you do work up a sweat the inner layer wicks it away through the outer membrane. Columbia, says that this new construction of waterproof works so well that they are planning 2 use it on their down coats.

If this new material is capable of being waterproof/sweat proof (we), need 2 be at their retail stores, charging and or stealing, robbing them to get them pronto. Popular Science magazine, posted an article in May of 2010, that inventors came up with or shall I say they have engineered a portable bomb sniffing tool. It said that when the underwear bomber passed through security no one noticed the (3), ounces of PETN, one of the most reactive explosives, stuffed in his pants. Therefore, they have kreated a new portable chemikil detector, capable of sensing explosive vapors at parts per trillion. They are using this invention at airports. The designers say the same way the aroma of freshly baked cookies fills a kitchen, a hidden bomb usually sheds trace amounts of chemikils in2 the air.

The device developed by Spectra Fluidics, sucks in these telltale chemikils trapping them in microscopic water channels supposedly a lazer then zaps the molecules causing them 2 vibrate and reemit the light in a signature pattern, which a built-in computer kompares them with a library of known substances patterns. In addition to PETN, it can identify less than a nanogram of other explosives, such as ammonium nitrate and nitroglycerine, as well as (**cocaine**), says their vice president.

Future applications of this device include detecting roadside bombs, food contaminants and cancer markers. At the 2010 publishing date of the article, the company was testing the device with the coverment's army. The company is aiming 2 get a $50,000.00, brick sized product 2 the transportation security administration for field testing. They believe that just like a dog's nose their device will even give dogs a run 4 their money.

Some of us should be familiar with Michelin's,Tweel airless tires. They are designed to not catch flats, but what a lot of us do not know is that there is a tire that's similar 2 the Michelin brand's, but these tires use honeycomb-shaped polyurethane spokes 2 absorb shock and withstand gouging rocks and broken glass without getting a flat.
These are the types of kreations in which we need 2 survive certain versions of attack. Even the Bose suspension system which uses electromagnetic motors in place of shocks and springs, it takes off payment travel easy while at the same time improving handling and

making the ride smoother. That's the new trend having a military grade type of suspension but in **Wolf Warfare**, it is solely necessary **because adaptation cost you nothing. EVERYTHING IS IN HOW YOU RESPOND!**

All these pieces can be obtained one way or another, yet keep in mind that they are producing online services 4 a reason. You can no longer raid the neighborhood stores if there are no more stationary stores to shop and or steal from. So to those of you who loot when the riots start, Sorry, them days are at it's end.

That's why it is imperative now 2 not take **4 granted** the time that we have at this very moment.

Stockpile while you still can. Bullet proof all glass, doors, panels etc. All vehicles like I said should be konverted in2 off road style vehicles, not vehicles that detect our mission, but vehicles that are made to be able to withstand the mission. The days of driving Lexus, is over. The times of removing the top of your cars to let the sunshine in is over. Fuck the Aston Martin, and the Bently, not unless it's to get through what the state calls society to be able to exterminate our targets. The Ford Excursion is definitely a truck 2 have in one's arsenal. It's big enough to mount the 240 Bravo, and anti-tank styled weaponry. They just need to be lowered, and reconfigured by way of axels etc.

Especially when it comes down to it's (2), gasoline tanks, this should be konverted into (1), tank not a merger of the tanks, but the utilization of only (1), regular mid-sized truck gasoline/ whatever fuel you choose to use tank.

It is also a must to redefine our fuel koncept, because we best to realize that our koverment will up the Annie on gasoline and diesel fuel prices. Electric cars will not be reliable enough so these options are and should not be permanently stained in our minds. Not saying that they can't get certain goals accomplished, we should have some at our disposal...they can serve as our everyday commute, regardless of if it's ethanol, biofuel, electric, etc., the thing is, we just need 2 figures out a fuel that we can use that won't be expensive and can be able to keep us functioning in whatever kontinent or terrain. If the peanut can be used 4 human consumption and also diversified 4 other experiments/projects, then the task at hand shouldn't be difficult. Alwayz remember that the terrorist is a thinker first, **so use your BRAINZ**!

We must learn to experiment with science, and technology 4 our self-preservation not just accepting what the coverment wants 2 stuff down our throats. People with no formal education or science laboratory have experimented with chemikils 2 make drugs better and harder such as crack cocaine, crystal meth, etc. These social experiments were formulated in kitchens, bathrooms, basements, and hotel rooms. So was the pipe bomb, hydro bombs, etc., etc. All of these were experiments that came from individuals and groups who wanted 2 provide technology and science 2 our general population/masses.

The terrorist revolutionary, was born with the knowledge of trial and error...and we still utilize this way. The known terrorist Johannes Most, in his book "**Science Of Revolutionary Warfare, formally known as (Military Science 4 Revolutionaries**), teaches the revolutionary terrorist, how to make Nitro Gelatine, Nitro Glycerin, and how to test it 2 blow up buildings, all because he experimented 4 the revolutionary cause. We cannot be afraid 2 experiment.

All terrorists aren't 4 partnerships, so no one should expect lone terrorist 2 follow group activity. But if there are terrorist who work as a unit there should be a core member who specializes in bomb making of whatever sort, should this be the case train your fellow members or if it's not.

There is no need to be alarmed about the kops patrolling the web/internet, for people trying 2 find such websites. Work construction, they have old DVD's as well as VHS tapes on demolition, mining, etc., these are all bomb making tools with many low budget techniques which can penetrate society and its way of life.

Study 2 prevent danger or accidents irresponsibly. The revolution needs a terrorist who knows that these wars and experiments takes time. How long, depends on each group/cell, and individual, as well as how bad they want 2 get that point across. So as long as it takes. The terrorist revolutionary is not an attraction, we have a war that needs to advance, the underground or off the grid mentality, needs to spread 2 any and everyone who no longer feels a part of their family, kountry, religion, state, etc.

Our wings should spread because they are our seeds that we alone farm in all nations wanting love, empowerment, employment, all without having to form unions with those not wanting 2 serve their fellow man and or G-d, as a duty with sincerity 2 fight against oppression and injustices.

This is true peace, 2 be able 2 fight 4 what **real** is. 2 be able 2 choose a side and know without any doubt that the decision you made 2 join the side that you're on, is one of real righteousness rather than the fabricated kind.

True peace is not in komfort, it is in work. Peace is a life that is alwayz being disturbed and attacked because of what it stands for.

Pride in the hearts of real believers...a higher consciousness that won't allow deceivers 2 come in and try 2 manipulate our lives like they did 2 Yeshua-Ben-Yosef, (Jesus), 2 you...when he had 2 go against his own friends, and family, along with the people of high position. The same with Moshe, (Moses), to you, Hitler, Muhammad, Martin Luther King Jr., Malcom X, versus the Nation Of Islam, and other countless people who formed brotherhoods or tried to form brotherhoods, to the individual task which they took with hearts who were ready 2 die as a kontribution 2 progression rather than regression and infinite failure.

CHAPTER 4

EXTENDING

No matter,
If you are a terrorist, revolutionary, militant, or a regular common person, one should pre-adventure that when it has come down to change and evolving or just complete separation from those who are unlike **us**, there has always been one man or one woman who came 2 teach a few people so that those loyalists could assist them in spreading their wingz. From the **Bible and To'rah's** perspective, the transformation started with Avraham, to Yitz'chak which spread **2** Iyaakov, who started the **12** tribes of Eretz Yisi' ra' el.

In the underground world, the revolution started with the black militant Malik El' Shabazz, which extended to Huey P. Newton, and Bobby Seale, which spread to become the **Black Panther Party**, which splintered into sects like the **Black Liberation Army**, which gave rize 2 **Tupac and his T.H.U.G. L.I.F.E., Outlaw movement**, which was a younger generation of **Non Konformist**, who were the actual children of these **terrorist revolutionaries**, and their groups.

These organizations were semi based off of the teachings of Mao, Lenin, Trotsky, Che, Engles, Karl Marx, Ho Chi Mihn, and Marcus Garvey.
Che, said it best along with Lenin that:

> "THERE WOULD BE BODIES OF UNDERGROUND UNITS ALL OVER THE WORLD."

But unlike these students, legendz, and bodies of belligerent illiterate trainees and professional **guerrillas**, the game has 2 be changed, along with the machination and playing field.
The gangs had, started something remotely clever. They created sets in

every part of the inner cities, and then extended 2 the suburbs, which by the way was and still remains a beautiful thing, but they got sidetracked and was unable 2 transition from a gang to a cell. Their founders and co-founders, listened to reason and chose at one point 2 be educated by the revolutionary klass and their politiks. Their predecessors were trying 2 establish true groundz with these gangs 2 provide uniformity.

Our enemies were the ones that 4bade our new outlook, and they planted seeds in our thoughts 2 create jealousy and internal strife between the **revolutionary** and **gang culture**. Here lies the issues that undermined the people all 2gether, because our koverment knew that if we united we would be unstoppable. The drugs were pushed on us 2 breakdowns that unity, and it continues to keep **us**, dysfunctional.

We began 2 emulate our oppressors, we **banned** under the cloaks of separate stripes of **red, and blue**, the same kolors of their **White Nationalist Flag**. These politics were in contradiction of the left's methods of operation. We tried to fight with this contaminated counsel which made our battle arrays cheap, and unable to withstand the **cold front**. The gang culture and organization were too criminal, by way of enterprise rather than militarizm. The gangs became **kapitalistik** no longer militant and revolutionary. We began to rob the establishment's banks etc., 2 become **fashionable**, by wearing skinny jeans, Gucci, Chuck Taylor, Nikes, jewelry, Bitch bags, colorful hairstyles etc., 2 keep oppression and oppressive meanz on as well as over the minds of those trapped in **Ghetto Amerikkka, Black AMERIKKKA, White Amerikkka, and the kountry's that want us to not resist, so that our outcome will always be Poverty!**

Revolution now means wearing corn rolls, naturals, dye in your hair, afros, mohawks, bald heads, bandannas, and khaki suits. The streets have become entertainment like Loc Dog, in the movie by Keenan Ivory Wayans, "Don't be a menace while drinking juice in the hood."

Loc Dog, asks his cousin Ash Tray:

> "How does this tec nine look with these house slippers, and high-top sneakers?"

While the Vietcong, Che Guevara, Kastro, etc., stayed in the jungles and trenches filthy most of the time with (1), or (2), changes of clothes which were the same in appearance.
The mentality they had concerning weapons was (we need these weapons no matter what), they are not 2 be played with. Our weapons are to counsel, structure, and for our rise and disciplinary issues. They understood the depth of killing the enemy and our own souljahs when necessary, not if necessary.

As revolutionaries they traveled 2 teach the vision that the adversary had to be challenged and overthrown. They gave this knowledge 2 those who they made komrades. They didn't go 2 sections of their kountry 2 infest them with drugs and rape or child molestation, and senseless violence against the people they needed to survive. It spread from Afrika, Jamaika, Russia, Cuba, China, Vietnam, Amerikkka, Latin Amerikkka, etc.

They gave the people who were disorganized, peasants, farmers, and mine workers revolution. This was the new hope because it touched the people and it valued the lives of the people, so that the people could bring themselves over to this people's liberation. That's why the people gave their time and talents, because it gave them freedom to understand themselves and what they wanted as a whole.

The people wanted 2 become revolutionaries through politikil education, not just occupational success. The people wanted revolution not Karl Marx's revolution, or Bolshevik revolution, 'but a revolution that really registered with the people. The red scare had someone else's ideology, but our revolution is totally designed by people who don't just want 2 be heard...but want war 2 show that we the people still exist in this world.

It's not just about money, because many people then, just like now, have and had money. It wasn't and still isn't just about being poor, politikily enslaved, or prostitutes of a politikil propaganda. It's about living life, simple, not over exaggerated, with morals and principles...seeing our fellow men, and women, as that, **human beings**.

It is not about who had or has more, it's about understanding balance...some will have more than others, but no one should ever have to worry about going without. Some will need a little more, but no one should ever have to go without. This is true equality…the balance is trying 2 keep us as each other's equals.

This equality which I and others refer 2 is that which compels us 2 design a system that gives true assistance and aid, and the kind of kindness that never goes unappreciated. Not that favoritism shit kapitalist speak of, or the reverend, Jews, Buddhist, an imam who says that Islam, is the perfect religion over all others like Jew's being the apple of God's eye. But real respect 4 those in compliance with life, to those that want 2 change their minds, outlook, conditions, etc.

People can try spinning words and the language like sisters and brothers all day long, but it doesn't kreate structured movements, or change entire kountries. It's just words and slang the people will throw away tomorrow. It will always be those who are set in place 2 lead, for the real, true leaders give the vision 2 the masses 2 spread it. The people must not fear that vision or message, they must coherently understand 2 be able 2 live upon the land and live within the life they've chosen 2 fight for.

This is what should fuel them...2 obey the criteria, laws, and challenge of destroying anything that tries 2 rebel against that **System**. Milika, is militant politiks...it is the order of operation.

An operation isn't kreated 2 stay contained within walls or in one or two distinct areas. It is to be **spread** amongst the born and the breeders.

Milika, is the Immortal Influence that the people should be guided by because it's this Influence that gives the vision and causes the masses not to be hypnotized by it, but gives it an interpretation so, that the people stay on one accord even while in turbulent times or division may try to peek his head through.

In the prophets' times in this case Muhammad, he feared the Milika that was sent down to him and the Arabian population. It wasn't sent down 2 him so it could stay in 'his heart alone, mind, nor his mouth…no he had to embrace it first then expound it 2 whoever wanted to hear. And whoever heard and or listened bared the power of transforming entire generations, kultures, and civilizations.

This is how Islam, became the fastest spreading religion due to this key factor, it wasn't new it was conformation of what was already instilled in the people outside of Arabia.

The people assumed the position, and they began recognizing the battle cry which caused them 2 fight the wars of men, in order 2 be considered followers and true believers.

Milika, has been moving through all parts of the world, since the forming of it. But now it has enhanced, and the people don't seem to see the uniformity or understand how revolution has encamped people's territories, rather they consider it religion, or underground cells, for it has all produced the same effect. It has shifted the course of history, and the roles that men/women, have played, in it.
Rather one says that G-d, is creating his kingdom here on earth, or people with higher consciousness, have decided 2 hear the call of

souljah hood, but no matter how you interpret it, it terrorizes the adversary wherever they may be. Our enemies hate the fact that,... people like myself bring forth that combative, image of influence. Man, can never keep his allegiance 2 humankind, or their creator. They fail to, due to the worldly desires and concepts of self-infliction and materialistic survival.

King Sholomo, or Solomon, became king not because he understood how to survive, for he had not the wisdom 2 do so, neither would his kingdom. This is what made him pray not just 4 himself, but more 4 those who were placed in his hands alone to protect. It was his father David, or King David, who was born with the appetite of war-hood, so that the kingdom of Eretz Yis' ra' el, could survive. And with a belief in G-d, and a strong constitution, in not 2 become a slave to a gentile nation he rose, and became immortal. Solomon, was only a builder or as we NIGGAZ say:

"King Solomon, was a 21 mason."

The patriarch Avraham Avinu, was both a general, and preacher, an also a master builder of his people. Moses, was also general, preacher, and master builder of his nation, the Hebrew Nation. As with Yeshua-ben-Yosef, or Jesus; and Muhammad, the prophet... (PBUH), and peace and blessings upon those mentioned before him. Yet this messiah, the anointed one called Yeshua-ben-Yosef, holds the immortal influence, in it's absolute form, more than any other because he is the only visionary, master builder, preacher, king, and general whose visions and leadership still talks literally 2 his nation of people the Jews and the gentile/pagan world. Some Christians, Muslims and Jews profess that this prophet did break the mold by not dying. Many Jews and Christians alike say that the power of his influence heals sickness, resurrects the dead, and converts people not to Christianity, but the triumphant manner of the truth. Mankind has not understood in depth the unique need 4 expansion, or freedom. And by this, kountries and civilizations have been crushed and have vanquished because they have tried 2 conquer the world through tyranny, magic, and arrogance. Those feeble desires caused those empires and leaders to be raped by those savage instincts and failed. Cesar, etc., who built their empires and watched them evaporate over time, between judgements, and space, even all the way down to lineages.

Alexander The Great, konfused the konquest of territory with an ill perception that his mighty forces and his glory was infinite.
All,
the examples provided thought that-prosperity was finite and not infinite, but these examples of conventional forces are kontinuing while in death trying to komprehend the infinite wisdom of G-d, and his established design. They ask while in death...how is it that his kingdom still stands, while there's no matter how strong and meritorious it was has crumbled under the feet of those same poor peasants that they penalized.

The revolution has crossed over into all seven kontinents, and as each new generation of revolutionaries come into understanding, it raises and evolves more into a people rather than empires.

It is these same generations who have suffered under the yoke of oppression who has slowly been taking over these kountries. Those dictators and oppressors who believed that they were supreme, are starting to witness more explosive rebels. More in tuned rebels, who are not satisfied with mere rebellion, no we have become compressed to be more hardened than, those who have come before us. They have given us(us), 2 be able to be more of an **Immortal Influence**.

The written words we find that causes us to tare up, burn down, infuriate with anger, and hatred 2 also, finding love in our voyages uncommon to man. This was 4 the nomad, or revolutionary who have always become inhabitors of dysfunctional dynasties.

Yet at times we were as they separated by fantasies but no more!

Here is the war kry, not a new language but still that same language which caused us to be united in battle but individuals, we kontinue 2 stand 2 be superior races no matter how integrated.

I am integrated with you! Milika, is uniting you...it is instilling in us the principle 2 overthrow those who think that they are all powerful. We no longer say that we the people are witnessing a konstitution, but are witnessing the latitude, and longitude, of revolutionary terrorist formed everywhere, out thinking, out growing, and outflanking these nations and profiteers who haven't learned real warfare.

The terrorist revolutionary war, will be fought at the same time but in different sections around the world. The vision has not just come down 2 lead the people, but 2 greet them, and 2 arm us as a whole, although it will only be a few who truly believe. Religion has destroyed homes, bonds, and love.

Mankind has desecrated G-d's earth, until we have found no joy to be comforted while in mourning. And we have found that there is no difference when it comes to viewing life. All the people have left is liars, and manipulators, mis representatives, and misprinted redacted dialogue that has been published 2 sow the seeds of discord and disunity.

These publications and oral announcements have been utilized 2 keep the people lost, uncertain, and at odds with those we need 2 love and who would love to serve us. No matter where you go in this world, rather 2 sight see, or pray...there will be us armed in prayer, and escorting our fellow men and women, young and old 2 the places that serves and protects them. **WE ARE THOSE PLACES, BECAUSE IT IS WE WHO ARE IN THOSE PLACES!**

A terrorist revolutionary is only a server 2 the service that's been given 2 us. When and once we comprehend this, only then will we be **unstoppable**.

Sad as it may be about our loved ones who will have to be put 2 death by our hands, it is of necessity, that we channel our kourage and energy 2 stay focus on our dedication, **compelling** our brothers and sisters in arms, **to do the same**.
Some of our best friends and family members have helped our foes and have helped 2 support this global world view of annihilation. There have not been any true revolutions, just internal wars 2 destroy us, the people and it's always been from the inside.

Let not blood cause you 2 cease these insurrections. May it cause not your anger to subside but increase until these kapitalist and destroyers of our love, life, and faith perish 4 their krimes against humanity. We pray 4 our souls as well as theirs, but let no believer in G-d, or otherwise cause you 2 indulge in anything outside this guidance. Don't let anything that's foreign or outside of the konfines of revolutionary terrorist teachings 2 cause you to doubt the seriousness of us surviving the odds of our enemies. That would be the injustice, that would be our deaths

The discipline must be there 2 hold the structure 2gether. This tests the wills of revolutionary terrorist. We obey in order 2 penetrate the **false illusions**, of our enemies, 4 the shadows, are a terrorist's best friend. Being discreet brings no disfunction or prying eyes into the fold.

ONE FUCK UP CAUSES THE DOMINOE EFFECT!

Teach this 2 every city rather major or minor, suburb, and kountry who has an individual that's willing 2 uphold the terrorist **BODY and MIND**. There will and should never be any hesitation when it comes to **wolf-warfare**. It is us who makes the difference. It is you who must concentrate all efforts and energy on destroying those who hate us.

You must tap into the revolution's mind, not the so called **revolutionary,** so that the unlearned can gravitate 2 that belief of triumph. It is our right 2 be people and politikil animalz, not domesticated or tamed followers who are led by bribery, falsehood, and cowardliness.

Our children must be taught 2 never lose faith in the realest doctrine ever assembled 4 and by mankind. That must alwayz be our ancestor's peace of mind.

Decades will pass.... generations will be passed over. Millenia's, and centuries will undergo konstant changes, but the focus is 2 stay the course no matter what we see, hear, or whatever.
Seek 4 strength, kry 4 the war that many have prayed and prostrated 4, 2 be that solution 2 whatever obstacle that should be thrown in our paths.

WE WILL FOREVER BE SOLDIERS OF THESE LANDS, EVOLVING UNTIL THE PLAN IS FINISHED AND IT'S TIME 4 THE IMMORTAL JUDGEMENT

CHAPTER 5

ADJUSTING

We are at odds with ourselves, and I do declare that this is the hardest part having to turn your back on your way of life and the people which you have birthed. These are the people that have been there 4 you, and have caused you 2 be the person you may be now.
This chapter deals with the personal side of revolutionary life.

When you've had children and have settled down, fought in Civil Rights Movements, carved out businesses 4 for yourselves or have become the face of a brand that people adore...it becomes very challenging 2 just pick up and leave it all behind.

From a religious standpoint, it is the same. A lot of times people think that their prophets just packed up and followed their G-d, without an internal struggle and the Cinderella story commenced, but that is far from the truth.

It took a lot of those men and women 2 be pried from their normal lifestyles rather poor, rich, or middle klass, 2 set themselves on a path that had nothing in it. There were no beautiful sights shown in their early stages conversing and following G-d, just their G-d, demanding that they adhere vigorously 2 his commandments and voice.

Families were broken up as a result to this adjusting period. Who in their right minds didn't stress behind trying to cope with these uncommon demands and disadvantages? The people that you have known your whole entire life now all of a sudden have no klue of what's happening and why.

They can't comprehend the person whom they've had beers, and hard liquor with. Some of us have shared sleeping bags, sleeping pills, beds, and bedrooms, clothes, shoes, emotional concern, as well as a laugh.

How great the tears are when you're told, not asked 2 disregard all that you've ever known.

Your identity is now in complete conflict with who and what you now have to become. Your dreams like the people say sometimes when they have had children have to be placed on the back burner but in your case which is rare, can never be reached now because they no longer fit inside of the vision of wing span, shadow warfare, and revolution.

For the most part the individual is lost, and now has become the buddy system and the buddy system, has now become the individual's accomplice. It is the evolutionary process of the shadow. It goes wherever, and becomes a part of whatever.

Your daily nine to five, or forty 2 eighty hrs., a week becomes days without sleep, and months without knowing the month, and as for the years, they are only clocks set 4 the missions. That small scale of protecting your environment and or family, friends, kommunity, etc., starts to change in illustration.

Those adorable little eyes that stares from their tiny sockets while you read them bedtime stories, or dressing their little bodies for school, must now be ignored due to it jeopardizing the real agenda of truly protecting them.

For you now it is a wish 4 them 2 understand, but a hope 4 them 2 forget you and life as it once was. Once the perfect little housewife who cleaned for the family, weaning and clinging to her family, keeping her home spotless 4 pleasure and to keep down ridicule from neighbors is now being swept 4 mechanikil bugs, and wiped down 2 erase fingerprints and other portions of DNA, that exist from daily movement and activity.

Those late night informercials and daytime commercials, teaching you about Febreze, no longer is paid attention to. The new television premiere, or the next NFL, game...**NBA-ALL-STAR-SHOW**, no longer catches your attention. That long-awaited vacation, money put away 4 private school etc., comes ata far healthier price than normal because at first it was so that you, our, and your families could someday become someone or something prominent in the world, but now it's 2 become something much more dangerous.

It almost feels like being abducted by aliens, but the kidnappers are yourself. No Amerikkkin on their own has ever signed the korporate konstitution; there has never been a citizen 2 do so...only the parties who wished 2 run the korporation.

They alone were assigned allotments, so why do we think that their korporate kontract doesn't validate our enslavement?

There is no breach of contract it was a notice, a simple note a word of undermining promises from kongressmen and women eventually, legislatures, and other members of their secret societies.

Just like the printing of the Federal Reserve Note, it is 2 keep business functioning and the slave secure in it's harvest, providing a process of elimination when the slave fails 2 function like a slave. It is we who are soooooo caught up with this kontract as if it is highly important but there is no real importance, it's a hoax 2 us rather than them just like **Santa Klause**.

It is us who believe it is (our), essence of survival, but it isn't...and the korporate owners know this. The real money is us and will alwayz be us this is why they secure us in the kontract...not with true benefit but with established schools of thought along with business proposals.

We lay in the actual vaults of our financiers. This is how they can play their weird war of psychology and its scientific experimental warfare. Politikil propaganda is a pig parasite just like the unlawful eating of the pig which was laid down by our spiritual advisors/ancestors, 2 us all that eating this filthy sub, beast would kontaminate and cost us our lives no matter if we thoroughly clean it or not.

Why do you think that they use the term "**Money Laundering**," or "**Kleaning The Money**?" This has become the ideology of all klasses of people...poor, middle klass, and wealthy.

Kleaning the money why do we feel the need to klean the money? Because it was krookedly gained...and the money has and will alwayz have blood on it which 4 ever keep it dirty!

The detrimental effect it has on the mind and body comes from this parasitik invasion. The pig is the symbol of innocence, but it is a deadly animal. The psychologikil effect is the same way when it comes to the money it causes those with and without it 2 stress, which contributes to breaking down the body, as well as the mind it causes the brain 2 malfunction and become warped.

Our politicians and merchants or businessmen/women, has this same symbolik attribute of innocence but they play games with the mass's lives. They are deadly animals with parasites killing the people 2 extend policies and plans building up economiks and vacation resorts while depopulating and enslaving us the people.

They horde multitudes of nationalities 2 be able 2 set up national and international korporations kontracted 2 kountries by konstitutions, 2 keep us under their kontrol.

We are the billions and trillions of dollars, imported and exported through the world union everywhere. It is considered the United Nations, a man-made submarket which smuggles the true gold, and manufactures the gold plated which they sale 2 us.

The same with the drugs, sliver, diamonds, oil, and food sources like wine and alcohol. So, washing the new Toyota Camry, Audi, Bugatti, etc., can no longer cross (our), mind.

The **strolls** in the evening hand in hand, with a whistle or pepper spray is futile. Your p.o. box, e-mail accounts, is also frivolous because you are still being utilized and korporate sponsored by our adversaries.
So now when you buy your car, truck, or SUV you start checking how many miles 2 the gallon, the tire pressure, and oil. You start doing it for the reasons of survival and strategy, not just because your vehicle has the latest camera, or voice activated features that nobody else has around.

Now you see clothes as clothes when you go out 2 buy them and the necessary shoes you do it because it equips you rather than just wrap you, or its trendy and worthy of being posted 4 comment on a fashion blog or the red carpet, 2 the hype of media frenzy. Now you bake and buy products 2 cook with or brush your teeth, deodorant etc., you study the chemikils used in them so that you won't become a victim of our foes scientifik konstruction. Hey, the cake may not be as soft, the vegetables may not taste like they had once upon a time, and they won't be supported by societies catch phrase "**organic**"...but they will have the necessary essentials 2 kontain and keep a balanced diet.

It's what we need 2 survive and that's all...nothing artificially added like they say. The bare essentials kills the will of the wealthy and the haves, but 2 follow this you wealthy muthafuckas and haves might as well burn everything you and your ancestors before you have known and have accumulated out of your thoughts. Terrorist revolutionaries don't believe in the non-necessities. And let your fame be the credit that gets you and keep you through the door of no return.

I'm not saying that you can't stay wealthy, we need you 2 do this but what I'm trying to get you 2 learn is that thinking this way, will make you healthier and more prepared because no matter what you believe the system will alwayz be penetrated and those who think they will fool us, can be found and exterminated.

You wealthy people know their politiks...this is what the underground calls the buy in. Today's success revolves around the buy in. We don't get our people 2 buy in... we aren't in to changing or trading places. You are information, the key 2 the konnected world, but it's us who reciprocates that world which the globe knows as well as cherish. I will not lie 2 you, many of us will die, but I can live with that, the question is can **yoooooouuuuuu**!?

Can you live with those same adorable eyes turning you over 2 the authorities because you couldn't let go? Or that husband/ wife leaving you and not following because they don't want 2 leave their komfort and blindsided beliefs.

Can you live with looking at drawings of your children alone? Can you live with not seeing their dimples and smiling, pudgy fleshy rosy red/pink cheeks...meaning physically everyday blushing and not be affected by the memory of a fading photograph? I say this because this is all you will have of them. .**you will only have endless memories**! Therefore, again I say, can you adjust?

Can you adjust 2 living your life intensely underground, or being two people at one time on and off the grid? No daily establishments newspaper, fresh cup of coffee. No doctor's plush offices when that time comes. Can you live with the constant raids by the **establishment's security enforcers** if your name gets dropped and you get placed on their world terrorist watch list?

Can you live with no trophies, massage parlors, and private 2 publik privileges, and the dead-end life of being nobodies? You will be konsidered the dead in the land of the "**living**."

Can you lie good enough 2 evade detection 2 persuade those specifically trained 2 get the truth out of you, most likely by some sort of scientifik engineered experiment? This is the life I am handing 2 you! Dirty clothes, possibly no fragrant shampoo that smells delightful and makes your hair have (bounce), to it, no phones 4 basik normal conversations...no address books 4 self only coordinates 4 assignments 2 carry out.

I'm offering you beautiful homes and luxurious lives 2 build factions within it's walls, housing and potentially nursing injured cell cadres who will be continuously in and out of our lives and homes forever more. What I'm offering you is the dirt 2 kover and throw on your own graves, along with the fire that consumes your body because a proper **burial**, will not be associated. When you can't pray five or three times a day, or when you can't go into a mosque, church, and synagogue, 2 pray... **I, ASK YOU ONE QUESTION CAN YOU FACE THIS VOYAGE AND ADJUST**?

Forget about the ballet recital, or your daughters first crush and kiss, dance, date, first baby steps, first words, first day of school etc., because most of us will not be attending and if you are the chosen 2 go it won't be to enjoy it.....it will only be 2 keep an eye on the target or you are there 2 murder the person of interest.

I know how some of you think,
no, it's not about being a hitman/woman, because we are not hit-men and women...we are however here not 2 be professionals like the establishment's trained personnel. This is only a manual that translates 2 the ordinary man/woman, not just a trained individual that there is a purpose 4 us to live and not just survive. This manual comes not by way of professional anything but those who have no special skill set, talent, etc., it is 4 those who don't necessarily know how 2 fight or go 2 war it was kreated 2 be in such a manner that you are overlooked,

unlike the armed forces or guerrilla bands.

I want 2 share this with you, even if you decide that you can no longer do this "revolutionary," thing as you try 2 back out of this way of life after entering, you'll find that you can't go back 2 being normal, konformity is konsidered normal reform is konsidered "**the normal life or another negotiated form of submittance to ideology versus the true outlook**. Nobody **will** be able 2 trust you again, not society as if it already had anyway, nor your cell. You will be looking over your shoulder 4 the rest of your life.

You can betray your right 2 life by telling your enemies all that they want 2 hear and know, but trust this, they will exterminate you…and we will exterminate you…G-d himself will eventually exterminate you.

The guilt will chew you up and spit you out like that whale did Jonah, and that guy that walked with and betrayed Jesus, Judas, (Yahuda), and you may even do what he did because of the guilt that will eat at you until you eventually kill yourself.

Can you live with that?
Will you allow our enemies 2 smooth talk you or finesse you in 2 going back to a lifestyle that's coming to an end anyway?

Time will tell...the pressure of time will tell if your children are more precious 2 you than life it's self. Heaven hides no coward, and hell holds no thief, which simply means that there is no loyalty 2 find in hell so don't expect 2 last long, 4 there is nowhere 2 run and nowhere to hide.

I am literally placing you in a box, so I hope that you are not clostrophobik. I'm teaching you how 2 "**DIE R.E.A.L.**," and can you blame me? There is no self-aggrandizing in revolution.

There's an enemy, there's a target, and there's a weapon 2 be used along with a decision 2 be made. Can you live with yourself after having 2 kommit a murder? Could you gird up the strength 2 kill, a life that's not life but a kreated experiment?

Could you bomb a child, a pregnant wife or mistress of your foe?

Can you eliminate them and then live with yourself?

Could you listen 2 your enemy discuss disdain, and racial hatred without showing the slightest bit of emotion while carpooling, having brunch, laboring over facts and figures, or pouring cups of hot coco/tea, in the board room?

This is adjusting going from one destination 2 another within seconds. Emotionally, and physikilly at the drop of a dime. This is adjusting when your kid is running a high temperature and you get that call 2 leave them 2 kill your foe…can you adjust?

If your about 2 say I do, at the altar, can you leave your fiancé, standing there looking distraught, while you take your position to kill the target? Do you think that these words and the cause can make you leave the most important thing 2 you?

Can you adjust?

Wife in labor, and your there in the midst of her contractions which are getting closer by the minute, she's having the baby at any given moment...can you up and leave just 2 murder your target? The baby is **crowning**, you see the head, she is screaming at the top of her lungs...can you sacrifice this at the drop of a dime and go to your destination and possibly your destruction?

Your parents or loved one is being buried and you are one of the Paul bearers, you may even be about 2 read and give the eulogy, could you adjust and go to the intended target which maybe there at the funeral? You can't let them escape, this is your only chance 2 leave them where they stand, can you be counted on to take out your foe?

You have to understand that you have speakers or orators in this world, and you also have men of action who are just as active as their followers. It's not just you who must adjust, we all must arrive here, 4 if the love of righteousness dies **than we all die**!

I ask of you is what I ask of myself, to exercise not only the mind, but the body, and spirit. This is my right 2 live even if that takes me 2 live in death. When all you have 2 your name is a photograph, or an old love letter, revolutionary book, of that **rebel's last wordz**, and that memory of that loss or wordz of redemption is all you own because the coverment, knew that they were selling contaminated foods, or that car company, knew that it should have **recalled their vehicles**, but didn't, and said fuck the people or consumer and your child or spouse's death was the end result, than you'll see that they cared more about lining their **pockets** than respecting those you have loved and lost...those pictures and wordz are what's keeping you going, while you're in that dark space of time, and your world seems 2 be growing dimmer, than maybe you'll understand.

As those pages stain from your tears, and begin to yellow over the years, ink fading and spreading...you'll start 2 come 2 grips about what the adversary has stolen from you, but don't hate them, there's no need to hate them because it is they who has given you a cause and a decision 2 make, and that decision which was handed 2 you is not due 4 you 2 just have the thought alone, but 2 follow the action 2 see where the line is drawn, and what side of that line which is not imaginary, by the way, are you going to see it as being meaning are you going 2 **toe it**, or **cross it**? It's that simple, will you see or ignore?

For the world is full of those that ignore, while the few not just see but understand what real misery do 2 those of a more stronger caliber. You die within yourself, and you live because you see those that are around you are dying. **2 Die Weak, and phony,** can never be accepted by a terrorist revolutionary, **We Die Real, Unbreakable and always as Non-Konformist 2 kultivate a kulture Thereof.**

This is what they hate...you who are of sound mind and it is they who fail 2 gravitate 2 what logik and wisdom guarantees peace. Your loyal but she's not, why? Because you are at peace, which is freedom within self. She is still searching 4 liberty and security that she hasn't realized that she already owns.

You work, he's lazy. You find peace because you understand the struggle which people dub **rainy days**, and those habits that give but take away. Yet even with this truth you are even handed, because you sacrifice or give no matter what it is you got.

Their body grows by kontract, and yours become feeble due 2 the war with them and the world itself, because that strain is constantly beating down on the mind from denying yourself what you know is falsehood.

Yes it is tempting, but that's just it, the temptation it doesn't need 2 be necessarily resisted because it's a challenge 2 you. It is not an unnatural thing when it's the trait of a human being. But once you become coherent than you resist because it is unnatural when it's no longer a part of your life and lifestyle.

We all are trial and error, we don't fall into a stage of it-we actually become the training because we understand the gravitational pull which wants us 2 either resist or submit. Kaos is necessary without it we're unable 2 see the truth within the lie, this guarantees our right 2 live.

To you biblikil thumbers, and preachers...Qur'an, Haddith, and Sunnah practitioners, there is nothing 2 read in the pages of plain language. All the Ayats and Chapters, Verses, etc., are nothing more but wordz numbered and prearranged 4 a falsehood that most people preach that the divine wordz are translating. Yet the believer is a believer not by conversion, but by what he or she already knows within what's wrong and right.

They don't have 2 say a Fatihah or say John 3:16; because obedience is not what is followed but what is cherished and pure of self. Life is cherished, and the spirit is that life which shows us the light in dark times. **THIS IS TRUE FAITH**!

To know and not guess, to share with others and to not be selfish. The understanding **is** the judgement that is what we find and accept as being righteousness. We all must keep in mind that the different degrees of the learned teacher is not what's being taught, but how it is being taught which causes tongues 2 speak in a variety of languages starting with the lower pupil which is man himself. So again, can you adjust 2 not just this argument but a truth that causes self-worth, and spiritual reflection pieced 2gether until the actual human form rises out of one state like Christ, or his proof and presentation of resurrection which people like 2 entitle reassurance.

Yoritomo once stated that:

> "The word is the most direct manifestation of thought; hence it is one of the most important agents of influence when it clothes itself with precision and clearness. Indispensable in cooperating in kreating conviction in the minds of one's hearers".

Dangennes, In Yoritomo
Influence

The Amerikkkin konstitution states that:

> "Kongress shall make no law.... abridging the freedom of speech or of the press."
>
> First Amendment

Which causes me 2 ask,
why than the gag orders? Why kontinue 2 keep people imprisoned or hold them/us, in kontempt of kourt when we speak the truth and the whole truth so help us G-d?

Why do the establishment kill the leaders who only want what's best for us as a whole? I'll tell you why, because it just sounds good and it's what the propagandized publik considered the population wants 2 hear.

Propaganda: or the essence thereof is said 2 be **kept simple and in konstant rotation**.

And like the statement Yoritomo wrote:

> "By wordz and speech, keep wordz and speech short and sweet, because too great wealth of wordz is hostile 2 konviction."

See pig propaganda in every kampaign, we will, we do every 4 to eight years...it's alwayz the same. Fix the budget, get the masses jobs, fix the economy, fight poverty, help assist in the black kommuniti, and our famous heart stopper **WORLD PEACE**.
Same objective like Malcom X, said:

> "Just a different face repetitively repeating it."

Yet us terrorist are silent. We are evaluating. We are moving in to enemy territory and the repercussions will be relentless. Yet we will not say a word, everything has already been said, and I am convinced and konvicted already yet hostile 2 the many wordz spoken by those that are trying 2 silence us.

CHAPTER 6

SILENCE

I know that you law abiding Constitutioners, will hate me 4 saying this but: "FUCK THE FIFTH AMENDMENT," THIS IS BY NO MEAN A REAL TRUE CODE OF SILENCE ANYWAY! From the Milikian standpoint, silence is the period of inaction, but it is still being totally active.

It is when your neighbor asks, just out of mere social conversation something that's politically based, rather about what you've read in the papers, in a book, or what you may have seen on t.v. or smart device. Silence is: Sorry I Did Not Catch It.

Silence is when the plan is in full swing, but nothing seems 2 be happening. Silence is not used 2 just throw off the enemy, but our cadres as well. Silence is when statements such as:

"Black Lives Matter!"
"Jesus Walks!"
"2pac and Biggie's Unsolved Murders!"
"The O.J. Simpson Trial!" to other political conspiracies, and farces such as those and this:

> "Congress is on the verge of handing over Amerikkkin ideas, jobs and innovation, 2 foreign competitors, soon they'll vote on H.R.9, sweeping patent legislation that will hurt the U.S., inventors, and embolden infringes everywhere. A broad coalition of inventors, universities, manufacturers, venture capitalist, start-ups, small businesses, technology and life science companies, oppose H.R.9, it's too broad and too flawed. Amerikkkins, deserve better, so vote no on H.R.9, and save the Amerikkkin inventor...4 H.R.9, is made 4 China, not the Amerikkkin people says basically the Amerikkklan Administration."

The terrorist Revolutionary, stays silent!
Meaning we do not call the news media 2 complain, and we do not make protest of any type under any circumstances. We can't march around like those negros, who marched on Washington, or marched at Selma. We are not seen, and never do we want 2 be heard, because we remain silent!
Strictly undetected, and unseen, meaning bringing in more attention than the situation warrants, again we are IN, AND OUT, even if we come under attack. When the terrorist revolutionary, attacks, there will be no emblems, 2 identify who we are. We don't buy and print up t-shirts 2 parade around in. The terrorist, has no slogans, or banners to show the public who we are. Neither do we run or walk in the crosshairs, of our enemy's rifles, like the youth did in Baltimore City, when they rioted, neither like those in Chicago, and Washington D.C., all seen goofing off skipping and running around high, and drunk, in our enemy's line of fire! The terrorist, will not be seen tear gassed, on live t.v. and the terrorist will not be seen getting our ass beat down in the streets like dogs, by these protectors of the establishment.

The terrorist revolutionary, knows 2 strike at the heart of the situation, for we know that there are three elements, in any revolutionary war, not just a revolution. For the (3), targeting elements are:

A). The Tyrant
B). The corporate-business World
C). And the Bureaucratic-petty-Bourgeois

For example: In the National Review, dated August of 2015, there was an ad that said:

> "At a Reagan Ranch High School Conference, the students can walk in former president Ronald Reagan's footsteps and learn about the ideas that championed or simply learn his conservative ideas."

Then there's a blue banner at the bottom of the page where there's a group of children/youth holding up this banner that reads:

(YOUNG AMERIKKKLANS FOUNDATION).

What this is pretty much saying is that our children will learn **Reaganomics**, and they will be brainwashed again through and by hisstory for they will be taught how 2 expand their knowledge of economics, personal responsibility, the triumph of freedom, and former president Reagan's lasting accomplishments through a series of lectures/dogma. In other words, the establishment is strategically training our integrated children in the knowledge of pig propaganda, 4 we know already that it has never created and will never create a change 4 any black person, etc., for it's only the privileged Amerikkkins of this kountry that will benefit and that train of thought, is what impacts our poverty and drug usage, that much greater.

Reagan the actor, and known cocaine gate keeper, flooded the 80's with the narcotics of Manuel Noriega, when they invaded his kountry and took over his drug operation 2 distribute it 2 guess who the ghetto communities of BLACK AMERIKKKA. Former president Ronald Reagan created the year of the young black hustler, or young black cocaine and crack dealers. And with this drug arsenal, they began 2 terrorize their families, neighborhoods, and neighbors. Which started turf wars where many of these young dealers died or got hooked on this dangerous product. All these atrocious gang wars, and turf wars came from the Oval Office, in the time of Reagan's reign. All this was under the watchful eye of former president Ronald Reagan, and his administration. We have to remember that while he had time in the Oval office, this man tried 2 wipe out the middle and impoverished klass, meaning the blacks, and Latinos of the ghetto. This is the man that we are pre-paring to teach our children about. For this is the only history that can be understood, because this was a part of his economic policy, and this was that part of history that he helped shape.

Therefore, it will always be silent on the real side of the social experiment, because those who have examined this misgiving has a different viewpoint of the president/former president's brain washing techniques. Speaking of past presidents former president Barak Obama, back in 2015, related that he would be releasing non-violent criminals, about (46), of them, and is seeking 2 reform Amerikkka's sentencing and penalties when it comes 2 drug offenders.
Yet releasing forty-six, drug offenders, non-violent or otherwise does nothing for the communities that they have contributed in destroying. That's not even a indentation in the over capacitated inmates in the Dept. Of Corrections, or prizon institutions here in Amerikkka.

Yet the cocaine traffickers, and drug lords/kingpins, commit more heinous crimes than murderers, or basic common crooks. Yet they get to be released before any terrorist, or freedom fighter, In the likes of Mumia Abul-Jamal, etc. That's very odd, that a person who builds a criminal drug empire gets exonerated, before a person who never pre-meditated anything within the crime he/she was convicted of. But this is Reaganomics. Use the fools 2 keep fooling, and glorifying drugs, and ignorance not giving a fuck about the people, their race, only the continuance of our downfall.

Yet the term non-violence, in today's political arenas has not the same definition as Dr. King's who was once a believer in its purest definition, and who once fought for it until he died. The new propagandizing of its meaning, deems it'self really hypocritical due 2 drugs and alcohol in its entirety, which destroys the people's way of thinking, and the people's way of functioning the right way. Look at the infamous Huey P. Newton, and his famous Black Panther Party. The criminality, and drugs killed Huey, and his party.

But Dr. King, with his keen sense of judgement and knowledge, embodied cultivating the truth and the seriousness that came behind drug and alcohol abuse and usage in the black residences period and communities. This 2, was his approach when it came down to embracing the real definition of **Non-Violence**. Like Gandhi, he embodied the philosophy's true sense.

Dr. King, never nor did his party, ever raise a fist in defiance, neither were there any form of weapon used 2 circumvent the white race or any other race for that matter. The koverment knows the effects of drugs, and they use them against us, as a ploy so that we the experiment, can undergo life and daily living without our full capability, and comprehension of these people's strategies and tactics. These are Scientific Methods Of **Psychologikil Warfare**. And it's purpose is 2 destroy and enslave the world's masses of people esp., those who are already impoverished, 4 they are guaranteed by this tactic that it will continue to condition the people 2 stay lost, ill-informed, and non-thinkers.

But lets get back to the former president Barak Obama. He continued to later say that there would be 30,000 convicted inmates released within the year, of 2016. At that time it was only state detained inmates, which by statistics show that there are at least 2.2 million, convicted persons behind bars throughout these stakes. And the Federal institutions have allegedly another 215,000, incarcerated. Thirty-thousand non-violent criminals doesn't even put a dent in the prison system's population.

The popular youth president should have taken notice that there is a problem here with this policy of his, and these two twin contradictive systems. These states within the U.S., have set up and violated more prisoner's rights than they have anarchist, and radicals around the world, for these citizens are priznors behind trying to earn a decent wage, and find humane employment, without discriminatory practices. Decent living quarters, a real chance at life not wanting 2 commit a crime but had 2, because of the rules and regulations that deprive a man and a woman from trying to enjoy a life that you are taking away from them.

There has been no real true **Due Process**, neither has there been any true protection under these undermining constitutional rights, so that the terminology and definition of **Equal Protection** satisfies an ambiguous foundation that keeps the total populous, contaminated, and not free from tyranny, and injustice. But there are too many violations of the people and their rights 2 keep on record, for they don't want the people to see their oppressive conditioning. But many of us, do. This is one of the things that the black entrepreneur, Marion Suge Knight, is or has filed many petitions and motions, because he was being denied the right 2 have visitations, (contact), etc., all because "THEY SAY," that in the past Mr. Knight, is known or has been known 2 use intimidation practices as remedies to stay free. Yet how do the cops when interrogating possible suspects, can use these tactics that a criminal use and get away with it? See the double standard? Yet we all should know that when it comes to past cases that has nothing 2 do with the current one taints trials, as the kourtz well know judges as well as the prosecution and that form of trial tactic puts the defendant in a bad light with the ladies and gentlemen of the jury. For this is damn near jury tampering.

Afeni Shakur, suffered with issues like this in New York City, under the Panther 13/21 kangaroo trialz, and her incarceration. She to was fighting not just 4 herself but also for the other incarcerated women 2 be able to keep their unborn children healthy and alive while pregnant and imprisoned. Like all resistors, of oppression, she was determined to free herself from the double standard and hypocritical laws that those who are in power misuse against poor people, and liberation armies considered terrorist. Think about George Jackson, Hurricane Reuben Carter, Mumia Abul Jamal, myself, and countless others who have been framed and hidden by these politikil riff-raft of Amerikkka. They've given us, titles such as criminal, terrorist, all so we can be treated like foreigners, by a kountry that we are suppose 2 be under it's care, but due to our resisting their oppressive ideologies, and because we speak up and out against their **crooked** policies, we have become targets in the eyes of the public, by this so called superior establishment. Lawyers are being given more power of say, than their actual clients, who are being brought up on charges and trying to assist in their case. But these lawyers by their new legislative laws no longer, have to listen to their clients anymore...for in their eyes we are nothing more but mere layman of their law, which justifies their meanz, and by this new standard, our input is considered unlawful, and un-necessary.

There are unqualified jurors now being allowed 2 sit on the panel or jury box, while the discretion factor of **Peremptory Challenges**, are being side stepped due to what the kourt in question feels that it wants to do because they are the lower power elite and they have been enabled to be the said rulers of the higher elite's politikil power. Judges are supposed to be neutral, while on the bench listening to the people's individual cases, but since this kountry has been founded, these judges have been found aiding the prosecution, and have conspired with our private and public attorneys 2 convict us, not acquit us! They are undermining the legislative intent, which by discretion of the judge shows the abuse that we take as blacks and the others who have been taught to surrender.

They have denied the people proper jury instructions, okay which is supposedly written to aid a criminal now it's for the kourtz 2 burry you with. It was supposed to help this so-called jury of our peers to be able to be guided correctly to perform the law as required of every citizen who has to play his or her role when it comes to deciding the right thing 2 do, but in many ways it no longer does. The object of the game is to abide by the law, not break the law. If these jurors are being guided by a misconception of the law the law is already broken, by ignorance and misapplication. The jurors might as well be us, the kourt made criminal. That juror supposed to individually take their own notations, to individually make their own assessments, which they alone need 2 render accurately, when it comes 2 the finding of a person being brought up on criminal charges guilty or not guilty, of the said verdict. The Constitutional Law, meaning the Federal Law, not the state's law, guaranteed it's citizens that we the people have these rights of passage written and documentized of how a person can be convicted. It must be with solid evidence, not circumstantial evidence, which is basically no evidence, or like the layman's say...Bull Shit, Evidence!

The attorney General, and District Attorney, Judges, our lawyers, these alleged witnesses, are all in cohoots. These material eye witnesses, are swearing falsely under oath, testifying 2 things that they have not seen, speaking of things that they heard, while these kourtz bend the facts, 2 fit their story or depiction of what happened, as if they were there. This method of trial strategy, as they call it, is similar 2 the cops tampering with evidence at the scene of the crime. These Kourtz Are Not Credible!

They with the establishment and merchants, are increasing their monetary, and political as well as social status. Motions aren't being filed, or simply not being submitted. Trial attorneys, are not properly advising their clients of their actual rights, therefore I ask:

> "How can there be a real trial, or real trial strategy, if the client is not in on the strategy and or defense?"

There can be no Fundamental Fairness, in these show and kangaroo kourtz. They are deliberately saying FUCK THE PEOPLE! They are calling major mistakes Plain Error, a mere justification that excuses our so-called lawyer's unprofessionalism. The legislature did not make the laws, for them 2 be ambiguous, and misinterpreted. It even goes to the inmate population, which there are certain rights given to us, but since the public don't know and can't see from the outside in, it's hard for the convict or politikil priznor 2 be able 2 expose them. This system that the establishment created keeps the public and our families, misinformed. Inmate grievances aren't being taken seriously by the overpriced babysitters dubbed correctional officers. Neither is the process of A.R.P.'s, which is the administrative remedy process, this too is being ignored, trashed, and not sent up to the higher ups or higher channels, so again it's FUCK THE PEOPLE!

The prison population is considered the Non-Society, because we as a result was written off by society. We are constantly being extorted by these music, appliance, shoe, and clothes catalogs. Many of the shoes being sold to us, priznors, are those that are brand names like Nike, Reebok, Under Armor, etc., but are considered their defective products, yet it's damn near the store prices. These prisons and these catalog owners/vendors have conspired with one another so that the jail can get kickbacks etc., while these companies price their goods way past retail value. With these murdering merchants, and other futile folks who know about this and the injustices that go on behind these walls, have kept silent in order 2 stay a part of a white klanned society, that don't even give a shit about them either, because if they did why do you correctional officers get pepper spray, a flashlight, and a walkie-talkie, in hostile environments that's 4 people of real profession and real experience, not farmers, and under achieved hillbillies.

They have teamed up with the politicals, 2 ensure that we are not eating properly and keeping up with proper hygiene. There's no nutrition in the meals that they serve here...everything is either canned or starch, except for the correctional officers, who without fail eat raw, and steamed vegetables three times a day. Yet they tell our families and the public that everything is alright, this game that they are running is all **pre-packaged** by our elected officials. These people are not our peers, and neither are they our representatives. These people are only puppets, and escape goats, frivolous intermediaries, yet Amerikkka wants peace, with the people here in it's kountry, and abroad. While it's cronies who call themselves world powers, are desperately seeking 2 keep the masses ' **safe** ' from world domination, or whatever threat in which they are in total control of.

How can they dare ask the people 4 peace, when they ha system that purposefully convicts, and kills it's masses lega[illegible]ed a what breaks up and destroys families and communities of all is is

Now there are no more pictures to be taken with families, who d[illegible]e most of the time hundreds of miles, and hours at a time on the road o[illegible]y to be harassed by these unachieved babysitters, than once the famil[illegible] gets harassed, they may receive one-hour visits, with that incarcerated member of their family or their friend. In many cases if the guard who is in charge of the visiting rm., that day, don't favor your particular color, or you are a mixed couple, meaning a white woman visiting a black man, it is an even stronger possibility that the party who has come to visit will get turned away, and spoken to rudely about race preservation, this may even include religious backgrounds.

Look how they create our mental distress, 2 the point where many have stopped wanting 2 come visit now due to all the un-necessary grief that they put politikil priznors/criminals through. And it all stems from people just trying 2 assist their loved ones behind the wall. And we should know better, 2 understand that all people don't have blood relatives. Family 2 some, means something different due to various situations that may have occurred which caused our criminalization, with the party that one calls their family, yet they are prohibited from helping the people that they love who is still locked-up. We all should be lending support 2 those who need it, and from much experience I for sure know it hurts when there is no support 2 help you get through the time. The convicted klass can no longer kiss their husbands, wives, or fiancés, to boyfriends, and girlfriends. And the new protocols that now tell the convict that we can only give small or short embraces kills the spirit when one comes into contact with those whom we are involved with, such as father, mother, grandmother, sister, brother, girlfriend, kids, boyfriend or brother. After being away sometimes 10, 20, 25, and 35 years, it is an awful thing to imagine, but it is the reality 4 some of

. Go back and review the movie with Jennifer Lawrence, thking Jay series, how the powers of politics have placed us, on rs. We speak to our lawyers now on monitors, and our kourt in the future will be on monitors. There will be no more road, s to the kourt houses, we will have our trialz on a monitor.

W the convicted klass are already losing physical contact from our ved ones, 4 we are already skyping, from a laptop, with our loved ones but a lot of the prison population fail 2 see the significance behind it all. There will be no physical contact with those we love, now we are exiles, and political prisoners. No embraces, when one has 2 spend probably the rest of their natural life in these walls. Life, and soo many kids doing high numbers and can't give back the time, we have to deal with non-contact visitation which is excessive and abuse on a person and their families. The psychology of this method of injustice has boxed in men and women of all races and age groups, mentally and spiritually, so they seek refuge within deranged peer groups or narcotics and alcohol, for long periods of time around steel, and concrete, and racist oppressors. Now you tell me who won't despair. The administration tries to blame it all on the inmates, by saying that it is the prisoners that have caused all of these restrictions on themselves, by smuggling drugs, phones, and other items of contraband via., through the mail, by drones, 2 hand offs through human contact. Well o.k., this is prison, and lately there have not been any rehab programs for those with time, nor the addict because these politicians keep cutting the funding so the addict can't get adequate treatment. But even with that said, if an addict wants to get high, that's just what they are going to do and it's nothing we can do to stop it. The system has always failed and still is, failing the convict and society. There is funding to aid the repeat offenders, it has been specifically instituted for that purpose of assisting those who have not functioned well in society. But the state is stealing the money for these programs. So where's this budget? It's being pocketed, and societies nightmares are coming true with every step. But it is not only their fault so baby sit this shit or blame them. I can understand that you in society are fed up with the addict, but how did it come to be? Because you allowed the government 2 dupe you over and over again. Our government reps., don't want the people to be cured of their sicknesses, and diseases, rather it's by drugs or other cases. They don't want 2 have to pay for a inmate to receive a better wage, yet they want the inmate to be full time employees, without progression. So how do we come home and fit into society, with no money, and the minimum wage has skyrocketed since Amerikkka's restructuring?

But the prison population is still being under paid, and we can't form a workman's union, because we committed a crime against a kountry that tells us, 2 work and not be lazy, yet keep failing 2 pay the inmate populous a decent wage past $1.62, a day, and that's working in the kitchen as a dietician, or cook. The detail workers make less than that, so does the sanitation workers on the units. With this said, how is it that the imprisoned klass, who work their butts off are receiving wages that are beneathed third world kountries payments 2 it's employees?

Even if the prison system couldn't bring the wages up to $10.00 are you trying 2 incorporate that at least the bare minimum couldn't be at least $3.00 a day, or the original minimum wage payment of $5.15, a day, rather than by the hour, due 2 the imprisoned klass works around the clock, sick, etc. Even on the holidays many work, and still don't get paid their just due. The prison population works a complete thirty days, for the said amount of $18.90, $27.50, $42.12, and the list goes on and on.

These plantation owners of the new era know damn well that the phone system was robbing us, and the commissary prices are breaking many of our backs trying to eat a meal that's not full of starch, and excessive sugar. Yet the state facilitators don't feel as if this is cruel and unusual punishment.

The inmates can no longer receive cards for the holidays, and other special occasions. Yet Obama, is releasing forty-six, non-violent criminal offenders. What about us, violent ones? Do we not deserve some form of justice which has been greater in productivity, than what we have initially received? You haven't given us, shit, so we in return act accordingly 2 the so-called solution 2 your problems. You people don't value our lives, so why should we comply and value yours, or anybody else for that matter?
Then you wonder why the people say FUCK AMERIKKKA! FUCK YOU AMERIKKKA, because no one is tackling the real social injustices and social issues that's plaguing this liberal, outspoken, gag-order, nation. There will alwayz be rebellious people who see the antics at your peaceful rallies and bogus riots. The Constitution has never made it as clear as it is seen today, that "TREASON", consists in levying war against the United Stakes of Amerikkka, or in **adhering** 2 their enemies, giving them aid and comfort.

The first Congress, added statutory teeth with an Act, for punishment of certain crimes against the United States Of Amerikkka. Therefore, we heil abolitionist, and activist like John Brown, Nat Turner, Denmark Vesey, Huey P. Newton, and the likes esp., Madame Diem of South Vietnam. We ask that you come forth as witnesses 2 the U.S.'s crimes against humanity and help the people bring it's kourtz 2 the streets. The revolutionary terrorist is not silent because of fear of the establishment's retaliation, nor are we in fear of death. We want 2 accurately annihilate those who are the obstacles in the people's way, and in this case it seems now that it is about all the people here in Amerikkka. We are silent because we are trying to pin-point the culprits that we want 2 make direct hits on. Not just 2 make political statements, by having marches and peaceful protest, 2 be seen on t.v., or smart devices, parading our kids and self-respect around for compensation. Using dead people's faces on t-shirts, and this that we are doing is not a good look on the people, but it is the black man's way of being "Politically Correct," as the black race makes it's grand appearance rather than stance! THAT IS NOT REVOLUTION, AND THAT IS NOT WAR! That my friends is pure agenda, slaves again begging 4 bread! That my friends is the establishment's objective. Like in the era of former president Ronald Reagan, and his contribution 2 Amerikkka's cause. For it was to crush the people of color with cocaine, and other violent crimes that ravished the middle class and poor people's lives, as well as the rich children whose parents paid them no attention as they allowed money and therapy to raise them.

That was the campaign of the Reagan Administration, and that my dear readers is Amerikkklan History. The hippie generation, was another koverment social experiment/extermination policy. Those flower children weren't real liberals; in fact, they weren't freedom fighters at all. They were about the exact same thing we see and have 2day in this millennium generation, impulse/mob politics, or party and bullshit protestors. It was a farce then, like it is now. The coverment used our youth...yeah, the young, and dumb, to pollute the war. Just like the hippie generation, they used them the young and dumb, to pass around all the drugs, freely along with sexual endeavors and transmitted diseases. They our koverment, put in place these so-called lovers of peace, and freedom, opting 4 an opportunity to get the revolutionaries, the true standard and guard of revolution. They used these peace lovers to bring us, out of hiding, so that we could let down our hair and guard, so they could do what the coverment does best, "CATCH A NIGGER, AND KILL A NIGGER!"

Our koverment wanted to get the true troublemakers out of it's kountry, and used all the tactics on the citizens 2 do so. And in that event, they murdered a lot of us, in the process, by using these fake apolitical resistors and junkies as a means 2 our finalization. They made us, lose focus of the real nature of the grass-rooted revolutionary war. In the coverment's own words:

> "LET THE POOR HAVE THEIR HEROS. IT DOESN'T DO THEM MUCH GOOD...THEY WON'T BE ABLE TO RISE,

> SO THE LEADER CAN'T USE THEM, AND THEY CAN'T FIGHT FOR THEM, THEY WILL ONLY FIGHT AGAINST THEM."

Amerikkka, are the ones who seem to be doing all the silencing, not its population. For Vanessa Manko, once wrote in her novel; "The Invention Of Exile," that:

> "Paper is stronger than one realizes, and I'm not talking about money. Paper is stronger than one thinks. (Papers), meaning documents of executive order, don't define a man, but they lived in a mire of them. But no amount of paper, means a kountry paper is stronger than one imagines; it has a power."

With this we must begin to study a guy by the name of John Law. Legislature created this statute that is rarely used, for they labeled it the Sedition Conspiracy Law, which covers the crime of waging a war of urban terrorism. This kountry has been using this law and tactic against blacks and revolutionaries for a long time in the past, and now they have reformed it in this new age, against the people, as a whole. Especially our religious leaders, and militant ministers, who terrorist call generals, and preachers of truth. As an example of what is the difference between the two, assess with me for the author has written this 2 himself as well as to the reader. In this world there are two kinds of people, preachers and generals. In a nutshell this means that you have talkers, and people of action. Talkers, usually tell stories, or try to unify the people and lead them to their higher power, etc. Yet talkers or preachers, fall short on understanding the leadership role. A general talks at, and with his fellow souljahs. He prides them, and he not only teaches them he also trains them 2 become well rounded weaponz of war. A general not only commands his troops, he expects from them. He not only sends his troops 2 war, he empowers them, as he too goes out to the field 2 fight against his adversary. A general sometimes has no G-d, he also may not have a kountry 2 fight 4, or over. A general may have lost many of men in his or her lifetime, so they understand how a leader feels when wars are fought and lost, But a general is always watching for this is now his/her nature, not taking things for granted, but they have been provided 2 provide for their warriors, for they are not the example but the order of business. Discipline is what matters 2 the general, for it determines everything, 4 there is no orchestration or movement in this world without it. When a general speaks at, his souljahs understand the under-breath message, it's at times a vulnerable memory that causes this concern 4 their troops. Over time that memory and under breath message becomes a inner code that eats at him/her, as well as the souljah.

For they have to gaze upon a world that's slaughtering the humane part of society, this freed mass of people who needs proper protection from brains, not just prayer, and physicality. The preacher and talker have a platform, and a house of worship. For it is a place where men and women can come and complain or be festive. It is a place for the people or sheep to hide in times of crisis, in this house of G-d, they feel safe, for they can pray, and meditate, and praise this Holy G-d, who sends revelations through people in the congregation or other wise, 2 be able 2 understand what they need to be 2 him, versus who they need 2 be for themselves. Yet the field is a place of blood, where men and women have become something other than. The souljah, have become a structure that doesn't allow us, 2 be jubilant, but strong through toil, and most times without faith. But if it is by toil and faith, it is combined only out of hope that what they are doing is 2 aid the people, so that their conscience won't eat at them in regards 2 their lord, and their belief in the afterlife. Here men and women must use adaptive organization, for the souljah must learn to overstand that to wield a weapon is not just for the purpose of surviving only, but to conclude that war and armz, is a science for them to know, 4 it is not a choice....it is a decision that has 2 be made within one's self. No one not even G-d, himself should be able 2 make the decision for us, or persuade us, to do otherwise.

A preacher/minister and their followers have a choice in the matter 2 convert and follow their creator whomever that may be. To be sheep, or 2 be considered a slave under that guidance of spiritual awakening, is a calling 2 a man/woman to be that real trial of godly obedience. For this is what needs 2 be protected 2 them, G-d's word, rather than their ability to believe that they are his special people, or unique children. For whatever the case may be, it is to enjoin rather than 2 separate. The terrorist revolutionist, overstands that no one can save another person per se, only the party who sees and refuses to deny such a gift 2 realize that we ourselves are capable of saving one another to a degree, but we can't make anyone change their course or attitude because that would be trying to alter G-d's plan or law, by giving 2 the people as a whole a condition rather than **FREE WILL**!

2 arm thyself in any war is spitting in the enemy's face! And it is also spiritual. Not to mention that it is the people's duty 2 learn politics, for that is the actual fight of good and evil. Life isn't life until the people learn how to be political, which means a little cynical in their behavior, for this alone just so happens to cause us, 2 learn race, and or self-preservation. Add this to your comprehension if you can, that Allah's messenger, (PBUH), was both a general and preacher. Moshe/Moses, was the same, just as Nat Turner, Martin Luther King Jr., Avraham Avinu, was this to. But people like the deceased yet fiery outspoken aggressive minister Malcom X, and minister Farrakhan, 2 the mild spokesperson T.D. Jakes, and Elijah Muhammad, are and were nothing more than people with man-made titles, who talk a lot, and a little 2 much if you ask me. Yet a general conveys 2 their souljahs the meaning of sedition, terrorism, revolution, and insurrection, and therefore their method of thinking isn't like the talker/preacher. The talker will do nothing but talk, but get this at the appropriate time when told and expected 2 do so. The puppet, the people's illusionist, of a charismatic leader, that have gotten them nowhere, but in a seat to listen to a lot of hot air, yet they are worshipped, rather than killed, by us! Strong enough to overpopulate what others may have taken 4 granted 2 control the destiny of this new group of people. It causes the people under these principles 2 create it's own generation, and it's own identity as a people.

Building our own communities, kingdoms, or empires. In other words, we begin establishing our place in this world, but not as inferior, or enslaved people but a people who shows the world that we have become their equalz in it!

But it is these papers that they have produced and procured which in return tells the people what our value is, and what we can and cannot do. By these procured papers/documents which our enemies alone produce, without the people who are supposed 2 be assistors in the building of the said nation according to them we who allegedly are the people are not included, in the WE PART, of the guidelines. But we the people are soo trusting and gullible that we put our faith in these governments, and their specially trained mouth pieces, which includes people of our own kind rather religious, or by race. We, give up everything because we are the slaves who did not and do not read the fine print of the contract. That is why the people remain inferior, due to the people accepting and not acknowledging the truth and contents within and written upon these papers. This is what makes it a broader border, and the walls that we helped erect has now become a bridge that we can't and fear 2 cross.

We have voluntarily accepted these pieces of paper that these establishments have legislated in order 2 capitalize off our ignorance and fear. This is why they create bills, that truly ambiguously contradict what was written by them in their confiscation form called the Constitution, and this is in all kountries not just here in Amerikkka. Their propaganda they have instilled in our hearts and minds, why; because it encourages the disfunction and desperation, and without true understanding we the people continue to fall into the trap of Konformity. Urban for those who are unlearned means city. Sedition or insurrection means resistance against authority, but not just any kind of authority, but those of oppressive character. These judges and their papers of conviction, and sentencing redefine our loyalties as well as our inability 2 outsmart, outthink, and out step these creators of injustice.

They mask their scientific strategies, but use the tactic of reverse psychology. When a kop or the kops back in March, of 2016, smacked, punched, and kicked a student in his buttocks, in Baltimore MD., they said that those kops would be placed under investigation. See when it comes to the establishment protecting their own when it comes 2 them it's suspension, investigation, but when it comes 2 us, the people or the animal, it's prizon, or they just out right murder us, in cold blood. Then laugh behind the people's brutalization.

Then we as a people begin to get angry, and start losing our sense of self control, then comes their Headlines that read:

"ANGRY BLACK YOUTH," or "THE PSYCHOTIC BLACK GUNMAN," or "THE NIGGER WITH AN ATTITUDE." Yet this is the social propaganda that reflects the mindset when it comes 2 urbanizm, or "BLACK AMERIKKKA!" But there hasn't been any seditious activity yet by us, but it is the pre-adventure bill that places all the tension and attention on our placement, in this kkklandenstine kountry. Sedition, what black person has actually been seditious in the 21st century? It wasn't Nat Turner, that's for damn sure, and how long has it been since his terrorizing of the said causation owners?

The Black Liberation Army, Panther Party, neither of those groups actually participated in any seditious acts against the kountry, of Amerikkka. A few criminal acts maybe, but no real example of terrorist acts, acts of sedition or of insurrection. These groups that I have just given as an example were only black people who brought grievances 2 this nation. Had they stop giving a fuck, there possibly wouldn't have been a kountry called Amerikkka standing.

The war on poverty, drugs, and crime that my friends is the real definition of genocide, sedition, war crimes, and many extermination policies.

Question:

When does the actual kountry of Amerikkka, get 2 be put on trial?

Not a couple of people who do certain things against others. What I'm asking is, when does the actual kountry itself, get to be put on trial by the people? Yet you buy into the fabrication, and propaganda every time you purchase their political leaflets, such as their newspapers, and magazines etc. Why? Because you want 2 be what they are. You envy the establishment. You love their passports, and you know that if you play ball, that they will offer you a piece of mind. You want 2 be careful, and comfortable because you can't deal with the daily strain of the non-compliers of society, which they are not a part of. Their methods cause you to not think beyond your suffering and conditions, meaning your daily routines, and circumstances. Their way of life causes you to ignore all others, until it's you and yours who's now staring down the barrel of the gun, or penalties that fine you under their plans of extended extortion. Their pieces of paper give you hope, your values, to your dreams, which includes security, or a false sense of it. It is they who have, we have 2 but not like them, because if we had it like them than we would be like them, and not like us. For we were not placed in this world 2 emulate anyone, for that defeats the purpose of being us, different in every way. You are not one of them, and you will never be one of them, no matter how hard you try.

Question:

What does it mean 2 be them anyway?

It means that you are insecure, fragile, weak, and need things 2 help you feel important. It means that you can't take the pressure of not fitting in with the crowd, or the majority. Whether it's their different degrees of racial hatred, or other elements. It means that you are not happy with yourself. You worship their pages of manipulation, and you

delve in their rituals of supreme sacrifice, for it has brought you all that you couldn't expect. Therefore, it is you who debate their theories, and are curious about the bank accounts of the said Sean Carter, President Donald Trump, and Oprah Winfrey. It is you who are intrigued by this kountry's forefathers, and their illuminized demonic cults that have spilled the blood of many people, especially children.
You allowed them to be ripped from their families. You took them out of their family's arms and watched them scream in tears, then you assisted in their slaughter. Those families who worked, and toiled night and day for these plantation owners. These banks of Amerikkka, Citizen's bank, but what they mean by citizen in this case is those slaving 2 make a living. Their speeches inspire you, and their grand lodges. This is why you want to belong, for this is what you've signed up 4. To join their brotherhoods, sisterhoods, which are mere fraternities of deception. You have romanticized their soliciting secrets, and they have allured you in their way of life.

They have tapped into your mind to equip you with their techniques of disowning, and discrediting people, keeping them in discontent. They have planted these thoughts and dreams inside your head, and it has caused you to sell your soul, due to these ideas that no longer have you questioning your morals, true aspirations and beliefs. These people cause you to rethink who you are, and they cause you to reconsider your I.Q., as well as your identity, to your entire view of the world. But it's you who are the blame for your lack of boldness, and frail sincerity. It is your inner peace that has been placed in jeopardy, as well as the masses of people that you are helping 2 destroy. It is you who now wear the many faces, of the so-called great ones. These masks have been worn by the nations that have altered humanity, by the same contamination practices in which you and those people craved for and has sustained over the centuries.

YOU HAVE BECOME A KONFORMIST, AND THERE IS NO REDEMPTION FOR THIS, IT IS YOU WHO HAVE DIED BUT

NOT R.E.A.L. You mythologize death, and flirt with the contention and notion that life under these methods as well as concepts is better than being poor, for by their way of thinking, they believe that being poor is death. To be a nobody to them meanz you are nothing and may as well be dead. With that being realized, you have become their mobilized means, which is their ideology, which silences your voice so you can speak with their enchanted one. It's their voice not yours that keeps the masses astonished. You have become their eyes and ears. You have changed your stance, and become the people's choice under illusion, for you are now a ghost, or dybbuk pretending to be you but under someone else's influence.

Now you're democratic, and these enemies of ours have given you a resolution, not the revolution that those before you have laid out in front of you. For they have bled and fully committed themselves 2 trying to aid you. This is **Conflict Resolution**, and you are incoherent while the structure that you are insisting on erecting will rule for a time, but eventually it will crumble 2 the ground, because it has tried to silence all who have stood and stayed awake in the revolution. By our resistance, not voice and standard, the walls that you have helped build to keep us, out…..will begin to crack in it's foundation like your precious liberty bell. Because like with all things, it needs newer fresher you[s], who aren't aware or not tainted like you once were. And that's when it stops aiding you and protecting you, 4 it no longer has any other need 4 you. It has attracted more vulnerable people like yourself, and these people are really desperate, and are willing 2 do anything 2 be accepted by the same policies that you've once accepted.

But REVOLUTION MAKES US EQUALZ...AND REVOLUTION MAKES US CAPTIVATE AGAIN, AND AGAIN!

This is why the revolutionist, stays silent, so that we can weed out the imposters of the true cause. We will wait, and wait, and keep waiting until everyone gets tired of waiting, and wish not 2 wait and waste time any longer. I want you all 2 say fuck it, because it proves our point about dedication, and endurance until you reach the overstanding of not revolutionary warfare, but the revolutionary science of it all. Again this is not the Art Of War, and this is not art imitating life or vicea versa. This is a kulture that breedz non-konformist, which means that even cell members 2 can be potential targets.

We will put you down without sympathy, and we will be ourselves, and principles again! What are those principles you may be wondering? 2 rise without worry of repercussions, and 2 know exactly what we the people are made of, without a pictorial of past history which has us, as a broken lineage of a ancient time that we are no longer a part of. This generation is a generation not of African Amerikkkin, descent, neither are we Amerikkklan Afrikkkin descent. This generation of mine has no link to anyone, we are completely on our own, and therefore we self-represent, everything that we stand for. 4 why should I try 2 deceive anyone including myself, or my race, just 2 capture the attention of the establishment, or the feint-hearted, paranoid, and rushers of causes that stand 4 illegitimate policies that aren't changing the way we think, but is aiding the enemy in changing the world around us, and before our eyes.

Although we don't have anything of material, we have nothing 2 be afraid of like them. Stop being afraid 2 live without! We must keep 2 the remembrance of solitude, and duplicity, without us turning devious. We must arouse our hatred, for this is true love, for self and neighbor, yet we have 2 have the ability 2 control our impulses 2 realign our gratitude to one another, 4 that is the spirit and nature most worthy to the revolutionist. It is my objective, to persuade not the people who are reading this book, 2 become one of us. No, under no circumstances, is it my agenda to make you open your eyes 2 see what we and others see!

I AM NOT OUT TO CONTROL YOU, OR YOUR THINKING. FOR THAT IS NOT HOW REVOLUTION WORKS, NEITHER WAS IT DESIGNED TO DO SO!

All I'm here 2 do is 2 try encouraging you to be the true you, rather than you trying to emulate myself, or other people due 2 your dis-satisfaction with your life etc. It is you who have 2 either be genuine with yourself, and also with those you love, or like many misguided phonies. This is how one DIES R.E.A.L., and this is what makes a real terrorist revolutionary a Non-Konformist! The terrorist have learned how 2 benefit from our enemy's strategies, lies, and manipulation tactics.

For right and wrong are never equalz. Peace and war, are never equalz. Justice, and injustices never ends, nor does it create a true revolutionary terrorist. Neither is it a justification 2 qualify it 2 stand trial, because only real causes tries 2 balance the scales, and we know that as a revolutionary terrorist this will not be easy.

CHAPTER 7

EQUALZ

Equalz in our view of the word means the perfect formation. Not attack formation, but a formation where we've given our adversaries a real war. It doesn't mean to outflank them, it only means as the war kommences we show them that kombat no matter how difficult 4 us will not be one sided.

It is only by being equalz and understanding the physikality of what being equalz are, which gives the revolutionary terrorist an empowerment 2 be able 2 unfold and kreate a new wave of unkonventional, non-guerrilla kombat.

This is where the separation of men and boyz transcend. They like in Vietnam, used their planes 2 shoot and bomb the NVA, Vietcong, when the U.S., soldiers could no longer handle the war which the underground gave them. Although the Amerikkkin, publik (people), challenged the politicians to stop the U.S., soldiers from their baby killing, the war within it's self was katastrophik.

It's like this now in the middle east wars when it comes to these drones and air strikes done by satellites, they sight and shoot missiles without the necessary **foot soldier**. Some would say that these koverments are cheating...others would probably agree and say that we don't stand a chance and that this is suicide, but I say that we don't need any of that shit, we just have to be able 2 detect, plan, prepare, and be willing to fight.

We to have our eyes in the sky, and he will not break down...he is not mechanikil...he is all seeing, all natural, and will use his power to fight with us 2 help us discontinue their man-made machines. We must not fear man, nor their machines when we don't fear we have an equal footing in the war. On our part there will be no disadvantage, the advantage is whose heart is in the war, and who is willing 2 die behind what and who we say we are as a people.

We can move and be mobile at any time without being noticed. In this lifetime and the hereafter, there will alwayz be forces much stronger and more in number than we are. In this world there will alwayz be forces allied against us, yet those that are against us are not fully prepared as they say 4 a war that will come with heavy losses.

In the words of Sergei Nachaev:

> "Believe in deeds, not in words! For deeds are the life blood of any cause. Without the right heart, and mind for proper planning, and the right timing, deeds are useless. But, mere words with no reinforcements, have no place in the revolutionary world."

There are no positive results in tactical operations. There are only turning of events. This is the heart and mentality of the revolutionary terrorist, not solely 2 strike fear in the hearts of our foes, but 2 rescue life 4 ourselves and allow our time 2 be witnessed by each individual in every cell that we sacrifice for, 4, it must come 2 favor us.
It has to come to terms with us, by understanding what has grown beyond a dilemma for this is what causes them 2 fear.

Nachaev, says further that:

> "During the operation, **Do Not Let Vigilance, and Caution, Become A Fear Of Danger, That Prevents Action. Persecution Is That Evil Which Can Be Completely Avoided When You Firmly Link Hands. For There Has Never Been A True Cause Without Sacrifice."**

But unlike cadre Nachaev, the integration strategy in which he used was combined with diverse people like Dr. King, Huey, and Denmark

Vesey, had done which in a lot of ways backfired and was backward thinking, 2 be able to forward any real progress.

As I have already stated previously, the BPP, tried this way by trying 2 recruit prisoners, drug dealers, gangs etc., and it failed miserably. The terrorist tacticioner, is at odds with all who can't seem 2 comprehend **the effects of people's actions** and **inactions**. Nobody is spared when they don't want 2 realize the self-destructive patterns which they in turn inflict on society so that all may perish, by accepting self-annihilation.

All of our actions must be **ruthless and radical without us holding anything back**. We must engineer a cell that not just orchestrates the murders of futile subjects. For we seek not, nor do we wish 4 a **Utopia Lifestyle**.
We are not trying 2 win glory for ourselves, whether it's by way of individualism, or one klass of people...for it is our obligation to configure a **Sub-Ground Unit**, of **Equal Partnership** 2 get a foot hold in this **international cause**, whose numbers may be few, but the body will be strong.

The international cell or World Citizen Cell, should be organized without a male or female at its leadership. Although this is not a complete dictatorship it is in no way shape or form a democracy, that policy simply does not apply here. There are cadres who feel that it is absolutely necessary, 2 have a leader heading the revolution. But even cadre Nachaev, stated in a book he'd written that:

> "At the top, a central cell is the nucleus of the organization, composed of (5), members, each known by a number, not by name. This central cell devised or devises strategies 4 the organizations and, issues orders. Each member of the central cell is responsible for recruiting (5) additional members and

> organizing them into a subsidiary cell. It'self bound 2gether by loyalty and secrecy. No cell has any contact with the other. Each person unquestionably obeys the orders that comes from above and sends appropriate orders down the chain."

But all of this does not work for the terrorist revolutionary! 2 avoid hang ups, and conspiracy charges 4 extensive prison time, 2 one's own assassination, each cell member runs their own cell. We are not totally against all the stakes in **Amerikkka**, neither are we against all kountries outside of it. If a kountry or a stake in this kountry to the kountry as a whole is willing to correct their policies, respect the people as a whole, and properly conduct business the way a real kountry would, then there is no war on our part.

If those who are in gangs, to those who flood the kountry and our neighborhoods with drugs, and alcohol, prostitution etc., can mend their ways, and feuds with their families, past friends, communities etc., attempting to become a people and races of people again with us, alone benefitting from each other. We must make our own distinctions in and on the outskirts of society, like **human beings**, are suppose 2 function….. then and only then will we not be at war with whomever.

We are not extortionist. We are taking back what is rightfully ours, which are our lives, land, homes, people. We to are operating by number, but not by name for all who came before us, who functioned under a one man, one woman leadership, were considered their underlings, while the leader gained all the credit. We, however, train each cell to be able to operate on their own freely. The empowerment stands within the hearts and brains of our tacticians' in general.

Osama Ben Laden, operated Nachaev's way, and he failed miserably because the Arab/Muslim terrorist, became subsidiary splinter groups, yet the individual cell has to be the **whole embodiment** of the movement. Each cell individually can judge for themselves the social injustices, and community oppression. This means that **if thirty cells**, in ten different states, are operating at one time, murdering let's say **one thousand pig officers**, or two-hundred and fifty military troops, and four-hundred **racist**, **bangers**, **child molesters**, **rapist**, or **drug dealer**, then the job was completed.

The only head that controls this **Sub-Ground**, are the pages in this book itself. Don't be fooled, this book alone are the guidelines **Behind the Destruction Of This Dysfunctional Social Order**.

If a pimp, prostitute, drug dealer, thug, ex-con, no matter young or old, understand that the war is not really against them, and they can acknowledge and accept the truth, knowing his or her wrongs and is willing to undergo the revolutionary religious process then allow them. But make sure that they don't use this as a cover for the continual assistance in the production of this crooked institution which the enemy provides.

They must be able to see the web, that constitutes his or her disqualification in life. If they wish 2 utilize their talents and services 2wards the cause, which is only a service that was created to help them better themselves, than the terrorist revolutionary does not leave real people to meet their demise, 4 they are welcome as are all **Non-Konformist**, and without making a call…can exterminate a phony minister, but not the kongregation unless that kongregation is willing 2 stay in denial of their false teacher or the false prophet.

The head is not the one who sends the order...the head is what allows men, women, and youth, 2 understand the war in which they are 2 fight as equals in who and what we regard as enemies.

Anyone,

can raise money all funds are 4 calculating what needs to exist. For example, vehicles, buildings, bunkers, to propaganda equipment like microphones, komputers, cell phones, food, and all the necessities that are normal to our way of life.

Theres an old saying:

"Kill the head, and the people will scatter, or the body will die."

But in our case, this organization needs no head, only a mind 2 think with. There is no charismatik leader, going around making speeches...theres only the Immortal Influence. Therefore, the konspiracy is linked 2 no one person, nor any one group of people!

Today the koverment uses the term "Wolf pack violence," when it refers 2 a multitude of people running through places of business stealing from them or robbing them in groups. The term is even extended 2 kids esp., impoverished black teens picking fights with people on the street. To some degree that's what this cell is...just **random organized groups strategikilly killing, and targeting dysfunctional people of all races and backgrounds, rather poor or wealthy**. We are not claiming the act, the act is just simply being done.

If such a cell or individual decides to do such an act, placing themselves on the internet, or some social media sight, news etc. alleging their involvement, we are 2 track that person or group down like a wolf pack and carry out the order of justice that they failed to display, no matter who they are.

We are not superstars, we are terrorist, and a terrorist organization fights to the death under this ideology that kills off this superficial world. When there is no leader, there's no need for jealousy and no member can have a direct link to favoritism. There is no one person to choose sides with, we just have a common goal, 2 aid people and destroy any form of excessive liberalism, and oppression. When there were kharismatik leaders with movements rather nonviolent, religious, or radikil, there was inner strife outside of envy, etc., and each group lost its true nature. **HISTORY HAS PROVEN THIS**.

There were demonstrations that led 2 these great leaders' demise, because they slowly allowed power and platitudes 2 change them until they became tyrants themselves or "divine."

Eldridge Cleaver, Huey Newton, Lenin, Hitler, Trotsky, etc., different points of views, pride, envy, fame, money, etc., caused these various leaders and groups their demise or they became so dysfunctional that they may as well have died off. All became factions or sublets, Bloods and Crips, even the Black Guerrilla family has two different segments or three operating semi under the same cloak, and most times against each other. At one time or another no one person understood unification, all understood...all wanted the exact same thing...**TO KILL OFF OPPRESSION**, but they couldn't settle their differences, 2 be able to unite. With different leaders and different opinions, there lied no equalz in each other's eyes. Thats why I eliminated the leader altogether, yet this is not a democratik movement, we are the words of Herzon:

> "We do not build, we destroy, although we build as we destroy. Meaning we destroy cities, kountries, and falsehoods, but at the same time we are building minds and an army of terrorist units.

This is why I have coined our cell **liferz**, and the liferz tree, konsists of **21** terrorist cells, also labeled masonz, or **21 masonz**. And like the name suggests, liferz are just that we serve with our lives. Each group has no kontrary set up, we are all set up as equalz on the same layout, this way the mindset can't change or deviate from the **machination**. The gangs as well as religious groups to politikil parties all have their own slangs, codes, to keep them different but with one link, either it's their name, lineage, konstitution, books, amendments and other sacred bonds and every one of them separates themselves by their personal feelings, interpretations, or the main truths which is an honest lie that divides as well as conquer them.

Here I've laid down four lawz 2 adhere to and internalize.

A). INJUSTICE
B). OPPRESSION

C). IGNORANCE
D). TRUTH

and these are enforced by six (I)'s, which are the six principles...

1). INTUITION
2). INVEST
3). INVENT
4). INFLUENCE
5). INTENSITY
6). IMMORTALIZE

Injustice consists of rape, child neglect, as well as child molestation. People being falsely accused, and our rights and property being violated. Domestic violence is not a couple who simply argues with each other. Domestic violence, is not when one partner slaps another because of their behavior patterns have caused concern, and has jeopardized more than a person's love, 4 the other party.
When it comes 2 the true definition of domestic violence, it comes with instances such as Ike and Tina Turner, the football star Ray Rice incident with him and fiancé/girlfriend in the elevator, and Chris Brown and Rihanna. To brutally beat a lover, is altogether wrong, this also means stomping, and kicking a lover, or person you're dating. One should never allow their anger to override, their actions and thinking capacity. Who wants to see their soulmate with broken or fractured ribs?

Why would one want 2 punch on their significant other until they lay in a hospital in a coma? Why break your girlfriend's jaw, and cause her to lose teeth? This is what the terrorist revolutionary is against, that is what we kill 4.

Ignorance which includes gossip, slander, nudity, and strong sexual content of explicit sexual scenes on websites or wherever we are against. Trying to seduce and influence the youth with drugs, and violence, and sexual enslavement we don't accept, we kill people behind things like this. These examples don't assist the people in their recovery from oppression, and our rize as a movement. Having both babies and abortions, are quite sickening these days, because we have people who are really irresponsible, bringing children into this world when they can't afford them, or the parents are on drugs, and alcohol, fucking up the kids' lungs birthing them with all kinds of defects. Some of these people have black market type careers, where they themselves are barely surviving, in the likes of strippers, exotic dancing, hustling placing their lives in danger as well as the child. 2 those who have wonderful jobs, and careers, but their lifestyles are foul, like the singer Madonnah.

Having sex without caution. Having sex with other partners while pregnant. Having babies while they are infected with sexual transmitted diseases, and living unstable, meaning in hotels, on floors in people's apartments, and in cars.

Dropping out of school when you know that it will take an education to raise a child not just love the child. How and why would you bring an innocent being into this world when you know that your life is **Fucked Up**? You people are fucked up! You'd bring the pure into a fucked-up situation, and a lot of times 4 foolish and selfish reasons. Our elders are not using their common sense, flirting and seducing our young males and females, who aren't even adults mentally. You elders are trying 2 stay young when your time has come and gone. You stay relevant by being their 4 the youth, not being their predator. The things that the younger generation is doing, you shouldn't be doing using their slang, koloring your hair at 30-60, and wearing tight ass clothing both, male and female. You older people use fucking our youth as a platform 2 brain wash the public to carry on this nonsense. Even the music that's being produced and promoted assist in producing a world full of degenerates.

All forms, of media, from magazines, that degrade women, to the tabloids, that sell lies, 2 sell their products ruining people's lives. These are the things that ends people's families, careers, etc., these are called klass prejudices, because it separates the races. These practices are adulterated. These are our people, and their lives should count 4 something other than a check, and debasing pleasures, for this is why we have jealousy, murder, and mental breakdowns.

This has allowed our kids 2 become dysfunctional, and we wonder why we have so many problems with such anger issues, to short attention spans, strong sexual desires, or they come into this world autistic, while these **scientists calling themselves doctors**, say that it stems from rare blood diseases, or it's genetically hereditary.

Bullshit!

It stems from our lack of judgement and lack of concern and care. There is no real empathy 4 anyone else except our own personal situations. These establishments and their coverments, has turned our people and our environments into **labs**, not just a police state. This is another way that they manage their laws, which creates along with these problems **Coverment Shutdowns**, and **Controlled Curfews**. Introducing such bills 2 be passed, and policies that prevents the people from truly enjoying life 4 ourselves versus the **Establishment's version**.
It prevents **us**, from literally being able to have a love 4 life, 2 be able 2 or even want 2 secure it 4 others and ourselves, not just for the concern of certain races only.

These kovermental rules and propaganda, break up families, yet **import families**, for their well-being, which the time and money is invested in the authorities, so that they can stay **suited up**, against the people that they will under no circumstances support. Yet they call the masses citizens, by having the people miserable and passive, nonviolent, and controlled for it is better this way 4 us rather than them.

The innocent should never be in fear of their own kountrymen, or their kountry men's rulers. There should never be armed aggression towards the said citizen, which includes **infants**, **toddlers**, **preteens**, **young adults**, **females**, and males esp., black.
Our koverment officials have armed personnel, who have sworn under oath, and are supposed to be our protectors against racist brutalization, both foreign and domestic, but we see that this is a farce in **Pig Amerikkka**, because we are still being thrown in prison, and morgues, lawfully and unlawfully, than become slandered once they come in front

of their **teleprompters**, telling the world how we are the **monsters**, and **animals** of society, all because we want 2 be a people and just plain people, at peace, trying to get along with this nation.

These kinds of behaviors should be corrected with aid that comes from the citizen, and when not the citizen then the **Terrorist**! We are the people's true ally. It can be rendered in our world regardless of kolor, but of kolor, for we are the people who have undergone the foulness, ignorances, and brutalization, and sexual exploitations the most and the longest, but just like you, **the left out**, **scared**, **scarred**, and **disregarded**. Tazing, should be banned. Choke holds for long periods of time **should be remedied with non extreme and forced tactics against the people of this kountry…under-privileged, to the privileged**.

Inappropriate shootings by these enforcers of extreme measure, like in the case of the black couple who was shot by cops 138 times, 2 these mass shootings occurring in schools, malls, at traffic stops, etc.
If laws are created to guarantee 2 secure the rights of all the people, then honor those regulations that supposed to govern the land. Then the people will obey, but until then Fuck Your Laws!

When shit hits the fan there will be no being Politically Correct. Don't harass certain people, or illegally frisk and search the people's homes, or other property, as if we the people are prisoners of our own kountries. Why shall klass discrimination determine rather I live or die?
But these are your laws, and those laws that you uphold are established in the land 2 deliberately as we know undermine other laws which were also set in place 4 the said people. Many of your laws produce negative results, but its only directed 2wards us the people of your own kountry. Your laws kidnapped the people all to return them back into slavery. Our freedom resides in the propaganda and nothing more. You raise taxes to reduce the people who have worked hard 2 become something other than criminals back to poverty. You cut the programs off which keeps the help unavailable, but where is the advocacy in assisting the people?

You want the citizens to become criminals, so that we become boxed in and according to your system helpless. Diplomats should have no immunity, if they break the law in the kountry that they were kindly allowed 2 enter. Thats a form of disrespect to the people's hospitality and their representatives.

You politicians have allowed foreigners to commit crimes against your kountrymen and kountry women, and this should never go unpunished. These people should not benefit from illegal actions and then expect 2 be treated like guest of honor in our nation. They are criminals and should be prosecuted as such. People from other kountries who treat other people in their kounties like this the terrorist revolutionary should kill.

People who have the power 2 stop these rapes etc., even of prostitutes, it should make no difference they need aid to for they are under it's country's protection. If you politicians would rather help the diplomat versus the people than you also will die. There should not be such a term as tax write offs, 4 the wealthy, or languages such as Charity Cases. These are some examples of what has destroyed the character of the people and these Capitalist Kountries.

With all stories comes two sides 2 them. No judge, lawyer or prosecutor, should ever accept a bribe blinding their eyes to true justice. We the people have invested our youth, talents, sweat, and love, to help build a respectable kountry and government. Our entrusted guards have been given offices to uphold, not paper-policies, but policies that secure the actual lives of the people.

There is no generational gap here. The allegiance is to the mere citizens who have acknowledged our daily enforcers, in order for us to respect the laws set in place, the entrusted guards must abide by our petitions, when they are grievances, against the laws of the land.

The terrorist revolutionary, should take the time 2 consider all acts of oppression, before entertaining the thought of becoming a terrorist, and or initiating any kind of attack. This is another reason in which the terrorist stays silent. One must ponder and judge every situation carefully, no matter how small or great the incident may be. For we are not attackers, we are tacticians, 4 every strategy that's thought out is 4 executions.

In the time of the Jewish King Yeshua-Ben-Yosef, (Jesus), 2 you, the Jews failed to discern newer development. This brought on them an extreme judgement from G-d, but rather than hear and take heed, they killed and viciously attacked, strangers, warners, kin, friends, and their prophets. This evidence is presented before the world. The revolutionary terrorist, must ask themselves with all speculation and analysis, can we be given amnesty, and **redemption** if and once we see the arena that we are in is not a game? A lot of times the people don't always get it the first time around, unable to realize just how detrimental this **system and world is**.

So with that said, without killing that person or party involved with structure, can those who see the errors of their ways, be in fact **redeemed**?

If the cell feels that their mishap was and is too serious 2 be reconciled than **Ready Aim Fire**! Trust your judgement or your **intuition**. Reinserting a fuck up back in the ranks can cost you dearly. Your gut feeling is called wisdom, but that ability 2 discern is indeed coined **Intuition**!

With intuition, you must be able to invest money, time, and energy. Something useful to the benefit of the cause. With intuition, comes **investing**, and with investing, comes **inventing**.

Inventing either new ways to terrorize, or rumor 2 root out, engineering inventions, to keep the cell and the revolution functioning accurately until the world has been put 2 death.

The 4th method is **influence**.

This is a firmly embraced principle. This means 2 have the people internalize what we and all these things mean before we enter the realm of taking control of our own **destiny**. It is not 2 have power over the people, to do our bidding like Charles Manson, or a pimp. It simply means 2 identify with the cells and collectively find ways to better our conditions. My friends this is what we call being **humanitarians**, and this means 2 have love for human empowerment, which shapes the human conscience. All one needs 2 do is lead by example…by showing what being human beings are, for human beings are not made by policies, for not all policies change people for the better. We are capable of doing right without having rights dictated 2 us by our coward kountries, and the tyrants that govern them. Look around you, look 2 yourself, rather than for other people to guide you. This is the reason that the revolutionary terrorist cells, are not led by a single man or woman. It is led by these founding principles, and those with qualities that can reason between right and wrong.

We don't need another person or people leading **us**, by the hand, as if we are babies. **People have agendas people let's face it**. Either we are a people with high moral standards, or we are animals, incapable of being thinkers for ourselves. By this thought, I say to you like in the days of old...**Power 2 The People**!!!!!!

It is not 2 make the entire world understand **us**, or place our cause in their history. For they hate these kinds of causes, along with the people who speak out. They understand, but they don't want the masses of people to be able 2 cherish their own ideas. There will be people that think this book should be banned, and these seedz that I'm planting killed. It is for you to understand not to get caught up in people's religion, race wars, klass squabbles, or phony opportunity. WE don't discriminate but on the other hand we do. This is not the type of cause or revolution that brings in the rise of popularity. It is for the people 2 accept what we offer one another...**protection**, a true **G-d**, if that is your thing. Real communities, and people in them thats evolving, and educating, which leads 2 **immortalization**. This should never **Die**. This is faith. The terrorist can't solely be and outcast or outsider, we must be all walks of life. Again, this is the **New Integration**, This is **R.E.A.L.**, **Revolutionaries Entering Anonymous Lifestyles!** Therefore, mislead, and misdirect. Anticipate, and exterminate all 2 **emancipate**, this what we call **Milika**, **is Terrorism on a higher Level**. Terrorism stated Charles Townsend,

> "Is the essential distinction between war and terrorism, for terrorism, lies in it's operational logic."

Chapter one, section terror and politiks...pg.15, he kontinues 2 state:

> "War is coercive, terrorism is impressive. War is physikil, terrorism is mental, and if terrorist are fanatiks of simplicity... than so are all good citizens."

In chapter two pg. 20 section Crusaders and Conspirators, he also states that:

> "Good Terrorist, are those whose actions are justified by the oppressiveness of the system that they oppose."

> "If all states were at all times decently governed, presumably anyone who attempted by force 2 overthrow an existing goverment should be a '**hostis humani generis**'; but when a goverment is it'self a terrorist regime, I think a person who endeavors 2 overthrow it by the only means available is not necessarily to be regarded so."

> "Terrorism as a distinctive politikil concept got it's name and much of it's unattractive reputation from the actions of the holders of state power. Goverments since, have been on any quantitative measure are the most prolific users, of terrorist violence."

> By the 20th century, states have routinely **branded** these resistance methods as terrorist acts. Considering people that resist, unlawful rule as extremist outlaws, of public moral and the politics that control that (**Public Moral**)."

> "When people decide that they will not beg or be guided by fictitious principles they are regarded as **rebels-against-the-established-order**." Pages 22-23 section (freedom fighters)

So before we go on NOW DO YOU GET IT?

Why be finalized as if it's a fascination? Why not be immortalized, to give life to people around the world? This is fuel for the fire. It's not the physikil fire that's going to burn down your residence, or people. It will be the eternal flame that burns within us revolutionaries who kontribute 2 this breed of terrorist cells.

Revolutionaries are killed because they bring the people 2gether. We are united by the kause, and this guideline. The fire doesn't burn out, just because you die, it only burns hotter and the flames go further.

The cell, brings us unity...it unifies the underground way of life. The cell hands us a mind on a silver platter, along with a spirit, rather than a society, religious body, or koverment. Just you and I inkorporated into one mindset.

No face, just weapons on the field of war with one goal. . . . .
K I L L OR BE K I L L E D! ! ! ! ! ! ! ! !

The organizations structure contains business minds, militarik embodiment, which I entitle **MILIKA**. Eventually you'll know who is a cell member. The music will say it, without telling it. The entertainers will show you without mocking it. **Watch the signs**.

They'll be no konsiderable tension…all street wars will be faked, all to adjust the warfooting, alluding the establishment. Looting the establishment...penetrating the publik, shaping the underground as well as society forever more our enemies EQUALZ.

In a nutshell a terrorist revolutionary is one who separates themselves from those that fear being broke, unpopular, uppity, and misguided. Milika is against those who don't want to change.

IT IS AGAINST ANY DICTATORIAL REGIME, TOTALITARIAN DOGMA, AND ANY OPPRESSIVE ESTABLISHMENT'S DOCTRINE.

> "IN WAR IT IS BEST TO ATTACK MINDS, NOT CITIES, PSYCHOLOGIKIL WARFARE IS BETTER THAN FIGHTING WITH WEAPONS."
>
> Mao Tse-tung

CHAPTER 8

MASQUERADING
THE PERFECT FORMATION

This section of the book will help the **sub-ground**, get acquainted with how our adversary's system is set up 2 a degree, along with certain aspects of training of our own 2 understand and counter their measures.

Our enemies use these forms of surveillance and tactics.

- **Dolphin Surveillance**
- **Waterfall**
- **Cultural Chameleon (this is not surveillance)**
- **Riot Control**
- **The split department of the C.I.A**. (which are **D.O.'s and D.I.'s**)

Dolphin Surveilance:

"Now you see them, now you don't strategies."
For two or three days they'll be everywhere, all over you. You won't be able 2 miss them, and then the following day, you won't see them for a while.

Waterfall Surveillance:

This team of surveillance agents will walk directly at you, rather than following behind you. It requires hundreds of people and cars, as soon as an agent passes you (**the target**), or what they label as **the**

rabbit, he then walks 2 a parallel street, no better yet he **turns down the first street, which is a cross-street**, then he walks to a parallel street, catches a coverment van that drives by to pick them up than they drive the agent or agents up ahead of you so that they can rejoin the flow, **often wearing a new change of clothes**.

The objective is to wear you out, so that you are forced 2 make mistakes. Day in and day out nonstop, with newer fresher teams and fresh techniques. They also pick locks of cars, etc. They rush computers and the files and hard drives, but with these you can beat them.

Anytime that you are in motion, whether walking or driving, there will come a point when you will be out of sight. This is called **The Blindspot**. Rather between buildings or some type of dip in the kountry road, you only get a split second 2 slip them. "**Preparation is Everything**!"

The tactic of **Cultural Chameleon** is 2 be able 2 anticipate and understand the actions of terrorist who are **different**, than one's self, "**Except The Dedication To The Cause**."

This is the coverment's job. It is 2 inhabit the minds of us terrorist and adopt our ways to see the game through our eyes.

This method is the **number one tactic of our coverment**. They have been doing this since the creation of this and other kountries. They have taught **us**, up close and afar; and once they learned **us** and how our way of thinking worked, they came and started picking our people off.

It was once said that, and I've also kept 2 this slogan 4 some years now that:

> **"The opposition is always out to get you, and they have the resources 2 do so."**

That does not scare me though, it only enhances me 2 push 4ward like it should be doing you. It should encourage you to study, train, and make plans 2 kill off, rather than assassinate characters of the said foe it'self but let's get back to our adversaries, and their tactics.

In riots the police, army, state trooper, national guard, MP's, highway patrolman, park police officers, you name it, are trained by **What Ever Means Necessary**, 2 control the situation.

Rule-1:

- First-they fire tear gas
- Second-they use horses
- Third-they use shield blocks, and move in attack formation.

Then theres: **Wedge Formation**

Which is an assault platoon formation. This is a classic formation, in **Riot Manoeuvering**. A show of force designed in a flying geese formation, as they thrust their night sticks, or rifles back and forth.

When trying 2 disperse a mob of rioters, it is ordered 2 first **use the gas, then shoot**, over the heads, meaning our heads, and then at our feet, and if all else fails...at the mob's in defiance, which means **at the mob it'self**. Yeah, they will be deliberately shooting at us at close range.

Next is the **Slow Riot Shuffle**:

Which consist of the establishment using a **Stomp Bayonet Thrust**, in a repetitive manner, and this is all written in their Riot Control Manual.

It states that there are four stages of a riot, or 4 sequences of how a crowd transforms into a riotous mob.

Step-1: The weakening of the forces, holding a crowd in check. This keeps happening as the crowd gets larger, and the Marshal's force proportionately grows smaller.

Step-2: A single piece of audacious violence successfully carried through, is achieved by multiple attacks on journalist.

Step-3: A harangue by a fiery leader or charismatic leader, which simulates by impassioned announcers blaring **Anti-Federal, Anti-Coverment**, or whatever incentively over the megaphone or whatever radio transmitter, sound system or transistor.

Step-4: The appearance of a conspicuous and hated figure or figures, even the so-called greatest president of the **United Stakes of Amerikkka**, John F. Kennedy, stated during the James Meredith riots that:

"**Amerikkklans, are free to disagree with the law.**" But then he says that: "**But they are not 2 disobey it.**"

What contradiction, what a bunch of bullshit!

He goes on to say that: 4 in a coverment of laws, and not of men, no man however prominent or powerful, and no mob, however unruly or boisterous **is entitled to defy a kourt of law**, because if this kountry should ever reach the point where any man or group of men, by force or threat of force, could long defy the commands of **their kourtz, and constitution, than no law would stand free from doubt. No judge would be sure of his writ, and no citizen would be safe from his neighbors.**

Well, if you ask me, I think the crooks for killing that contradictive cracker, because he wasn't for our side neither was he for you all. He only associated with Dr. King, 2 gain and keep his popularity. Look around; how many judges cut the time of **Child Molesters, as well as Rapist**?

Come on you gotta start asking one's self, aren't these same **Child Molesters and Rapist our neighbors**?

Such b/s, yet this is the situation that we are in. We have no say so in our lives. Do you think that our time will be cut if we so happen 2 slaughter a couple of these muthafuckas?

No Way, Not Here In The United Stakes Of Amerik.k.k.a!

Do you think that these child molesters, and rapist live around or live in the company of Joe Biden, George W. Bush, or Nancy Pelosi?
Unless those rapist and pedophiles are one of their kids or grandkids, then I think you already know the answer. Yet it's your votes and tax dollars, whether you're a Republican, or Democrat, that places these kinds of freaks around our seedz, and in and around our communities.

How many times have the cops, killed in cold blood us, the so-called citizens? Or locked up the people who they knew were innocent, yet these **judges simply ignored the law**, and took matters into their own hands, giving people who deserve, rehabilitation and lighter sentences Life, to 197 years. Knowing full well that those trialz, and sentences were unconstitutionally unfair, and our people were disregarded according 2 klass and color.

That's why I can say shit like: **Fuck That Writ, And That Warrant**. This kountry began doing this shit as it was coming into power. These injustices haven't just started happening in the 21st Century. We've already passed that point, while former president John F. Kennedy, was alive, and in office, on up 2 the current president Donald Trump.

I guess people like Kennedy, wasn't in touch with his era and time. The political north, the politicals in the south, west, and Midwest, don't give a shit about the under privileged, in the **United Stakes of Amerikkka and esp., it's Constitution**.

A lot of the slaves were killed right outside of the kourt room. Some of the judges back then even participated in the lynching of the so-called citizen. Many of these judges gave the order 2 **non goverment officials**, 2 murder niggers Therefore, if these are the landlords, and if these authorities don't obey their own **Laws**, after they make them into laws, **Than Why Should We?**

Samuel Adams, didn't obey, yet he's considered a pioneer/hero, of this kountry. And wasn't it Dr. King, that said 2 the people that:

> "In order 4 people 2 condemn injustices, that they must go through 4 stages?"

Stage 1.

- people must ascertain that indeed, injustices are being perpetuated

Stage 2.

- we must try 2 negotiate with the oppressor,

and demand justice

State 3.

- and if our oppressors refuse, then we need 2 regard self-purification, which starts with the question:

"Are we ourselves wrong doers, and are we ourselves oppressors?"

State 4.

- after this self-examination, and after removing one's own wrongs before demanding justice from others, is True Action!

Without this, we will be like what Karl Marx, and Engles, conveyed, regarding the proletariat, and the bourgeoisie:

"The proletariat, will no longer be that, once the reciprocation comes into effect; we will be them the New Oppressors."

We will be the **petty bouergosie**, and the true **bouergosie**, will still be in control. I, use these people like Marx, Lenin, and Engles, not as communist, or socialist, but as a teaching method 2 consolidate what I'm trying 2 get (**us**), to understand, not just you but myself as well.

I am no greater than anyone who reads this text the strength comes from (**us**), empowering each other, it isn't solely about unity, because even when uniting, if the army is not on the exact

same page, we all will perish. Movies like 300--
prove this.

John Dillinger, and his gang; also 4 example, You cannot be hot-headed and have a mind, not unless you have an education, for without it means that one has a futile brain. No matter how strong or **warlike**, when the time isn't in favor of the oppressed, and the masses are far 2 gone 2 comprehend that **there** can be no change, out of season, fighting against the current is foolish thinking and nothing will be gained 4 the revolutionist or the people trying to reciprocate their oppression.

Everything that our adversaries create is always by twos.

The **C.I.A.**, has two departments-

1. D.I., or the dept., of Intelligence
2. D.O., which evaluates information

They are: -**Analyst-Regional Experts-Sociologist and Psychiatrists**

The D.O.'s, are information collectors. They mainly work overseas and this same C.I.A., assassinated so many people even after former president **Ronald Reagan**, issued **Executive Order** titled: **1233, prohibiting** the C.I.A., from conducting assassinations and **assassination plans passed in 1981**.

The coverment doesn't give a shit about it's own agents and political figures, so how do **we**, expect

them 2 give a fuck about the so called **citizen**, or the **masses**? Yet again there are **laws** like **Federal Murder For Hire** charges, whose statute penalty no.'s are **1952**, and **1958**, which holds a **maximum sentence of Life** in prison, or death.
If we really think about it, we are already receiving legally life and death sentences anyway for petty ass charges most of the time trumped up charges, so the masses of people might as well **go all out**. We may as well start organizing 2 try to win something for ourselves meaning the terrorist nation, besides the damn lottery. Lets win a little dignity and honor 4 ourselves and our children. Then and only then can we give Dr. King, Che, and others the true benefit of death and life through their teachings. Those are our children whose bloodstains are soaking the concrete of Los Angeles, Chicago, Prince George's County MD., Baltimore MD., Detroit, Texas, Florida, New Orleans, and Washington D.C. The **toe tags**, are endless and we are returning our babies back 2 G-d, too soon, while this kountry is growing fatter by stuffing their pockets with our children's blood, and our parents and grandparents sweat, and tears.

Then theres that other great atrocity; The **2 Constitution's of Amerikkka.**

1) The Confederate Constitution, which consists of 42-delegates, from South Carolina, Georgia, Alabama, Mississippi, Florida, and Louisiana. These met in a convention at Montgomery

Alabama, on Feb. 4, 1861. "They," adopted a provisional Constitution of the Confederate Stakes Of Amerikkka, and elected good ol' Jefferson Davis, **MS**, as provisional president, and Alexander H. Stephens, (**GA**), as vice president.

A permanent Constitution, was adopted March 11th, and it abolished the African Slave Trade, but it did not bar interstate commerce in slaves.

On July 20th, the Congress moved 2 Richmond, VA., and Davis, was elected president in October, and inaugurated on Feb. 22nd, of 1862. This confederacy or Congress, adopted a flag first, consisting of a red field with white stripe, and a blue jack with a circle of stars later changed 2 the more popular well-known flag 2day which consists of the red field with blue diagonal **crossbars**, that holds thirteen **white stars**, for the 11 states in the confederacy along with Kentucky, and Missouri, but we were **born 2 believe that the Northern Federal Union's Constitution runs this Kountry.**

In the **Civil War**, the Feds, fought it's own civilians, not 4 slavery's abolishment, but 4 control of the economy. The original Constitution states:

"The war of independence was conducted by delegates from the original (13), stakes, called the Congress Of The United Stakes Of Amerikkka, also known as the **Continental Congress**."

In 1777, not 1776-

the Congress submitted to the legislatures of the states the **Articles Of Confederation And Perpetual Union**, which was ratified by New Hampshire, Massachusetts, Rhode Island, Connecticut, New York, New Jersey, Pennsylvania, Delaware, V.A., North Carolina, South Carolina, Georgia, and finally in 1781 Maryland.

The first article reads as follows:

- The stile of this Confederacy shall be the U.S.A. This did not signify a sovereign nation, because the states delegated only powers that they could not handle individually, such as 2 wage war, and make treaties etc.

The president **signed himself** (**President**), of the United Stakes of or in Congress mostly likely in Congress, who were assembled. But here, **The United Stakes were considered in the plural, and a Cooperating group**.

Once the war was won, it became evident that a strong **Federal Union**, was necessary, so Congress, left the initiative 2 the legislatures. VA., in January, of **1786**, appointed commissioners to meet with representatives of other states.

Delegates of Delaware, N.Y., N.J., and P.A., met at Annapolis. Alexander Hamilton, prepared their call, asking delegates from all states 2 meet in Philadelphia, in May of 1787, 2 render the

Constitution of the **Federal Koverment**, adequate to the exigencies of the Union. Congress, endorsed the plan on **Feb. 21, 1787**, and delegates were appointed by all states except Rhode Island.

The convention met on **May 14, 1787**-
George Washington, was chosen as president or (**presiding officer**) and the states certified sixty-five delegates, but ten did not attend. The work was done by **55**, not all whom were present during every session.
Of the **55**, attending delegates sixteen, **failed to sign**, only **39**, actually **signed on Sept. 17, 1787**, some with reservation. This is the **Konstitution**, that **we**, abide by, as well as quote in unison 2day, which states:

> "We the people of the United States, in order to form a more perfect Union, establish justice, ensure domestic tranquility, provide for the common defence promote the general welfare, and secure the blessings of liberty to ourselves and our posterity do ordain and establish this Konstitution, for the United Stakes Of Amerikkka."

When I first started 2 get involved into politics, I wasn't sure how all this verbiage, and assassinating tied everything into each other, which includes the propaganda, until I began reading this Konstitution.

By saying that they wanted 2 form a more perfect Union, 4 themselves, and **indicating 4 their posterity**, this was where the signs began to

caution me. Then it reads that everybody wasn't present, who was suppose 2 have signed it, for a perfect union, means the people being one and together, but they did it in separation, providing this thought, that the analysis of 2day, which is the year of **2016**, this Superpower of a kountry, has undermined the so-called united civilization, that they tell the people that was established 4 them, for here we can see that they propagandized the **phrase, The United Stakes Of Amerikkka.**

Therefore, **This is Why We Are At War!**
Again, this book wants you 2 understand not my opinion, but the irregularity of all who say that they are 4 us, but are not with us. I'm sorry to make you read such hypocrisy, but you've been getting slandered by your press, and we're being placed in **Double Jeapordy, jargon**, which your **Amendment's supposed 2 4bid**.

Amendment 1:

Religious establishment prohibited, Freedom of Speech, or Press, the right to assemble and to petition.

"Congress shall make no law respecting an establishment of religion, or prohibiting the free exercise thereof; or abridging the freedom of Speech, or of the Press; or the right of the people peaceably to assemble, and to petition the coverment for a redress of grievances."

But get this; freedom of the press, is this really a right, that gives the media, full authority and access to and over our lives? Can they bypass our privacy, by climbing into trees to snap photographs of us or hide behind bushes and then jump out of them? Are you saying that we have given the media/press, a full access pass to irritate the public's right 2 privacy, and what I mean by irritate, is **invade our right to space, even if a celebrity**?

They are doing this without our permission, but the United States allows this in their Konstitution. This Konstitution, has given total strangers the opportunity to treat **us**, like shit in the **public eye**. We have no say in our belittling, on **international** networks an t.v., programs like Wendy Williams, or TMZ, under the so-called lawyer who boasts that we can't basically do anything about these underhanded dealings.
This Amendment gives these people the right 2 **Spy** on **us**, and our conversations, while tracking and monitoring our every move.

This **is** unfortunately the case people. The Constitution has **FUCKED THE ALLEGED CITIZEN**, and we have given them the ammunition to do so. There are no rights of the people inalienable or otherwise. This kountry deprives its masses from being and staying human. Here in the **United Stakes Of Amerikkka**, I say the United Stakes because that's what the people are being placed on, **torture stakes**. As they abuse their authority by not protecting its people from being publicly humiliated and treated in a manner that is completely contradictive 2 the guidelines that are suppose 2 govern the kountry. This growing humiliation has been done to give the world a particular view of the false liberalism that has plagued this nation.

Jesus, the son of man, was not placed on a cross, like they had many of **us**, believing, but a **torture stake**. Dracula, the impaler, impaled his enemies and hung them up 2 be displayed so that the public could see the draconian laws in full affect, as well as the witches of Salem, who were publicly burned at the **stake** of torture 4 all to see, during the witch hunts.

Then there's Amendment VIII,
excessive bail or fine; cruel and unusual punishment.

So if this has already been established as a law, by the legislatures, and Constitution, which gives counsel 2 some degree each state, overseen by the **Federal Union**, than why is it that the Afrikkkin Amerikkkin, suffer behind these outrageous bails. And if fines can be paid rather than having 2 serve prison time than why are they continuously throwing **us**, and Latin Amerikkkins into cells?

The state knows that the people thats in poverty don't have $**1,000,000.00**, dollars to be able to post bail, thats unreasonable, at all variables. This type of intensity from our koverment is unlawful, and it's abuses should serve as a valuable lesson **that Amerikkka has practiced genocide and much more on the people of the nation**. This country has

failed the people. The **Amendment XIV**, which is the people's rights not being **abridged,** - which means that they are not 2 be **changed or rearranged**, under no circumstances. Yet it has simply been **undermined** and cut out of the people's lives, by our gov't., and their foreign and domestic circles that oppress it's natives.

I. All persons born or naturalized in the **United States**, and subject to the jurisdiction thereof, are **citizens**, of the United States, and of the state in which they reside. No state, shall make or enforce any law which shall **abridge** the privileges or immunities of the citizens of the United States; Nor shall any state deprive any person of life, liberty, or property, without **Due Process Of Law**, nor deny to any person within it's jurisdiction the equal protection of the laws.

II.

See the **Contradiction**, yet you say that you are defenders of the Constitution, and that you support it. I'm also speaking 2 the whites of this kountry, for I know you can't be that blind to the facts and signs that is **being** placed before your eyes.

You support a **Constitution**, that kills it's so-called citizens, you were the white privileged, now you to have become the **down troddened**, and your rights have been slowly taken by your kind, and foreign elites.

Illegal searches and seizures, people of foreign backgrounds like the Spanish Community, are being tossed in camps without their children, and illegally detained against their wills as if they are **terrorist**. The citizens of this kountry have a **futile** protection, and these things are done by these corrupt politicians and the corporations that they endorse, which steals the people's lands by pushing the natives off of their property, even if it is by pay-off, etc., these politicians, and elites, know damn well that their corporations will make four to five times more profit after that bribe.

As the politics hold in regard to **Amendment V**, it states:

"Nor shall property be taken for public use, without just compensation."

So when Walmart, or some National Park, or shopping center/mall, is trying 2 buy up the property of the citizen or buy off, the citizen in order to take their home etc., isn't this in violation of the term/phrase, **Public Use**?
And it damn sure ain't just compensation when they make four to five times as much than what they had offered you for **compensation.** Backgrounds are being scrutinized 2 bar those from future furtherance. So I ask aren't these background checks illegal searches, for seizures that have been designed by our coverment officials? Infringing on our rights under this guise?
Why does the coverment need to pry into the lives of their **citizens** who are under this **guaranteed right to privacy and warrant**?

No one should be legally snooping around the lives of their neighbor, that's what sabotage is. Your coverment is undermining the people, yet the jargon remains In G-d We Trust. Yet isn't it in your Bible that G-d, said:

> **"THOU SHALL NOT COVET THE NEIGHBORS HOUSE, WIFE, MAN SERVANT, OX, ASS, PROPERTY THAT IS WITHIN THINE GATES!"**

If I'm riding in my car, or another person's vehicle authorized by that person, or legally obtained through hard work, then why do the police feel as though they have the right 2 stop me and ask where I am going, and where did I get this particular style of car that I'm driving. Or where did I get the money to buy such a nice vehicle, and if I decide to or not to tell them what gives them the right 2 remove me from the car, or truck, that I paid for to be harassed, and put under question rather I'm the driver or the passenger.

Even if I am in the wrong 4 lets say speeding, or I ran a stop sign, hell maybe even a red light, what happen 2 the relevant questions of excuse me sir or mam, **are you alright, is everything okay, this morning**?
Or, can I assist you with anything along your travels, as well as **license and registration please;** This is suspicious behavior from the terrorist revolutionary's point of view, versus the police accusation of **probable cause**, which brings about in most cases **mis-understandings**.

How does this 'probable cause,' term, validate the illegality of searching my person, or property, at the officer's discretion, which by the way forfeits the people's right 2 turn down the officer's request of can I please step out of the car, or can they search my vehicle etc.?

If I choose to say no, that the officer cannot search, or no I am not **stepping** out of my car, by Law that is my right, which doesn't consist with **resisting arrest**. Saying **No**, by my right under the protection of the **Constitution**, should be enough, 4 if it's enough for them when they speak the law to **us**, than why not when we speak it 2 them?

Yet I am penalized for this while they get the humane treatment from their **kourts of law**, and their chiefs and captains which allows them the opportunity of an **investigation**. This is not **equal protection under the law**, which allegedly guarantees all citizens this right.

What do they mean when they say:

"The right of the people 2 be secure in their persons home, papers, and effects, against unreasonable searches and seizures, **Shall Not Be Violated**?"
How can anyone misconstrue this?

Amendment IV-
Continues by stating:

"**And No Warrants Shall Issue, but uponProbable**

Cause."

What is probable cause?

It is suspicious behavior, by those who's standard, is in reverse of the said people. We have one sided laws in this kountry. It takes away the people's right 2 have a say in govermental affairs and against their coverment. A man or suspect was black and fits the description of guilt due 2 the hatred of racist, and behind circumstantial evidence do time.

Warrants cannot be secured on the spot, esp., at a random stop 4 traffic or otherwise; but it's done, and we are sent 2 prison.

What this constitution is specifying is that it has a **double standard**, one 4 it's elite, and the other 4 the slave. There are phrases within its language that cuts out the people, 4 there is no rights for the people, only laws that govern them to protect their upper echelon. Unfortunately, We The People Have Been Brainwashed **To Believe What These Oppressors Have Taught Us**.

> "In all criminal prosecutions, the accused shall enjoy the right to a speedy trial and public trial, by an impartial jury of the state and district shall have been previously ascertained by law, and to be informed of the nature and cause of the accusation; to be confronted with the witnesses in his favor, and to have the assistance of counsel for his defense."

But if you can't pay, then this same **Assistance Of**

Counsel, will fail to keep you **free**. How can the prisons be overpacked by **Spanish Amerikkkins and Afrikkkin Amerikkkins**, if there is and was such a equally balanced system? There should be a new word added to the dictionary, legal, to collegiate, and that term should be called **Ass-system-ance**. Which pretty much means that the system makes an ass out of it's citizens by using such methods of assistance which is **Anti-Assistance**.

Who then sets the true bar, is it the **Constitution, or the Attorney**?

Is it the constitution, or the **businessmen and women**, who are the real **Authority in Amerikkka?** Assistance to them isn't the same definition that was given 2 **us**. Assistance 2 them means someone that has their back and best interest, a **Representative**, in layman's terms. So who is suppose 2 be keeping our asses out of jail? Surely it is not them, but don't take my word 4 it, give it time.

Just like there is **Public Defenders**, who pry into our business and throw the people 2 the wolves, the **Public Assistance**, policy is structured the same way. You get nosey ass personnel of the social system, telling you who to report to, and how you have to live your life while on that system, or you will be cut off of **Welfare or the new phrase State's Assistance**.

Therefore, you better do as they say or you will **starve**, because the government will let you. These people want 2 run background checks on **us**, before

they decide if you **qualify 4 adequate, housing, and food**. You are under **conditions**, that they force you 2 meet before they **stamp or brand you property of the state**.

When placed in positions like this, the government isn't there 2 help you get on your feet, or 2 be able to gain success, they have become **private investigators**, in other words a **police state**. Little parole officers, and probation officers that's making the people check in with them as if they are **Still-Cons**. This is another way that the establishment keeps the people **institutionalized**, and under constant **surveillance**.

Lawyers and prosecutors and judges are **officers**, but of the courts. The definition of the word assist means:

A.) 2 cause 2 stand, 2 give **usually, supplementary support /aid**.

B.) 2be present as a **spectator**

Assistant:

helper, a person who assists. Webster's definition, not the authors. Just 4 a moment think about those in these insane asylums, and nursing homes, to your day care centers. They are hired to do a service for you or for your family, yet a lot of times you **find** that the hired servants are taking your money while mis-treating members of your family. Not all of the time, but there are more than a few. And like any average commoner, they if they choose, are only there 2 witness what is going on in our homes and our surroundings. What we do, what we say behind closed doors, who we have in our houses, they are spies, and my favorite **spectators**.

There are the people that we have entrusted with our lives. We have paid 2 have this system assisting **us**, in our keeping out of their way, by way of our captivity, and our downfall. Either we pay or the state pays 4 them 2 do our jobs **4 us**, which is 2 become **konformist**. You will not and cannot defend yourself by law in **Amerikkka**.

See when you don't know the law, they throw you 2 the mercy of the kourt, and in front of the constitution, which tells **us**, in black and white that our attorney is there only 2 assist you, not 4 them 2 do the job **4 us**.

Can you grasp this, are you now comprehending the **double sidedness** of this **kountry**? There used to be an old proverb that said:

"**Never place your life in someone else's hands.**"

Hold your own, learn 4 yourself, educate yourself. Look at all those who have money, trusting in their lawyers. Made Men, etc., throwing these mafia **giants** 2 the constitution, because they believed in using other people's smarts, and not their own to relieve them of the **stress** that they were encountering from the law and their enforcers. These mafia men, believed in a false safety net, by making and allowing others like their lawyers 2 do the work for them, without these millionaires studying any of it 4 themselves. Such fools, learn from the past, you are entrusting your lives with everybody but yourselves. **Take The Time 2 Read**, because arrogant people hate a **Smart Asssssssss**!

This is what makes you a terrorist revolutionary, rather you believe me or not. It is because you cannot and will not be duped. You will not lay down, because you are a **challenger**, not 4 rights, but 2 separate yourself from this intoxicated world, in which they want **us**, 2 help them create. Stand firm with **brains**, and with your **Armz**, ½ cocked no...but pointed at them, at their head, not in their direction. The revolutionary terrorist sees their masking, the revolutionary terrorist, knows the army that they have at their disposal. They are one behind the other, just as they have said in their constitution. The **Perfect Union**, the **Perfect Formation**. Recollect about the entry and introduction of this book, about how the war in Boston, and Britain, was waged.

Let me break down the story 4 those of you who don't know it 2 end this chapter.

The **Boston Tea Party**-

in **1773**, Britain's East India Co., on the verge of bankruptcy, **possessed** large amounts of tea that it could not sell in England. In an effort 2 save the company from bankruptcy, the goverment passed the **Tea Act Of 1773**, which gave the company the right 2 export it's merchandise directly 2 the colonies without paying any of the regular **taxes**, that were imposed on the colonial merchants, who traditionally served as the middlemen in such transactions. With these privileges, the Co., could under sell **Amerikkklan Merchants**, and monopolize the colonial tea trade. The colonist, responded by boycotting tea, unlike earlier protest. This boycott, mobilized large segments of the population. It is also linked or helped to link the colonies 2gether in a common experience of mass popular protest.

Particularly, important 2 the movement were the activities of colonial women, who were one of the principal consumers of tea, and now became the leaders of the boycott.

Various colonies made plans to prevent the East India Co., from landing it's cargo, in colonial ports. In ports other than Boston, agents out of the Co., were forced 2 resign, and new shipments of tea were returned 2 England.
In Boston, the agents refused to resign, and with the support of the royal coverment, preparations were made 2 land incoming cargos regardless of opposition.

After failing to turn back three ships in the harbor, local patriots led by Samuel Adams, staged a daring action of disobedience. On the evening of **Dec. 16, 1773**, 50, men began masquerading as **Mohawk Native Americans or Indians**, went abroad the three ships, broke open the tea chests, and heaved **9,659 lbs**. worth of Darjeeling, into the harbor.

As the electrifying news of the Boston, incident, spread, other seaports followed the example and staged similar acts of resistance. There is a couple of things that I wish 4 you 2 see here in this historic passage.

Samuel Adams, the patriot, is the same man that they made and named the beer after. **Beer**! This so-called patriot and his band of resistors, if that's what we would like 2 call them, created a beer, out of a revolutionary act. Tea I guess wasn't good enough, so they concocted alcohol, or a name brand alcohol beverage. These people took a healthy product and pushed it 2 the side, 4 a drink that would later cause health issues and death.

But lets not stop here, lets explore the difference between real, revolutionaries. **For there are a few names in which I would like 2 use as examples**:

I. Nat Turner, and
II. Samuel Adams

Both led two resistance demonstrations, but only one came in a true **revolutionary terrorist stance**, the other a cowards stance. Samuel Adams, was the coward, because he posed as someone else along with his men 2 resist.
Nat Turner, stood up 4 what he believed, **that the slave was not going to fear the whip and his oppressors any longer**. He nor his cadres hid behind a mask, **4 All Terrorist, Confront Their Fears, Being All Man and Woman.** Therefore, his rize may have been brief, it was true, and he and his cadres died real.

Nat Turner, couldn't be called just a regular revolutionary, he was a **Revolutionary Terrorist**. His party struck fear, in those he waged war against and Made the history books not because of **propaganda, but because of him being a threat 2 the slave system as a N.I.G.G.A.!**
Samuel Adams and his band of brothers never did this, he and they are and were used as a propaganda tool.

The names Nat Turner, they will never consider a patriot of Amerikkka. This same Nat Turner, the **Martyr**, and true terrorist **left** a legacy that can never be masked or glossed over. Neither will it ever become misleading or commercialized like the coward Samuel Adams, and his beer company, because Nat Turner, was the one who physically put 2 death **The Slave Mentality**.

His mentation, avowed 2 his heart's belief, unlike Samuel Adams, who may have sparked a resistance to the opposition, but never **struck fear**, as did Nat Turner, who caused so much **terror**, that his captures placed him on display hoping that the view of Nat's tortured body would deter other slaves, but it didn't. How can I say this, because I'm writing for **us**, and fighting 4 **us**, in this day in age like the people fought and resisted the system before I began doing so.

Samuel Adams, gets called a patriot for his resistance, but Nat Turner, is considered a **wild nigger**, **a murderer**, **an animal that had to be put down**, not a patriot of revolutionary duty, yeah a real insult.

See how they wear the mask in formation? It's a perfect cover up of what suppose 2 be a raw revolution. It is us, who must begin to learn what one behind the other means. Let this chapter open and broaden your mind. One Behind The Other, is how soldiers march, and are born in real causes, which we embrace and dubbed Terrorist Revolution. This is how our generations keep coming. No war chest, which means we've started this movement with no monetary. Some of us, had 2 steal our weapons. The real grassroot Sub-Ground. No formal military training, etc. We are one behind the other Shocking, Bombing, Shooting, and Killing, not Maiming, but Terrorizing!

The sound of the bomb exploding on our terms, not bursting in air. The **rata-tat-tat** you hear from the **AK-47**, and **AR-15**, is the terrorist revolutionary cadence, it is our **War Song**. Now it won't just be called an assault rifle, no, now it will become a **Murder Weapon**. With us, combined, we will take the hearts of our adversaries, 4 it was them remember that enforced the con. It was them who were the artist that drew and painted our pictures in blood.

Now is the time for a good question 2 be asked:

"Will The Assault Rifle Genuinely Come 2 Life?"

"Will it really infuse our rize, or will these registered voters, and victims, keep protesting about their acts your precious 2nd Amendment, waiting on permission for somebody to tell them o.k., or have they just plain and out right accepted keeping the gun/weapon in poverty? "

Amendment II: The Right 2 Keep And Bear Arms

"A well-**regulated** militia, being necessary 2 the **security of a free state**, the right of the people to keep and bear arms, shall not be **infringed**."

See there are always **stipulations**, when it comes 2 the system.

CHAPTER 9

2
IMPOVERISH
<u>ARMZ</u>

How should one generalize the use of armz?

The mis-education of the **<u>2nd Amendment</u>**, the suppression of self-preservation, and how the **<u>Second Amendment</u>**, over-rode the human guidelines of protecting the peoples kountry, and freedom of belief to govern one's own household.

This chapter is a chapter for the people who are truly endowed with the politikil sphere, **<u>not the adaptation of the right 2 bare armz law</u>**, which takes away the people's moral rule 2 regulate one's community, household, place of worship etc., and how this misuse of the words **<u>gun, rifle, or weapon</u>**, has become oppressed in this police state an global war.

Formation of the people has become legistics of do's and don'ts, along with homicidal/suicidal detriment which diluted the aggression of the revolution. Thus, bringing in the constant injustices of individual safeguarding, 2 promote as well as bolster the **<u>defending of the Fatherland/Homeland. Meaning that the state comes b4 society or the symbolic nature of it</u>**.

The degradation of the community itself, supplies the fuel 2 these politikil kriminals, whose job it is to govern us with **<u>propaganda</u>**, thus encouraging us 2 try more peace, and love, remedies so that social equality finds and has a chance to contain (**us**), the **<u>people</u>**, as a whole, within the state, rather than outside of the political circumference. This what makes the "**<u>Social Structure,</u>**" not the academic, but the

pandemic, which causes the impoversation of the **Armz**.
This has been the world view of the establishment since empires have come into existence. Display the weapon, and use it as a force against the people, portraying a method without allowing the oppressed of their lands 2 **personalize, appreciate and utilize them 4 our own benefit, and individual purposes esp., the cause of revolution**.

The establishment or empire decrees a law, of how the people can **Arm themselves**, not by our standards, only theirs. Take away the **war weaponz**, which causes collision with the establishment, especially when trained, deprives the people of that true chance 2 stay free and liberate ourselves if one has been subjected 2 this falsified procedure of social benefit and right of **personal soverning and protection**.

Law, therefore, protects the kountry rather than the alleged citizen. Groups like the (**NRA**), help to determine civil obedience principles, 2 conduct business for the conditioning caretakers of the kon-institution/constitution.

These laws and defender groups were formed on the premise 2 socially build the kountry by placing the necessary tools in the people's hands, until the nation was built up to it's absolute power, then took those same **trademarked tools**, out of the people's clutches.
As with all **Ideologikil Education**, it takes and took, because again, it only benefits the state, when the **Home Front**, has these kinds of state of emergencies. By this you can then proceed to make such things as "**Citizen Arrests**," and aid in surface legislation, while the small print which augments a different agenda; **becomes Law**, and what is also known as **bi-laws**!

The citizen then finds his or herself a castaway, all 2 initially become more delusional by trying 2 recruit others who are in the same boat, to become some sort of **influential party**, that can impose on the people and can infringe on the institution's objective. Yet the institution has already considered this **mediocre mania**, and have opened its social plat form 2 entrap such vandalizers and treasoners of the said law.

The reciprocal means of utilization is one of the greatest methods of strategy used by every imperialistic state, because it invites the castaway, into the **Status Quo**, circles, but only as it's subordinates to do the social dirty work, 4 that is it's sole purpose, which brings us back 2 that old **Bloodstained Banner**, of **Divide And Conquer**.

This causes political drainage for grass rooted terrorist revolutionaries. For example: The Black Panther Party, primary elections, and literary forms of expression etc., transferring energy that downgrades versus understanding that this same philosophy was once their oppressors, until they embraced it and made it their own.

So now that the education of the status quo, continues 2 be the **ideological** dogma of all "**Enlightened**," because as a whole the protection of the present state is as valuable to us, as it is with them, due 2 the **criteria of privileges**, which brings us what we crave, which 2 everyone, is and shall remain everything! So shall it be 2 the enslaved klass, the propaganda is not looked at as being a privilege, but "**The Way Of Life**."

The socially acceptance of the propagandized, fail to comprehend politikil persuasion, so they follow blindly the opinions of those who have created the **frenzy in the 1st place**…now all of a sudden, but not out of the blue, that you have your **Feminist, Civil Rights Movements**, and **Homosexual Movements**. Yet these were your social outcast, or castaways who became not the **statistic**, but used by other strategical tactics of the state.

Without diversity, and versatility, the **social acceptance** would not be able 2 dominate the minds of the people who are the real **weaponz of society**, to those that truly make up the strength of the underground.

Therefore, the frenzy is again taken away, by saying **'Take The Assault Rifle And The Handgun Away!'**

Lesser ammunition for the magazine, including lesser grades of gun powder, 2 make matters worse. Background checks 2 stipulate who can purchase as well as own guns while inserting stiffer penalties to prevent not just the criminal, but also the actual citizens from acquiring them. **Weapon control**, dynamite and other possible chemicals that can be used as a fatal **combustive** 2 cause harm to the coverment, and be made as high-powered explosives, they don't want in the people's hands, but I must ask:

> **"Should I have 2 be in the demolition field or construction business, 2 have in my possession such explosive devices?"**

Yes, because they are in the **social circles** of the state. It is they who are the literal builders of the state, and it is by their hands that their **shrines are erected**, so that our eyes may feast on the icing on the cake, rather than the indigestible ingredients. This shit is not about being candid. The criteria, contains remote places that pinches nerves in those of (**us**), who fear.

It alerts them and reminds them of the places where having, is a determent, so in order 2 stay in the utopia, the work must be kept up to keep up **appearances** and that **dream world**. For after seeing death over and over again up close, rather by t.v. screen, in the **underworld** or **streets**, etc., the fear of not being or feeling safe controls the movements meaning the physical impulses of the people. **This is why the ghetto is so important**. It validates the fear of those that can hide, and can't fight.
It completely dominates politically, the minds, mobility, and characters of the people.

So the goal is 2 weaken both sides of the equation. This is the definition of **propaganda**, **2 repeatedly keep the idea in front of the masses at all times, while keeping that idea sooo simple** that it not just registers with the intellectuals but just as much with the fools. The establishment, keeps the upper hand by keeping contention up even when it comes down 2 **subjecting**, their own "**War Heros**," and our families, to all sorts of pain staking treatments of everyday, because of the combination of **Utopia**, and self-affliction. Yet it's not seen to the masses as **self-affliction**, the only ones who actually see is those who have an eye 2 see, because they are those who have supplied this philanthropy.

The evolution of this kind comes not figuratively, or imaginative, but in the literal sense, keeping the state active in **every** sense of the word. By sending these guns and or weapons into the impoverished zones, they substantiate the **criminal climate**, therefore the weapons are now considered the **predator**, of these incorporated environments. Guns with high-capacity cartridges, are secured 2 adjust more deaths 2 depopulate as well as plant seeds of hopelessness in the less curated minds as possible; because in the "**Fatherland/Homeland**," there is not enough room 4 all 2 grow and be happy…and "**There Never Will Be!**"

The **scientific-social-selection**, has taken shape. It grants certain key individuals' **positions**, in the state to give ideals, to the subjugated children around the world. The system is designed 2 give you your Shaquille O'neals, but never your Jonathan Jacksons. Its prepared to give you your Muhamad Ali's, never your Muhamad-Al-Sawws, the prophet of real Islam. It grants you your reverends such as T.D. Jakes, never your Huey P. Newtons.

It has the educated, and the uneducated belonging to its endearment, so that sympathy can support and supply the story. But, when you belong 2 true activism, you find your story in their headlines slandered, with an unsympathetic media, considered the **people**, who regard your story as an equivalency of a death certificate. In the ghetto, or poverty, the mind now wages war with almost every individual; and now that that mind is unable 2 be in control of the community, or 2 one's self, each individual fails to understand the capability of that community, and this is what the establishment wants.

It loves and needs protest for **Freddie Gray**! It wants these kinds of violent outburst. The establishment didn't like the kind of publicity that **Rosa Parks**, decided to enlist in. It wants such things like "**Black Nationalism**," it doesn't want the people of resistance with **internationalism**, which will eventually become a mass movement of international warfare.

The term **Black Nationalist**, or **Black Nationalism**, is just another label. It is a meaningless word/phrase, like the term communism. The Afrikkkin Amerikkkin, resents being set aside and dominated. It also resents not being allowed 2 enter the mainstream of Amerikkklan society. These people who form their own groups, because they have been **manufactured**, not rejected, start trying to create favorable societies of their own 2 make it seem as if resistance is their mantra and motto. Yet and still, this is a misleading comprehension, because the 1st thing that you must remember is that I am a **N.I.G.G.A.**, and I have been denied the right to enter the **main body of society**, not the commercialized mainstream of **Amerikkkan Society**, better known as the **United Stakes**.

As a **N.I.G.G.A.**, I am rejected, resented and will always be discriminated against. **The Masses and Terrorist Revolutionary**, are the **Excluded**, and due **2 Amerikkkinism** we are terminated the most **out-of-all-groups in the United Stakes**, and around the world. **THE KILL OR BE KILLED KLASS**, therefore this term or phrase of black nationalism/nationalist, is a hard scenario to define.

United Stakes, we are the most hated klass of people. As for **being** a black nationalist, this is a word thats hard 2 define. No, I am not a **Black Nationalist**, 2 the degree that I would exclude white people or that I

would-prejudice any other race.
I would prefer to think of myself as an **internationalist**! That is, I am interested in the problems of all of **mankind**. Whether they be of **Africa**, **Asia**, **Iran**, or **Latin America**.
I believe that we all have the same or similar struggles, with our own race of people and that of real liberation.

Discrimination and race hatred are undesirable, and I'm just as much against this in all forms, across the globe, just as I am against it here in Amerikkka!

And what do the negros mean by **Black Nationalism**?

When you consider the present **White Amerikkklan Society**, it can be classified as nothing more, but a nationalistic society based on color safeguarding. Yet as soon as an **Afro-Amerikkkin**, speaks out and up 4 his/her people, when conscience and proud of his or her historical rootz, as well as kulture, then black people automatically is considered **Black Racist**. Personally, I don't mind the labels, but I am a firm believer of not being a hypocrite.

In so many words this in which I convey is almost the words of political activist Robert F. Williams, in his book **Negros With Guns**. When a individual can't seem 2 comprehend this, than that individual is a conflict of true resolution, and conflict of interest of his or herself. These people have no understanding of our objective, and I say this because these people spread false and misleading information which causes our ignorance, which the establishment keeps in continuous rotation to cause our **Armz, 2** stay impoverished, rather than raising hell in the revolution where it belongs. The gun is no longer a ticket 2 his or her freedom. The gun is in a commercialized form and version of his or her life. In this unskilled untrained mentality, the gun has become a phantom type of protection. It is un-real, because he/ or she has begun to view the war as a pick and choose initiation, rather than realizing that this is indeed a **life-or-death reality**.

Survival to these people is second nature, while currency is their first priority! These people die fantasizing, because they don't comprehend how the German made Glock, or the Russian **AK-47**, that they may or may not possess changes situations in midst as well as around them, but instead they view this as a crime against humanity. But this is also a falsehood. These people simply dismiss this altogether until things come before them, people like David Thibodeau, learned the hard way. To their understanding, they try dressing the part investing in trend and trendy costumes and fashionable retro looks, versus investing in what is in their near future. Their radio breaks up their ability 2 hear the sound of the actual revolution that's stationed around them. The drugs oppress their way of judging, and in return they have become incompetent.

They have cashed in the real revolution for a mock one, in which they can never damage those that define their course of life, and for this at birth, was the reason why his/her life was preserved, to be a deserter not a challenger. They fight to give nothing back that's worth anything to and in their community, yet 2 their same like-minded community, they have made it.

To their families, they have resisted and risen to become that somebody whom they could never **be**. And their support groups cannot help them reverse this and their **psychosis**, because they are a part of these disbelievers' political front, that is why they are the **Front Men and Women**.

2 some, they are not black enough. To themselves, they just want **2** receive the fruits of their labor. Their prayers are the **church and state's recommendation**, and they are required not to use their own sweat and life's blood, like their Moses, Muhammad, and Christ.

They contemplate with deep thought, but their mind is too learned to grasp what it is that they must do. They are the black fearful, not the **politikil animal that dies in strength rather than in character**.

Their pride is in their clothes, hair styles, various products, certificates, residences, cars, and their mother who from the start, never weaned them from her blemished breast; this is the reason that they love those commercials about prospering, and statements like black excellence, rather than those special news bulletins, about their kind being killed, beaten, and sent to prison.

When they relax, they look at the world through the screen of their laptops, and cell phones, televisions etc., and they say 2 themselves:

"WHAT IS THIS WORLD COMING TO?"

They say this because even after **45** and **50** years, they still haven't come into their own. If they have come from poverty, they have pushed extensively hard to leave that part of their lives where they were, and out of their minds 4ever if they could hide the past, but they can't, and when they try, it is always discovered. They say to themselves that they are, or we are not them. Yet 2 say this they distance themselves from what the revolution and their people are all about. They **4**get what struggling had done **4** them and **us**. The black domestic is ashamed of their partnership with poverty and it's oppressed people, which is them, not the whites who aren't truly saving them, it is only the whites who are hindering them in the **society that only the whites are a part of**.

The gun scares them, they have conversations with their '**friends**' and or spouses about should they own one 2 protect themselves as a man or woman should. But once it is owned, it is put inside a drawer or closet, placed in a box because in all actuality they don't really plan to use it or truly want 2 use it.

It is just there, 4 decorations, put up on display like them-selves, because the **establishment** has taught them to display their weapons as trophies, keeping it displayed 2 show and prove that they will keep to the laws of the land rather than 2 the laws of **self-preservation**.

At one point in time, fathers would teach their children how 2 shoot and clean their guns, along with educating them on how to be responsible when it came down to owning their weapon. But now our kids are curious and therefore shoot themselves, by accident 2 shooting others for whatever futile reason.

There is caution to the owner, he says that he is not prone 2 violence, yet it is violence that has kept the institution's system controlling the minds of the youth and unconscious adults.

And is it violence to be in a situation or a cause and not be able to protect one's self, family, or community? The black domestic, never once ask themselves what am I doing, or what is this impover of the weapon? They don't see the regression within themselves. They believe that their spouses should be pretty, attractive, beautiful by image and appearance. These treasured souls they occupy the time of the black domestic.

They feel as though their partner must have a phat ass, and must be smart far as **I.Q.**, is concerned. They would rather have their soulmates **mentally meticulous**, not **mendacious**, or **militantly structured**. Once they have asked themselves should they own a gun/weapon, then they have immediately accepted the establishment's analogy of what they are, and who they are.

When they look back on their lives and accomplishments, they think that they have helped people to stick 2 their guns, and individual dreams, separating themselves from the entire ambition of the whole. They honestly believe that by paying taxes, and accumulating

accolades that they have assisted themselves and others like them, but they can't phantom for some reason how their inactions have actually humiliated and hampered their well-being.
Here the **generation gap widens**, but it no longer makes the **state's student**, seem socially awkward in any way, but all the while they are in every way. But non realizes except those who are truly committed 2 over coming the oppression. The black domestic is the **establishment's investment**.

The **Black Domestic**, argues when their time comes around to voice their-opinion about their race still being **socially**, **and economically stagnated**, as they always have, but in a outdated dialogue.

But when do they and we ask: "where does Al Sharpton live?"

Where do people like Bill Cosby, stay? In prison now obviously, but surely, he doesn't live in the same vicinity as little Murda, and lil Mookie. The good ol' reverend isn't in arms reach, nor are any other domesticated negros who are dubbing themselves "**BlackisH**," and not the **Black Masses**. These people are only in our lives 2 entertain us, with the establishment's ideals. They exclude the fact that when the **state's enforcers**, which are consistently paid and constantly trained to assassinate people of color, they begin 2 rally with us, but behind our backs, they are siding with the enemy.

But as they start seeing their oppressors sending out their enforcers, those same enforcers who have been in every state **shooting kids**, they say when does all this end? Yet in the behind The scenes moments, they whisper amongst themselves, **at least it wasn't non of our children or their social circles kids**. This is what the black domestic and others like themselves, have secured since adolescence.

They defend the kountry, but not their own people, and that's why we hate them, because they are weak, and have always been weak, inside of the environments in which we come from. We hate them 4 who and what they have become, and have remained. They hate us, and the very places that have birth them, yet they forget what poverty has actually done for them. They argue in the media, proving how they truly resent our outlook in regards 2 overthrowing the system, and it's **psychological, and physical conditions**. They feel at home here in their comfortable abode. Meaning that they have been conditioned to accept their plight in **Amerikkka**, while they say **Fuck ours**...and 2 support this assessment, they speak for themselves proudly of how they **do not** wish to cause any disturbance, because they don't want the institution supplanting their **security**, and they are fighting tooth and nail with all they got, 2 keep away from those of us that **resist konformity**. These people believe in amending their survival, in this theoretical **Liberal Society**.

But how long can they be able to function this way before betrayl?

They are crucifying themselves not their Christ, all to be some **sort of idol**, and **glamorously glorified**, well written about character that went down in hisstory.

Their religious beliefs are not centered on the precepts of the lord and master whom they swear they serve. Their lord and G-d has a mistranslated name, which they seem to care nothing about.

Yet they say that they know the **sacred texts** of their spiritual 4 fathers, but they do not know the truth, even though they have many truly dedicated followers, that are following behind them blindly due to their **slave master's ideologies**. They clap, stomp, and sing glory, praising G-d, falsely, as well as foolishly, because this is what their **enslavers** beat into them until they submitted 2 the **Good News**.

They sit in front of cameras in a congregational styled unity, and preach that they are the kingdom of heaven, and that G-d, as well as his son

Jesus, came to bring peace, grace, love, and joy to the people. They preach that Jesus, wants all humanity 2 love one another, and be **festive**. But I want you who are reading this book to research the scriptures 4 yourselves, and view what the man called Jesus, truly said to his disciples in regards 2 his mission, and most importantly **Armz**!
G-d's word never changes, please I beg of you to read the Good Book; starting with Mathew 5:17-20, where it states:

> "DO NOT MISUNDERSTAND WHY I HAVE COME, I DID NOT COME 2 ABOLISH THE 613 LAWS OF MOSES, OR THE WRITINGS OF THE PROPHETS. NO, I CAME TO ACCOMPLISH THEIR PURPOSE. I TELL YOU THE TRUTH, UNTIL HEAVEN AND EARTH DISAPPEAR, NOT EVEN THE SMALLEST DETAIL OF G-D'S LAW, WILL DISAPPEAR UNTIL IT'S PURPOSE IS ACHIEVED."

Sooo If You Ignore The Least Commandment And Teach Others To Do The Same, You Will Be Called The Least In The Kingdom Of Heaven. But, I Warn You...Unless Your Righteousness Is Better Than The Righteousness Of The Teachers Of Religious Law, And The Pharisees, You Will Never Enter The Kingdom Of Heaven.

Mathew 6:1-3

> "Watch Out! Don't Do Your Good Deeds Publicly, To Be Admired By Others, For You Will Lose Your Reward From Your Father In Heaven. When You Give To Someone In Need, Don't Do As The Hypocrites Do, Blowing Trumpets In The Synagogues, And Street To Call Attention To Their Acts Of Charity! "
> I Tell You the Truth,
> They Have Received All The Reward They Will Ever Get. But You When You Give To Someone In Need, Don't Let Your Right Hand Know What Your Left Hand Is Doing."

Luke 22:35

Then Jesus, asked them:

> "When I Sent You Out 2 Preach The Good News And You Did Not Have Money, A Traveler's Bag, Or An Extra Pair Of Sandals, Did You need Anything? "No His Disciples said."

Luke 22:36

> "But Now I Tell You Jesus, Said, Take Your Money And A Travel Bag, And If You Don't Have A Sword/Armz, Sell Your Cloak And Buy One! "For The Time Is Coming. And Already Come For This Prophecy About Me, 2 Be Fulfilled."

Let's not forget that the **Gospels/Good News, states that Jesus, himself was counted among the radicals, rebels, Revolutionary Terrorist!**

Here the precious beloved Jesus Christ, and also known as the coming Messiah, of G-d, the Catholics, protestants, Baptist, gentile nations, and Jewish savior/king. Son of the Almighty, lord of the Christians. The peacefully mischaracterized, anointed of G-d....the loving, gentle, soft spoken prophet as we see tells his own students who are also his personal guard 2 go purchase **Weaponz Of War**. He didn't say casually to them oh go arm yourselves whenever trouble arises; **Hell No**! Jesus, told his cell, to sell their possessions in order 2 get them, because he knew a threat was coming to them after his demise. He knew that the fight was on, he never told his cell **not 2 arm themselves**. The people called 4 the uniting of the people, so that they could be governed by G-d alone, not mankind's tyrants, who they were already under the yoke of. The people called for **War**, and that is what they got a **revolutionary; the violent**, Jesus, said:

> **'Will Come To Try To Take** the kingdom out of the very hands of the people.' These people sponsor these social stagnation systems and groups that globalize the containment of these social

outcast, using them as markets 2 **mobilize the methods** that target us to become peace makers, and these methods are to ensure the state that we will be totally transformed.

Their taxation programs deduct our wages as it **is** collected to generate these groups and their foundations along with their donations go, 2 bringing in these protectors of the state 2 our front doorsteps, and this is where they propagandize these state **trainees** as terrorist! They have indoctrinated the people **globally** to put down the **gun/weaponz**, and we are supposed 2 follow their every word which they **enforce as law**, not that which is supposed to be already the law which is the word of G-d.

A lot of them know that they are being duped by their politicians, and these state holders have taken advantage of our stupidity, and fear. Some well after seeing what their donations and taxes have paid for and endorsed, yet and still they remain seated.

They begin rethinking their actions and faith in their state's system, even in regarding their purchases, and the owning of weaponz, but to no avail, **their ideologist**, tell them let's try another tactic and this will-bring the masses of people under total compliance. Let's **promote nonviolence**, but this is only 2 keep in subjugation the gentiles or goy nation which are black domestics, and other nationalities, their purpose is to keep them legally blind, and non-aggressive, so that non can injure their plans and empire.

They caused the black domestic 2 disarm, their people, by promises of a better **future** etc., that if the masses of people begin to arm themselves, this would most likely be the very thing that saves their lives. Work the slaves so they can never think about **insurrection**. And never keep them idle no matter what! They want to always work the hell out of the slave, all 2 make employment their/our culture.

Finding a good man or woman 4 the Nobel Peace Prize, isn't hard, and why should it be, when the state has birthed and bred every candidate. It is they who have created the **Prizes**, the current terrain, and those who have procured as we proclaimed as their responsibility... "**THE FIGHT FOR SOCIAL INJUSTICE!**"

So now we have **65 years of talking, and 50 more years of staying as far away from Arming ourselves as possible**.
Poverty: means poor, deficient, in need, scarcity. Now think about my reason for labeling this chapter the way that I did.

Understand that our armz, is in desperate need of us! Getting our hands on them is getting harder and harder, and the way that we have been utilizing them has been in extremely toxic ways that have made them and our conditions even poorer. We are **treating our weaponz of war like shit**! There is no life without them. And there will be no **real liberation without them**!

There is no freedom without fighting for it! And the state knows this...the establishment is not going 2 hand you a manual and train you in order for you to put an end to their system. It is solely up 2 the revolutionary terrorist 2 regard, secure, and keep our **armz** in combat, appreciating it's worth "**BY ANY MEANZ!**"

CHAPTER 10

3rd World Psychololgikil Training

You do realize that this is what this book basically is right? It is a scientific method on how to make the political animal, that I've alwayz and we have alwayz needed as well as wanted **2 be**.
This,
is not about 400, or 500, years of slavery, it is solely about breaking that fear, and oppressed mantality. It is **thee**, fundamental **principia**, 2 destroy the opposite **us**. 4 I have taken the necessary pieces of the world, and broke down individually their concepts which control the people's actions, in society, as well as with their religious beliefs.

The dynamics of these pages provide the following....it feeds us, insight on how to prepare and how 2 punish, rather than see and do nothing more than pray; because like it or not, our enemies see **us**, as **prey**!

You may be asking yourself, does this revolution, bring us, closer 2 G-d? Let me not be the judge of that, but what I will say is this: **What This Does Is Bring The People Into The Realm Of You And I, Spiritually, Providing The People As Whole With True Things 2 Value, And Appreciate Like Humanity.**

For in this earthly realm, it will take a real upholding of G-d's word, which gives the people a united guidance 2 be able 2 fight against these forces of evil. Therefore, what is Affirmation?

It is the expressing of approval. So does your lord, approve of you confessing his way of life no matter the cost, before the unrighteous of mankind? Yes, **ABSOLUTELY!**!!!!!!!
But even more than that, can you face the fact that even with or in the absence of Ha'ish, or whomever you deem 2 call him, do you approve

of the establishment and their framers of our downfall, telling you that you must abide by their laws, rather than your own, or G-d's lawz which are not just the laws of Moses, **4 G-d's laws supersedes the laws of Moses**!

Here is an example of what I mean: In Oregon, a lesbian couple asked a bakery called Sweet Cakes, owned by a married couple by the name of Melissa, and Aaron Klein, 2 bake them a wedding cake. The owners the Kleins, said no, 2 the gay couple. The Kleins, said that they were happy 2 sell items 2 anyone, but would not bake wedding cakes 4 same-sex couples, due 2 the fact that same-sex marriages/couples, goes against their religious beliefs.

The lesbian couple filed a complaint with the establishment, while purchasing their wedding cake from another baker called Pastygirl, which they also accepted another cake **free-of-charge,** from a Duff Goldman, star of the t.v., show Ace Of Cakes. Goldman, of course another Jew...had heard about the Oregon, debacle, and began to launch a non-discrimination protest with other gay activist, and same-sex couples posing as activist against the more observant orthodox Jewish couple and business owners the Kleins. Their campaign or methodology used against the Kleins, was the manipulation of "**Civil Rights**," and "**Equal Rights**!"

Boycotts, death threats on the Klein's children, etc., occurred against this religious couple who believe in their right 2 practice their own religion under the constitution, was forced 2 close down their bakery, and was ordered by the kourt to pay this gay couple $ 135,000.00, for emotional distress which the gay couple said the Kleins inflicted on them.
Yes, right here in your beloved Amerikkka!

The same Amerikkka, that you defend, when voting Democrat, or Republican. The same Amerikkka, that specifies right there in its

Constitution, or Amendments there of:

Amendment I:

> "Religious establishment prohibited, freedom of speech, of Press, and the right to Assemble and Petiton. Congress, shall make **No Law**, respecting an establishment of religion, or prohibiting the free exercise thereof:
> or **Abridging** the freedom of Speech, or of the Press; or the right of the people to peacefully assemble, and to petition the goverment for a redress of grievances."

This article was in the National Review, August 10, 2015, this is the edition with Hiliary Clinton, on the front cover. The article didn't say that the Kleins, were disrespectful 2 the same-sex couple, it just says that they declined them as was their right 2 do, as it states in this double standard quack assed Federal Constitution. I say this because the Constitution, states one thing, while our representatives say another, 4 these twin systems are totally at odds with it's said kountryman, and women. The To'rah, and the Bible, prohibits lesbian, or same-sex anything, the Sunnah, and the Qur'an, as well. Yet because people have opinionated views under liberalism/Democratic rule, and are pagans, they are allowed to encroach on true believers in Ha'ish, the G-d of our ancestors who 4bids **us**, as his followers not to indulge in other people's or to foreign doctrines, which he alone sets **us**, apart from. See the falsehood in the United Stakes Of Amerikkka? Theres no Constitution, there is only contradiction. There is no true support for the believers in G-d, here in Christian Amerikkka.

These same-sex couples and gay activist tried to manipulate the late prophet Dr. Martin Luther King Jr.'s words, by saying that he was a champion 4 liberalism, broadmindedness, non-traditional, for the people including pagans, which he bled and died for, as a firm believer in Ha'ish, as an old fashion slave reverend, that's what they say or are saying in regards to his beatings, and jailing as a Civil Rights Leader. We all know that the southern Baptist minister was G-d, fearing, so their teachings is a false accusation, and they have viciously lied on this western prophet.

These homosexuals are trying to use Dr. King's platform, to open more doors for things that are not of G-d. And what the so called coverment is saying, is that, the opposing view of foreign doctrine can politely move or remove the alleged foundation of this kountry.

The gay couple could have just kindly moved on 2 another bakery like which was done, was gladly to take on more business. It has now become a factor that the offended couple and people these days, can't accept criticism, and the use of the word **No**! Today the people have become soo sensitive, and when people stand up 4 their causes, or themselves, or beliefs, now they want to use words like **bully**, or **bullying**.

The Amendment clearly states:

> "No Abridging....and Congress can make No Law that prevents its citizens from adhering, and practicing their beliefs."

Regardless if this world around us, hates it, this establishment is hypocritical. These gay apolitical activists if that's what one chooses to call them threatened the Klein's children, but no one seems to think that anything is wrong with it. These kourtz swore to uphold the law and it's Constitution, but are not caring about the people and their **rights of passage**, because if they actually regarded the people, they would not be enforcing a law which is not a law which forces people like the Kleins 2 fork over money, ordering them 2 abandon their beliefs, for a **man made doctrine**.

Yet these are the signatures that was inked on a sheet of paper displayed 4 everyone to see, and learn as well as put our trust in, believing in a fictitious right that actually doesn't protect you from harm or judicial

injury.
Goldman, I'm sure has understood Jewish Law, amongst his friends, and household. I'm absolutely sure that this man heard the Mitzvots of Ha'ish, which forbade Jews, from inter-acting, and interfering with homosexuals and homosexuality period....yet, the Jews, like Adolf Hitler, warned **us**, were contagions, sneaky, little rodents of a people who pride on destroying all nations.

The lesbian couple was very high strung and selfish. They were awarded by two different bakers and bakeries, two totally different wedding cakes, but they allowed ignorance to seep through their disgusting pores, out into the hemisphere of society fabricating their alleged pain and suffering.

What pain and suffering was this? They really wasn't being discriminative when they politely declined the same-sex couple. It was the Kleins, whose children were threatened, and it was the Kleins who were forced 2 close down their hard work, established name, and their business which they kept Kosher, according to their laws and teachings for the Jewish people who observe Ha'ish, their G-d. And it was the Kleins who were intimidated into forking over $ 135,000. 00 for being true 2 their right to practice their way of life in G-d. These **citizens** are infringing on our way of life. They are rising 2 divide us, up in our homes, businesses, neighborhoods, and religious groups and marriages. They want to control **us**, and our dreams, ambitions, faith, and bloodlines.

But I say 2 you now and forever more to **Refuse Them No matter The Consesquences, Difficulty, Refuse Them; Dot Konform, Die R.E.A.L.**!
Refuse their doctrines, because they formulate distortion of the true teachings of revolution, and what a revolutionary terrorist is. Refuse them because you see that what I am saying is the G-d, honest truth. Some may see it and still refuse to recognize that we the people are

human trials!

The terrorist realizes this, understands this, and knows these things as a fact. We know that there can never be the white picket fence dream for **us**, nor the Mercedes Benz, BMW, and so on and so forth. The terrorist revolutionary comprehends that we can't own any land, or property with the belief that we can carve out a destiny for ourselves and our families if we have any. That konformist dream is prohibited 2 **us**, for that is the enemy's standards for a world which they by themselves are killing off.

The terrorist revolutionary knows that what they have seen and heard 4 themselves by the writings of other resistors, that there can be no civilization, in the midst of those who are **un-civilized**.

Stale bread, and contaminated water supplies, are ours to have not theirs. Border patrols, are preventing us, from eating off the good part of the land, as well as the real essentials. Our balanced diet will be distributed by the establishment, for they are behind these so-called vitamins, which aren't vitamins but some form of scientific grown experiment producing what we the public are not aware of, but will be given out for the people 2 eat and die in the process from food poisoning, and malnutrition. All these things will come upon the poor, and the wealthy, along with the resistance pupils also known as native terrorist.

Hear me that guy David Koresh, of Waco Texas, the man who went around telling certain people that he was Cyrus, and the Messiah better known as Jesus The Christ. His cult before his demise, back in February, of 1993, the 28th 2 be exact; were sectioned off on the Davidian compound, which it was called to learn the teachings of what G-d, had given him. He began relaying his revelations to these groups of men and women, that G-d, wanted the married females to stop sleeping with their husbands, and 2 sleep with him to have G-d's special kids for his kingdom. David explained to the parties involved that they would have 2 leave their husbands and wives, and the husbands would have to live out the rest of their lives in celibacy, while Mr. Koresh, alone would be the only person having sex with all the women on his compound.

Koresh, was also having sex with the under aged girls on his compound, practicing child molestation, yet did, not one of his disciples confront him about him committing acts of adultery, and pretty much raping their young daughters. Non opposed him or said that these practices were against the teachings or word of G-d. He got away with these things because he knew that these people he recruited were not rationalizers, neither were they devoted readers of the religious books, which in their case was the Bible, or Torah. Instead, they went along with this persuasive leader. Rumors begin 2 spread around that these things were happening, and the coverment started 2 raise their little antennas towards this occultist group, and began doing an investigation on the Davidian compound. They learned that David and his disciples were weirdos, but there were children, as well as teenagers on these grounds, many fathered by this persuasive leader/messiah. Yet they found no evidence of these children being starved as rumor had it. There was also no evidence to further their investigation that these kids were being kept from school, for they were home schooled, and well educated, and well mannered. This is what kept the coverment at bay for the moment, until rumors began again that these cultists were now stock piling artillery, which got the ATF, involved, but as it turned out, Mr. Koresh, and his disciples only had a few legal armz, and a couple of rifles that were all legally registered with a Federal Fire Armz license were Mr. Koresh, could legally sell these armz as he did to earn funds for his compound, and his disciples' upkeep.

Again, there was no criminal act being done by Mr. Koresh, or on his disciples part. It was told many years later that a lot of the followers of

David, on his compound didn't like guns, or even using them, but their leader insisted and assured them that one of these days the establishment they would have to fight against, because the law of the land was eventually coming to raid them, and that the law did.

The raid on the divine compound of David, was dubbed showtime, and as foretold by their leader, both the eager koverment, as well as David and his cult, began firing away at one another. Yet it was the koverment who they said started shooting 1st, while the cultist were firing back allegedly out of self-defense. It is a must that I say this; that David and his followers had a standoff with the agents of the goverment 4 approx., (51), days. The media camped outside of the compound 2 keep this story running throughout the kountry. And this is documented as public record, that this standoff had some (2,000), press covers. No one 2 this date has ever had that much media covering their story, not even Hitler, himself could boast this and he and his warlords created their own news.

With all this press in and out of their tents, setting up on the outside so they couldn't miss a bullet hole or a baby's cry, due to the intense nature that was occurring inside and outside of the walls of the compound. People started regarding it Media City, because the news pre-occupied such a large area attempting 2 cover this highly publicated fabricated in certain instances story. By themselves it was confirmed by the ATF, that they alone couldn't stop David and his cult, therefore the FBI, was called in 2 help reenforce the penetration so the electricity of the compound was shut off, and the agents of the gov't., began shooting holes in the Davidian compound's water tower, 4getting that the compound it'self were holding children within its walls, not just their parents or religious gaurdians who were shooting back at the law. It is stated that Mr. Koresh, and his cult which included (21), children and (54), adults, ended up dying as a result of a fire that the government agents caused, at the word of the Attorney General, and the top elite brass of Amerikkka. Before they burned the compound down the fire got out of hand and caught flame to an entire block. See even a false prophet can tell people the truth, 4 David's followers, all agreed I mean the ones that didn't die stated to them relentlessly that their government was not a gov't., of the people, but one that would disregard them as people. He is said to have stressed 2 them that they would be treated like animals, as well as their children. Why, because they separated themselves from society and spoke the honest G-d truth.

That as long as you act different, they will hate you, and those in power wish to control the populus, and will exterminate whoever they feel is not worthy of living in their kountry, and as it turns out Mr. Koresh was right and they seen it with their own I. Seventy-five people died in that trajic incident of Waco Texas, all behind rumors for the most part. It was never said that David Koresh, was a violent man, but it has been told that he was uniquely humble in character, and would try 2 mediate any hostile situation that arose against him or anyone else for that matter. Yet for this and his twisting of words, and false testimony of being the messiah, etc., to his teaching people a way of life of resistance, and training them 2 stand up to their coverment even if it claimed their life they were targeted and annihilated by Amerikkka, who burned these people's pure innocent children, yet they the U.S.A., tell the Amerikkkin public that: "No Child Gets Left Behind!"

When we read text like the To'rah, and the Gospels of Jesus, it teaches its readers and believers that there would never had been a Moses/Moshe, if his parents weren't resistors, along with the Hebrew midwives, who lied to Pharaoh, about how Hebrew kids were born. And there most likely wouldn't have been a Jesus, or Yeshuah-ben-Yosef, if Joseph/Yosef, the stepfather didn't listen to that voice in his dream.

Martin Luther King Jr., and those who were truly apart of the real Civil Rights Movement, were never awarded $135,000, and they were beaten with night sticks, spit on, attack dogs were sicked on them, and they were hosed down with fire hydrant water, and their cause was

legitimate.
Religion did not bar blacks from being citizens and having equal rights as well as justice, no....this warped establishment did that. Even in our fight 4 human rights, blacks are still subjugated in our plight here in Amerikkka, no matter how rich, we become or have become, and still remain **indefinite servants**.

Regardless of our education, or our inventions, it is, and we are still the "**Property Of Every State In which We Reside In The Great United State Of Amerikkka**!" We need 2 get the police to understand that they need to give up all the files and records/reports, of each and every rapist, racist, and child molester, in Amerikkka, and if not; then you protectors of these contaminators of the community, will be **fair-game**, and we will declare war on you for protecting these defective mother fuckers who have been fucking over our families, schools, marriages, businesses, along with friends and associates for centuries now.
The attack will be on you ATF, FBI, and Homeland Security agents 2 you assaulting female soldiers Armed Forces**,** local Police, and this will include you Correctional Institutional Officers, in whatever prison that you all work in here in Amerikkka and elsewhere!

And unlike David Koresh, and his occultist...we are not going 2 wait for you to come striking at us, we are bringing the war to you, night and day nonstop. Our past ancestors warned you that this was going 2 take place, and how the masses of people would not remain a mob 4 long. They/we are leaving that identity of your pet names, and peasant offspring 2 accepting this terrorist revolutionary science. We will be firing upon you uniformed, and plain clothes detectives etc., leaving you with the message of Mohammad Abdulazeez, teaching the establishment that there is no such thing as "Sanctuary Cities, and States!" Charles Darwin once stated that:

"The truth will not penetrate a preoccupied mind."

So the terrorist revolutionary request from you that you release the files and every address of these predators also known as citizens, who are equally if not more protected than the actual people who are law abiding. For your constitution undermines real moral law. For it is a guideline that infuses racist actions, and the terrorist revolutionary, refuses 2 accept such treatment of its people any longer. Turn over these records or else! Obviously, we can get them ourselves, but we rather that you do it, you who see the daily corruption in the workplace. 2 those behind the scenes banding together 2 brutalize innocent people, while safeguarding those who are literally destroying and altering the we, which is that nation of people that know what we stand 4, and stand against...for there is no kolor line here. The line we are drawing as a people is against capital crimes which we deem oppression. Free your hands from the handcuffs, and your feet from the fetters, that you alone are carrying and walking around in. For what have you proven but a pointless point.

Liberate yourselves from those that also treat you with disdain. How can you say that you are trying 2 give the people an opportunity, without giving us, real respect and justice first? If it were your borthers-n-arms that was shot and killed, or raped, kidnapped etc., by whatever class of criminal that you classify many as: you and those that you made bonds within the workplace, would break every law known to man 2 avenge that partner, or brother of the honorary badge etc. You know that you and your brothers would band 2gether and become outlaws, and vigilantes, for you and yours, but not 4 ours who you victimize?

Think of your wives, friends, and children. Fuck the job, 4 that can wait. THE WAR WILL BE AGAINST YOU ALL NO MATTER WHO YOU ARE, AT THE PRECIENT, THE BARRACKS, OR WHEREEVER! Whoever you are, and whoever you belong 2, there will be no peace talks after fair warning, for this is your last and final warning. For this way you can't say we weren't fair, therefore it'll be K.O.S.! It'll be hell 2 pay. Many un-necessary people dying, and hurt because you failed to recognize and take heed 2 fair warning. Don't be phony with your racism, put your chests out and be proud. Don't hide behind the badge, or the judge's bench, either aid the people of the kountry or just flat out and tell them FUCK YOU! But ask yourself do you really want 2 see your loved ones hurt, which includes those neighbors on the weekends that you have BBQ's and beers with? Think about this, your kountry is barely standing as it is, do you want to fall with it trying 2 protect what can no longer be protected? Confessing your sins at Sunday's mass, won't end your horrors. Those above your paygrade have designed this problem 4 you, and thanks 2 them, they have put you smack in the midst of a people whose mantality will not change, and have no intentions to. Your police chiefs, Lt.'s, Sgt., majors, colonels, mayors, and govenors, all have been bribed to cover up Congressional, and Presidential hits. You are not truly apart of them, you are their puppet. It is you who they have out here playing step and fetch it, 2 murder those you all say that you are in the line of fire trying to protect. But who you really are protecting is the true criminal element, the politikils, not the people, for the people remain poor, lost, and like you fear to be the cast out, that individual versus the status quo.

Infants, toddlers, and teens alike all have died by your hands 2 open McDonalds, in every kountry. Men, and women have died due 2 you wanting to open Taco Bell, franchises, and Starbucks, in everyone's kountries, these coverments and business merchants got you running around the world to save their corporations. So the war goes a lot more deeper than just nuclear missiles, and fake terrorist plots of poorly trained believers in G-d, and militant aggression. The terrorist is a thinker...the terrorist regards education for that is revolution, and it is it's survival. For we do not assassinate it, nor do we assassinate it's character. The revolutionary terrorist assassinates those whom call 4 our destruction.

The terrorist revolutionary is a Field Manual. The world is what has hardened the terrorist revolutionary. For we have lost a lot, and this is why we do not hope for mankind, just those that we know will be the remnant of it. The terrorist, doesn't try to stick it out, 4 we h been conditioned far to long 2 know the process of what four hundred rs, and plus, does, 4 it produces cheap labor which relinquishes our e quality for goods of no real capital to us. Only the people have sh their blood, sweat, and tears for the scraps that we are fighting the dogs for, while the establishment gets all the wealth.

We are considered that cheap labor, used to build this enormous system that never gets over-capacitated. We are that authentic product which has been reduced to nothing more than fabrics, and slaves.

The revolutionary terrorist, provides not brotherhoods, but humane structure. We are not killed in action for names, and titles. The revolutionist dies accepting their roles as martyrz, and people who stand up for themselves. We the terrorist, have come to realize that faith has fallen, and life has become famined; and no one understands what is at stake in this position for us but us!

There is no tomorrow for the people or the terrorist unless we cadres make one for ourselves! It is clearly up to us, because it is you and I, who must give our last dollar, our last drop of blood, and last thought to the cause, 2 uphold the armor which is the principles which causes if not ourselves, others to survive. And although our children may have to grow up parentless, the terrorist revolutionary, and our cell-, communities will have to step up a whole lot more in order 2 provide the courage that our kids will need to help them understand how to be **heirs of the rifle**, and how we carry on **our legacy**. The books already had their examples, but where are we after the history has been made and the pages of our heroic valor has been written?

The examples need 2 be us, a live version of these and those past pages. The terrorist, dedicates without asking or needing unity. We well know just how strong individualism/separatism is. Unity to the terrorist, only means fighting 2gether, at different stages of the war in separate units, nc e the guerrilla bands, and those who still practice conventional v are. **Wolf Warfare**, is a battle strategy and tactic of the mind, ich breaks up into little atoms on the field, not as people who call nemselves generals barking down orders to the little man. No, Each individual is his/her own general and makes the decisions to carry out the machination that it has created at first glance and through the study of that target. Guerrillas, don't do this and can't do this, because everyone in this war ideology has a top ranking officer guiding the unit, and those who still practice conventional warfare, are only practicing lengthy layers of un-necessary physicality, which these two groups split down the middle as if they are 2 different theories.

These theories are considered orthodox and un-orthodox tactics, or styles which they have to abide by in battle. One follows the technique of forward engagements or head on collisions, while the other semi-makes up its own rules. This technique can also be compared to just about everything that exists in this world...for example:

> Duke Ellington, vs. James Brown. This is a wonderful comparison for the lay person of the grass rooted terrorist science. James Brown, was an un-educated man who could harmonize a note and blend sounds together, this was his method of creating the music in which he called soul music or funk music. While Duke Ellington, used the normal concept of music through notes, such as A-sharp, C-minor, B-flat, and C-sharp.

The underdog or the have not, always has the ability not 2 just compete tough as that may be, but they also have the ability, to practically destroy conventional methods and traditions, such as it is with the terrorist revolutionary. We see things and hear things that the establishment can't. The haves and the have nots or the theory thereof; has it's origins in this field of defying customary beliefs, but the establishment wants the people to believe that we must be like them and their ancestors, rather than we alone comprehending 4 our damn

selves that we are just as good as they are if not better.
Both Mr. Ellington, and Mr. Brown, were pioneers in the music world, and many tried to emulate their talents, but it could not be done on their scale. Both un-matched in talent, skill, as well as entertainment. But Mr. Brown, took the understanding of music and transformed it's concepts of utilization. His methods were not systematic, while Duke Ellington's was. James Brown, saw that music is brought to life not by just using a note, or harmony, not even by mere instrument, but by the musicians themselves, because they internalize and hear in ways that can't always be understood, or elaborated. 4 it is how your great ones are pushed to the forefront to raise the bar with or without the technological devices other people may be using for them to be able 2 try to be competition. Need another example: Jimi Hendrix.

Even the almighty creator G-d, himself believes in this...how can I say that because he gives the Islamic World empowerment, as with the Judaic World, as well as the Christian World. Every one of these religions came from an old teaching from the past, of those who had and had not. Once those who came into being then started to go contrary to G-d's established teachings, and saying 2 themselves that they were established for they alone established themselves, and had it, it was removed from their nation, and a Goyim, or Gentile nation was given the opportunity to show that they were of better character etc., for G-d, equips them all, but uses diabolical or un-orthodox strategies against the people he set up, which no matter what is his people 2 either bring them back into consciousness, or raises another so that the ignorant nation can be provoked to jealousy and beg for his 4giveness, or he just simply destroys them altogether. He may even create a newer form of these same laws, but possibly replacing them with different components, unique in functions which may seem 2 contradict the other forms of his other religious nations, but as we look deeper to see...they don't.

The body of the terrorist combines all persons. With this being understood, this allows the individual to be a part of a system in general, yet we pretty much discussed this in detail in Chapter (7), entitled equalz. Third World Psychological Training, in a nutshell, is a prisoner inside a prison. He/she isolates, as well as meditatively communicates. He/she studies their surroundings from the television, books of various kinds, 2 the daily prison inmate, and guard population.

The terrorist revolutionist, propagandizes themselves by routine and he/she distinguishes that the world it'self is **systematic**, and every so often the establishment injects certain things in it to shock it, all to get the people to buy into what they are creating which is confusion and chaos, keeping the masses feeble, throughout the months, days.) and years, don't believe me look at Covid-19.

Yet the terrorist revolutionist, is tailor-made 4 this way of life because he/she, builds it's future analysis in letters 2 other cells, and cadres, texts, and unique acquaintances, whose worries of what car one should buy, changes over time. When the rulers of this lower world as they call it for the people, starts creating panic, and scare tactics which includes economical depressions etc., it causes the public to run to the stores and buy up more food to store away, bleach, water, and the daily life essentials, while we see the bullshit, for the terrorist has pre-pared ourselves for these issues already they don't scare us.

This is the vision that we have already come into contact with. The terrorist, has looked inside of their sheet metal mirror, or the little plastic ones with the glass looking tint on it they sell and witness the **shadows**, and silhouette of a face not full of features that has partially or fully grayed, or wrinkled. The terrorist, learns how to be the meanz at all times, rationalizing our portions of meals, from full sized to baby spoons of food, fasting off of the knowledge that we experience because there is no comfortability, and nothing suits us more, than the breaking of the oppressive cycles of the "New World Order."

The terrorist revolutionary, is in the midst of a world that is revolving around non-thinkers, and brainless machines. The revolutionary terrorist, has begun to transport time; meaning that time is valued in two ways...(iced), and (decaying). To expound on this, one must appreciate captivity, 2 undergo this particular training, and studying one must recognize in its entirety or as an individual what it means when we view self-preservation, and humankind as a collective for preservation.

After collecting the data of one's own capabilities, our hypothesis, seems necessary to apply these scenarios on both the youth, as well as elder groups within the populous. This suggests the analyzation of spiritual growth, mental diversity, and possibly the start of our physical deformity/physical health. To master all three functions is a beautiful thing, but here the realization of it all takes shape, knowing that all can't function with all three, only a select few. For many these capabilities can only be broken up into splinters, which means that they can perform either one way, or with two functions, but never with them all.
Mastering the higher essential qualities, allows many to struggle with the lower ones. Most who adhere 2 intellectualism transforms a more active belief into a series of events. What I, mean by this is that they are more productive in seeing their visions come to fruition, dreams etc.
Yet, over time with more and more concentration on success, and better ideas, and ideals, it causes those individuals 2 lose its normal physical capacity, or physicality. This shortchanges their abilities to challenge those who are advertly dedicated to physicality, or adhering to the basic physical needs like Albert Einstein, being one of the greatest scientists that ever existed, but with all his high intelligence, he wasn't even, able to tie his own shoelaces.

When people forget how to use their mental strength, which aids them in their awareness of the establishment's schisms, this part of the intellectual nature places strains on the lower muscles, until they begin to become brittle, which causes tares, due to their lack of understanding how vitamins, and nutrition works. When one forgets these, than the ailments come and the body can't heal nor the bones, or one's mental stability, as the way that G-d, and nature intended them to; and if we seriously look at the establishment and how it uses this form of propaganda, and psychology against us, the masses we see that it is done to keep the people 4ever broken so that we can't stand against them, neither can we as a people, withstand life in general.

The propaganda that they are promoting are crippling those who fail 2 comprehend, which the people don't see is causing us, 2 continuously gravitate to the "Sporting Events," which indeed produces/ manufacturers, physical champions, or fighters, of arenas who neglect their other senses and abilities like their spiritual maturity etc. And if they haven't; then they are still bound to their false beliefs, which focuses on prayers, that bless, rather than teach them the gift of wisdom, unless some G-dly, intervention causes a phenomenon, which is a miracle that occurs for some, but not all. With this the bacteria can never be cured, because it is always bandaged by testimony, etc., which is again mis-applicated. Once the program of such propagandizing is up and fully running, it contaminates everything in which it encounters. When it comes to assisting the people who see the festering blisters erupt before our eyes, we overstand that it is the people who should be the germophobes, rather than our enemies.

They combat us, with their evil gossip, rather than the true Gospels, of the messiah, and they use their anger 2 override the Ayats, stating that Islam, forbids other forms of religious beliefs. This isn't 2 say that certain parts of their ideology isn't correct, but what they fail to see is that their religious dogma, is going contrary to the true guidance of Allah. It states that the Al-Qu'ran, is a confirmation of what has already been sent down in the earth 2 the people of other religious beliefs.

When one can't comprehend this than we see that Satan, Iblis, Lucifer, has been whispering in their ears, yet they comprehend it not.
Therefore, the terrorist revolutionary, identifies with the animal that

has lost four legs to become an adaptee of two legs and a brain. The terrorist revolutionary, can't sympathize with just a simple kulture, and the environments that are responsible 4 peaceful protest, which are eating alive all who have participated in such demonstrations and have unfortunately unraveled all that the resistant forces have done. For again we don't burn down our own places of residence, as if we are stupid shitting in the houses that we sleep in like animals that have no brains.

The terrorist revolutionary, stays a student, of physicality, as well as intellectualism, along with spiritual incest. The terrorist revolutionary allows all points of warfare breath, so that when in that war, we are fully nsync in the process of thought and scientific tactics and strategies. By listening, this brings all points of warfare into existence, by both space, and time, as well as isolation, for movement is not necessary, until it is time 2 build, such a movement, of mental, spiritual, and physicalness. This is the environment of a terrorist. He/she, buys in to the common man's claustrophobia. The terrorist revolutionary, sleep with eyes that are in the back of their heads, not just those that peer out of it solely. The revolutionary terrorist, sleeps when we can, refreshing our minds with what can always be reflected upon at any given moment. There is no actual down time, the evolutionary period, which can be at times associated with the stagnated period but under a process of incubation, because as a student we grow along with the experience and experiments, that give us our rise. Fucked you up there I know, yet everything is growing around us an in us when we perceive the war correctly.

The terrorist revolutionary political scientist, has to come 2 grips that, time has placed us, in a box, where we cannot move forward before our time. The time juncture corresponds with the methods of warfare. If our data goes beyond the minds of the people, then the revolution fails to be proactive. And since now we can semi-view the incubator/ evolutionary stage we can begin 2 recognize that old saying of how we

reside in "**The Belly Of The Beast.**"

Non terrorist fight against the incubation period, for they rush to make a statement but never an indentation in the rules of engagement. These are not terrorist; for time is the terrain of the tactician, and it guarantees penetration, once released upon the world. Look at Communism, it's authors, to it's activist these key figures such as Marx, Engles, Trotsky, Lenin, and let's not forget good old Stalin, and Castro. Socialism, became stationary after years of inner growth, and external evictions etc. Even Amerikkka, it'self before we entered this era, was a kountry that underwent mass protest, from whites, as well as blacks, atheist to religious pupils, and such leaders. And once established, the sequence followed in order 4 us, 2 see for ourselves the forbidden fruits fashioning it's way through our social nexus, which caused us, 2 no longer be at the forefront, but taking window seats, as—Observationist, and partial rebels.

Not just the pedestrian/civilian, but the revolutionary as well. The initial revolutionary terrorist, needs to trash or do away with it's old outdated orders of business, and strategies, because although the technology is brilliantly crafted 4 the time your creativity, tactics, and thinking compacity is frivolous.

It doesn't lay out plans that assist in the overthrowing of the establishment, or the extremism of mob retaliation that only sets the people further back than what we need. Neither does it help the people who have undergone the process of a revolutionary, and have altered their way of life to see the fruits of their labor. For this kind of revolution only benefits the people in power, 2 those of their kind. Hitler, transformed an entire German kountry mindset, until it became Nazi Germany. In the times of Lenin, he allegedly dethroned the powers that be, but even his reign was assisted by the puppet masters pulling the strings behind the scenes, all to bring forth other commis, like Joseph Stalin, and his control over "Mother Russia."

We are not designing articles of war, however, we are designing combat zones, to increase our sub-ground population of celled terrorist revolutionaries. We than can fertilize the necessary seedz, that can't be genetically modified, or soldered with metals and plastics to make super soldiers, and brainless soldiers that are the manufacturing of the establishment. The revolutionary terrorist is being kultivated rather than being engineered 4 eradication purposes. The terrorist revelations or the Manchild Mantality, increases our momentum, and it carries our makeshift schedules over the united stakes so called fortified establishment. This is where mental meets machine, and mind versus mantality. For our weaponz of war are not sanctioned by the coverment. These are fuedal lawz, not 4 establishing the land, but for us, it's new land evictionist. THIS THIRD WORLD TRAINING, in the terrorist sense, requires those who need to comprehend instructive indoctrination!

Instructive: meaning the value system of the way we need 2 view our lives. The terrorist revolutionist again doesn't believe in slaughtering innocent people, for that is against our teachings, as well as G-ds. It is also a humanitarian crime, for we know that children are innocent and those who kill them without rendering a real justification of why...even with why you will pay 4 what you have done. Unless it was the children of our adversaries.

If it is their kids and grandkids, than the innocent blood of a child is not the blood of guilt and that individual or party can be excused, and will be excused. Our children's blood is on our hands when and if we do not protect them and educate them, 4 it is as if we have murdered them ourselves. These people who get a kick out of murdering innocent women, and babies, the elderly etc., think that they are the ones who are in control, and proving their point, 2 the people who fear, to the masses and the Creator, but you and your kind have initiated 'Dar Al-Harb,' which in Arabic means, The Territory Of War!

For we do not suggest, we insert the idea into the minds of our cadres. We value our hope in a Monotheistic Structure. For we understand the importance of a smile, tear, laughter, hardwork, education, and building a real nation thats built for and by our people.
There is no racial discrimination in the revolutionary terrorist movement. It will not be a Islamic Nation, Jewish Nation, Buddhist Nation, or Christian Nation, or whatever one is into. This is a NIGGA NATION, not a sect of various religious groups. We the terrorist revolutionist, are the restorers of the people's faith, and spirit which carries us, on. 4 it is the center of all believers, and people of moral principle and action. We do realize that all people do not regard followers of faith, or monotheism, and we can and do respect that. Yet all women, and men respect privacy, friendship, community, etc. We are the govenors of ourselves, and no matter the kountry that we reside in esp., Amerikkka, we will not konform to their policies, and they will never be able 2 counsel it's resistors. There are No Negotiations When One is A NIGGA, for we are the keepers of the new sub-ground/underground. We are it's work force, and we will not be dictated to, by our oppressors, slanderers, and contradictive communities and society.

If we can't eat, you can't eat! If we can't cross state lines, you won't be able to cross state lines. Comfortability is over. For if we can't have you won't have. You may be asking yourselves how are we to invite destructive idealism into positive hearts, and minds, in which we as a people regard as life, love, and liberty which are positive teachings and of honorableness. It surely is and it is also the sign of the times from the creator. The revolutionary terrorist, overstands that all persons religious, or otherwise, are not fighters of physicality, and thats alright, for it is well understood that some people fight with speech, 2 assure the hearts of many who are preparing for war do not feint, and they speak 4 us, to be able 2 have stability in our faith, and hope in our victory to overcome the difficulties at hand.

Others provide the security which protects us, and push the masses further. Then there's those who gather intel or information 2 help the terrorist revolutionist, come up with better detailed strategies so that we can transition in the war so **that** the security force can come in strong, to destroy the foundation of our adversaries. We need the people 2 use their homes, etc., 2 hide the fugitives which we will become, in the future when we start this war. There is room for all kinds of aid in revolution, and have we forgotten that the prophet Muhammad, (PBUH), was virtually a humble man, and was this way until G-d, himself told him or granted him permission 2 fight in the cause of Allah, his G-d, and our G-d!

The prophet (PBUH), didn't just take it upon himself 2 just start murdering people. Islam, as with other religions I'm only concerned with Judaism, and Christianity, when I say this, that it is forbidden 2 do such things.

Abraham, didn't just train his warriors to fight....no, he trained them in G-d's word first, and then taught them how to protect themselves and the teachings, of their creator. The same was with the meritorious Huey P. Newton, 4 Mr. Newton, overstood that fighting physically before mentally and spiritually would prevent his Panther Party from reaching it's nationalistic goal, and that was 2 feed the under-privileged, and to educate them, because he knew and taught the revolutionary that it was indeed the people (Black) people, who are under attack.

The slogan still remains "Power 2 The People," but once the slogan and principles began to change hands due to others who weren't on the same page as he, the organization started to become dysfunctional with others wanting to establish the physical first, and not the mental, and spiritual, which were the foundation that it was built upon. Don't be fooled, the people that's already in power is creating our power the riots of George Floyd. So to say that you are dying 4 a cause, or a belief, but can't comprehend that cause, or belief, than it is not death 2 the enemy, it is only death to oneself, and one's people.

There's no real war on terror, that's just the enemy's way of planting false thoughts and fear in our brains. It is a war on the strong, and those who believe in honesty, family, love, and everything else that mankind was given at birth since the beginning of time.

This is what is being turned against us, and this is why we fight regardless of what part of the world we are from. Whether one considers this revolution, Jihad, or Armageddon, it is all a war which is pretty much the same.
It is men and women going into battle 2 stay true to who and what they believe in, which by moral standard is being pure men and women. Not homosexuals, transgenders, rapist, enviers, addicts, prostitutes, strippers, drug dealers, and gang members. Therefore, we repeat this saying until it begins 2 register in one's heart, and mind. To those of you who are contemplating becoming a terrorist revolutionary, let this really sink in your spirits.

Death Before Disarmor……
Never 2 believe that our oppressors, is going 2 grant us, black, or otherwise Real Justice, Equality, or True Representation, 4 this we know is a futile belief.

We fight, No matter Who Wants 2 Be And Remain Our Enemy …

The Terrorist Revolutionary Knows That True Immortalization **Comes From The Creator…And It Is His Teachings Alone That He Causes His Believers 2 Spread, And Protect……….**

It is you who are your neighbor, as well as neighborhood. And we the revolutionist of terrorism, are the real representation of our own war, for we are not rioters, which is a waste of time. Nor are we the kountry's citizens, because we are not this konformist kountry's property, neither it's priority.

We are their end and they know it. The revolutionary terrorist, is not a fabrication, nor are we fascinated by their **mail-2-order-brides**, and **grooms**. We are not their runway models, walking their Hollywood stages, being paraded around by these indoctrinist. The revolutionary terrorist, are what the few call **Real Role Models**, of life and legend!

Liferz, Militarized, Revolutionist, but most importantly when you describe us, we are nothing more than servants of each other.

Fight, No matter If People Unite Or Not...for the Message is 4 **All**, but only a select few will truly comprehend 2 defend such a thing!
We are at war 4 others 2 live. For isn't this what it means 2 be souljahs, followers, and believers?
Isn't it 2 aide the people who want something in this life besides tears, and grievances? When do the oppressed/victimized get the opportunity 2 rize up and end their misery, 4 it is completely up 2 us, to help them and them helping themselves 2 put an end to death… so strike out at the establishment, and those who oppress locally help put death 2 death!!!!!!

We don't go inside churches, or mosques, and start opening fire on people who are praying whether their good or bad...we have faith to the end in people. Even if they are wrong, we still try 2 educate them. This is why G-d, sends down revelations, and prophets to correct the issues that are in error.
This way gives people the ability to understand G-d, believers, and other things which can possibly change their heartz, and minds to one day become a convert.
Don't go shooting up a mall where children are being children, buying mother's day or father's day gifts, or birthday presents for their friends and or families. Don't go shooting up schools, where education and

those educating truly aid kids and parents on how to be good parents, and successful, because G-d, gave these people such tools to be able to teach. Yet, if these teachers who supposed to be guiding are sexually harassing men and women or fondling our children then we catch these people and terminate them. Rather they have child pornography on their computers, etc., Target these degenerates.

TERRORIZE THEM! This is the shit that the establishment is against, they protect these, because they are the force behind their way of thinking. They use these individuals to cause our fears. Thats why Terrorist Propaganda was born, this that I write is Terrorist Propaganda. People like Che, Hitler, Assata Shakur, Geronimo Pratt, Tupac Shakur, Bobby Seale, etc., all taught terrorist propaganda, EVEN DR. KING!

They like we tried and is still trying to instill in the people resistance of oppressive dogmas, and oppressive ideology. They committed their lives to uplift the people, they gave us programs that was of necessity…and they like we demand answers from their/our coverments.

They organized us and the movements, and when they didn't get the right answers…messages like BLACK POWER 'KILLED THE UNDERGROUND, because it is not kreated for just blacks it's designed for all mankind who are the true empowerment of MEN, and Women who are strait and nothing more.

BLACK POWER SEPARATED BLACKS FROM THE UNDERGROUND. There are no real representatives advocating for the people just races, but what the terrorist are acknowledging is the universal suffrage of **m**ankind as a whole. Man has no color, he/she is only flesh by nature, and spirit by way of understanding not by conquering.

The establishment still owns our way of thinking because we the people can't get past kolor! Therefore, tactics like coin-tel-pro will always in the end keep us bound and blindsided along with separated.

Unification has no manufacturer's warranty, or manual, so its definition can't quite be assembled. For unification is a form of communication, it's more of a formula, rather than a formulation, if that makes any sense to you readers. We as revolutionary terrorist, understand that separate corners are vital, and necessary because every man can see something that the other may not or cannot see. We also respect the fact that other races and nations had things and situations that many haven't, so we assess this and analyze it until we find not only the similarities, but the many weaknesses in the areas of our lives and ourselves, and this includes our enemy forces and their multiple minions who break their backs 2 protect this World Watch Tower, which these so-called world leaders have built up.

To you white supremacist, I just may have 2 marry one of your daughters, etc., in order 2 continue your bloodline. I, just may happen to be the savior that keeps your people/race, in history and thus you just may have 2 protect my thoughts 2 further the progress of our people, and our plight! No one book can teach the many different races of people everything thats why we all contribute 2 our survival, 4 we can admire those who came before we came into the picture, and come together not 2 fight a race war, but 2 understand uniformity to fight against those who are responsible for tricking our ancestors into believing that we must fight against each other and not against those who are cherishing their weapon of divide and conquer.
In order for the cells, 2 be the best that we can be as terrorist revolutionist, we have 2 participate in the war that is costing those who are true 2 remain true 2 everything. Many races or nationalities have raised from these pillaged, rather than pilgrimed lands. FIND YOUR BROTHER IN ME, LIKE I, IN YOU, WHILE FINDING OUR FAITH AND PLACE IN THIS EARTHLY REALM WITHOUT US HAVING

TO KILL EACH OTHER BECAUSE THIS CAN ALL TAKE PLACE IN SEPERATE BUT EQUAL CORNERS!

What seems to me as the bigger picture is, what we do separate brings the people or races of people closer 2 understanding the real nature of a cause, and we don't really have 2 be close to get ourselves closer 2 the goal. Dealing drugs, pimping, banging, being false guiders of G-d, 2 simply staying criminals are all done separately, yet the funerals of our beloved, and glorified, bring many 2gether 4 the most part, because like it or not these people have like any other have people that love and care about them. The time is now, and not 2morrow. It is truly kill or be killed. We know that the koverment want the masses of people dead and in jail, yet we allow them 2 do it and we sit back and do nothing, 4 we don't even want 2 end the famili feuds. Famili also means race feud. The people have all accepted this inferior work, than want to cry when they deny you whatever in their world because it's their kountry, and they can do that!

This is not black pride or a call 4 black unity, when you murder and or humiliated the sister because they didn't want to do what you wanted them 2 do. It wasn't black power, or black lives matter, when you sold that junky who is also a person of color, that bag of heroine, or rock of crack cocaine. It was none of that when the little sister was high out her mind off that molly twerking in your club or at your V.I.P., table, or the little homie you sold that k-2, to, and you all knew that shit you was selling was bad and cut with all the garbage just to make a few pennies now was it?

You gangs' tie flags to get monetary, but won't do a home invasion on the White House. There are no more skeletons in the closets. The United States Of Amerikkka and other nations has renounced it'self, and pronounced it'self, 2 be some of the greatest killers of mankind, which we have seen with our own eyes. Make no excuse for dummies, or you'll find yourself lying dead beside them. Embrace Milika, and terrorism FOR IT TAKES A LIFE TO MAKE A LIFE BETTER, BUT YOU GOTTA SOMETIMES TAKE A LIFE TO MAKE RIGHT YOUR MISTAKES IN LIFE. WE HAVE 2 BE ABLE 2 LOVE LIFE, 2 BE ABLE TO FIGHT FOR A LIFE OTHER THAN YOUR OWN OR THE PEOPLE THAT YOU KNOW!

Donate to the cause, and help your fellow revolutionary terrorist get the weaponz that we need to go to war with our former slave masters. Forget about giving your money 2 these false churches, exhausting your time money and livelihood to these strippers. THESE ARE THE PEOPLE WHO ARE TAKING YOUR FAMILIES AWAY, by purchasing cars, and SUV's, high heels, and worthless relics, of a well-established profiting organization. Stop being so insecure, and being worried about being liked and loved. Thats the system, it makes you buy into the fabrication, and illusion, for the heaven you seek is you and in you!

The paradise not the paradox in which you can't imagine is in doing something totally un-selfish, 4 a cause that's trying 2 aid in breaking out of the boxes. We don't want war for needs, we go to war to bring one another peace of mind, justice, and a sense of happiness in this world, before we leave this earth, and if there is a hereafter as some believe and say, hopefully you play a part in helping someone along with someone else helping you get there, or like the Staple Singers, use to sing.....

I'll Take You There, but we still ask for those who are true to help.....

CHAPTER 11

REAL TRUE MARTYRDOM

We know that there is a G-d, a real true G-d, who lives and who distinguishes those with valor, versus the petrified and weak. I'm not here 2 tell anyone how 2 worship their creator, all I, can say and do is give you pointers of how to look at certain viewpoints which only that person alone can accept 4, his/herself to enter the cause which is our Holy War. All I, want to do is train you mentally, unless you are one of the ones that's under my direct tutelage. But I, want you 2 identify with what this terrorist, has already left you with. Whether it is by audio, immortal revelation, video, or magazine; I, need you 2 burn my images and paragraphs into your thoughts, until they are both your dreams, and nightmares.

Make your home-made explosives with pride, and strap them to objects, not to your person. That is not terrorism, that is a suicide bomber, for the terrorist revolutionary need you around. You are important to the cell. We need you around not in the ground. For how can we as a whole be effective, without you? If we blow ourselves up little by little, then how can we interrupt the adversary's plans? That would only mean that we are aiding the enemy 2 kill us, faster, which is not the attitude that win wars. 2 be a martyr, you would have to teach what that is. For it said that G-d, alone owns and hold the real record books of our deeds, which believers call the "Book Of Life," which has all the names of those who gave and are giving their everything. Not just in war, but also in charity, humility, bravery, and as a civilized people. In order 2 rize from death, or from obscurity, you must do something different from the rest. At times you will be doing things in single acts, but for the most part, it is what we do as a people who believe in such causes for that cause and belief is 4 a lifetime. This is what makes our demise worthy in the creator's eyes, 2 those who are with us, in the war. This causes the people to remember you and your dedication. It was the constant sacrifice due to love, 4 that is the true motivation and no true deed or act ever goes un-noticed. Anyone can kill an enemy, or a weak and frail person but to go through life excusing certain faults, or bringing captives to life while you 2 remain an exile uplifts the broken and teaches them that the spirit of a revolutionary is that of an ultimate warrior. We must at all cost, teach this will 2 our people. For this is the foundation of any belief in revolution, or religion, 2 just being merely human. Some of us, will go astray, but we have 2 stay the course. For we are the untainted, the unblemished, and not the misrepresentation. Either you are or you are not that person who will rize; 4 it won't come with cheers, but it leaves you as the legend, of Martyrdom, due 2 the aid we gave to those who were less fortunate. They sacrificed their childhoods, families, and everything that we can't possibly think of, in order 2 provide us, with things like the To'rah, the Gospels, the Al-Qur'an, justice, freedom, and equality. Their concerns were not for paradise, but for assisting their fellow man, and honoring their and our lord. They died to be able 2 rise in our hearts. And they gave us, faith, so that we could push forward through the adversity — that G-d, placed in front of us.

It took years in prison, poverty, loneliness, and feeling neglected, because there was no one who could understand the task that was placed upon our martyr'z shoulders. Yet this brought them closer to their G-d, and it also took them deeper into their faith 2 become leading converts. They were lied on, beaten, shot, and their characters were slandered. These believers in the cause really suffered behind what they alone had attached themselves to, which was a struggle 2 make them more determined to accept their separation from life and death. Can the Islamic Ummah say this? Have you been lost in this quest of belief and society?

Has your G-d, attached you to his will, so that you can embrace it in the physical, meaning your mind and body? Along with the spiritual, not the man's version of his will, but G-d, himself, who you say you love and are serving. How can an imposter compare or be compared to the true authentic martyrz, that fortified and forfeited their rights 2 stand among men 2 be considered sacred?

It is their teachings that you slander for glory, when they were murdered for you 2 have a life in and with G-d. How can you dare call yourselves martyrz, when your death denied the people a chance 2 convert 2 real worship? It took our prophets decades, and centuries to get the people on board 2 stop sinning. You people forgot the essence of the commands of the Messiah, Muhammad, and Avraham's real walk, faith, and worship. For obedience is the true praise and dedicated action of G-d's will!

It is you who have failed 2 comprehend G-d's enlightenment. 4 your enlightenment is the enlightenment of human source and Satan/Iblis. The prophet's revelations were of the finger of G-d, his divine revelation was sent down by his hand's only, and written by his finger alone. And their lives were shortened because G-d, alone shortened it. Men think they kill, and by these mere human thoughts that's what he wants you 2 believe, that human hands murder, but they do not. No person is allowed 2 take their own life. Not a prophet, nor a mere mortal, that's suicide and the creator has already 4bidden his people from committing such abominations. No revolutionary can believe in this either, this was also expressed by the Communist revolutionary, Huey P. Newton.

You are suicide bombers. You have become man-made devices, and paradise has been far away removed from you. Martyrz, see the good within the bad, not 4 ourselves or the side that we fight on but the higher cause, which has civilization at the forefront of our minds. It is here that we volunteer for the service of G-d's purpose. Death is bred in your kountry's established system, and it is falling apart due 2 you and your kind's hands. These same kountries that the creator has given 2 you and your ancestors so that you could prove your worthiness, and faithfulness 2 him and him alone, but you have disgraced the land and your G-d.

Martyrdom is a non-reclusive subject because it counters glorified thoughts. It is a man or woman renouncing what doesn't totally belong 2 him or herself. It is their life, and a hard life it will always be because one has volunteered 2 be singled out, to be the counter-kulture, of the world's way of living. This if we choose to study is the reason why there are not millions of martyrz.

There is this select few, who are whole heartedly committed 2 the cause at hand. And this few are chosen to open the eyes and hearts of those that have to understand these revolutions/evolutions in every generation. And to give those who have been waiting long to see for themselves that their faith in the creator was not in vain. For in all seasons there is a time and an era.

In these days and times, we use the term martyr, like we use the term N.I.G.G.A., but like all thing's mankind has watered it down. They have been persuaded to separate this and these terms, but the true meaning will never die, because it is not real, and it doesn't conform to the people's way of thinking. There are no words that can insult, or define a revolutionist in this terroristic science, because its depth means martyr. It is what we die behind and over. What the terrorist revolutionary sees and hears is the calling of true life, by being placed in the hands of fate, in which we embrace as our judgement call!
That call is 2 say 2 mankind who do you think you are, and what the FUCK, do you think you are doing? Cease your actions because you have been mis-informed of the true way. A life is being taken from you, excuse me, not a life but a presence, is being short changed 2 allow you to come 2 your senses.
It is G-d's, way of teaching mankind how to serve him and how 2 understand real Death, As Well As Sacrifice! For there are 2 kinds of martyrz, but only one that can be immortal. This is not intended to be a religious book, or religious doctrine, but there are too many examples that fit these situations, and the references being made are obligatory non-the-less. Nothing is by coincidence. All things prove its value in

due time, if it is purposed for the people 2 learn. This is why time is the central connection 2 unveiling. I know the phrase many say when they are sincere here in Amerikkka, that "I'm Willing 2 Die 4 Mine!" But death is death when there's nothing qualifying it 2 resume its life.

Does this make sense? For instance, if you died for lets say trying 2 rob someone versus you die behind pushing a little girl out of the street, preventing her from getting hit by a car. To your friends, life goes on… but to the little girl's family, you are a saint.

Your life is worth celebrating by people that you don't even know. Church communities, community activist, even your family now can be at peace and not look at you with a disgusted demeanor. Streets, and community centers, get named after you. But 2 those who have not a clue of what it means 2 die real, you only live on a headband, hat, jacket, or t-shirt, for a couple of days. Your name may get sprayed on a wall, or a stop sign; liquor, or beer, may be poured out on your behalf, but thats about it.
That little girl, will one day grow up to hear about the unselfish boy, or man-child who gave his life 2 save hers. You did not think or hesitate, it was a pure selfless act, and it had no praise, or recognition attached to it. This is integrity, and this act was in everyone's eyes morally correct. It was G-d, possibly testing you 4 a greater blessing, in the future. Thats a martyr, who must be immortalized! Some people in return for your action begin 2 glorify G-d, because of this brave act, and no matter the past sin committed or past sins, and no matter how fucked up your life may have been or still is, just before that incident occurred, all is 4given, and overlooked, and instantly you overnight become the Hero!

G-d, rather you understand it or not, took your life's bullshit away, by calling this blessing into your life, to now be seen, and known from now on as that town or city's beloved saint, no longer the loser, and that little girl along with her parents are grateful, and in debt to you forever.

Martyrdom cannot be scandalized, although there are people in this world who have tried 2 shaden it's beauty. But it shall always be looked at as the sign of hope. Yet 2 be martyred, the battle must be won from within, before the actual war can be lived through and fought outwardly. I can say this because I myself am a martyr. Not by man's hands, or his thoughts, but by this way of life that has been allotted 2 me, having been surnamed Daniel Khalid Shahid. Daniel, which in Hebrew translates to mean G-d, is my judge. Khalid, is an Arabic name which when translated means immortal. And finally, Shahid, which is a mixture of African, and Arabic dialect, which translates into a parallel or the same or similar term which means martyr, but only the Swahili speaking Africans' write Shahid, as Shahidi. If you are reading this I, shall be in preparation of my demise, which by then my life should have expressed my soul's actions with no misgivings. My purpose of life was for you the initiated.

Personally, I hope that I have given you a sense of pride, and **faith** 2 accept these words and my deeds as a offering, or gift, not just a mere manifesto! And my belief of what a martyr is, is that:

> "I, WILL DIE, BUT WILL HAVE CONTINUED TO LIVE STRONGER THAN THOSE WHO HAVE CHOSEN TO MISUSE THIS CODE OF CONDUCT, AND DIGNITY. NOT TO FURTHER A RECYCLED POSTURE, BUT TO GIVE INSIGHT TO THE ESSENCE OF WHAT MY SMALL SENSES CAN ALLOW ME TO TRANSLATE TO YOU TERRORIST OF REVOLUTION."

I've always knew that I, would die at an earlier age than most, since I, was a child. I, was always in fights against friends, family members, girlfriends, the police, homosexuals, and those who stood for images of falsehood, rather than identity and being the face of authenticity. Yet I, have always taken the initiative 2 demonstrate action, and educate those that were around me. My time in exile, meaning prison, furnished me with thoughts that weren't of a condemned man, but a political animal that would one day be a service again to the revolutionary war. I'm no Malicai York, but like him in a way, I, AM SETTING THE RECORD STRAIT. I, require a method that Leads to the journey, not run away from it. For the martyr, your patience, must come to fruition, never decorate duty for a tribute. We are not tokens. The revolutionary terrorist, can't be bribed with opportunity, for that is what the opposition wants 2 celebrate. Why do I, say this? Because to be one person who's celebrated, while a million, or more others remain nothing more than convicts, and field fertilizer, is not doing the people or revolution any good. We all are compasses around the world, struggling to find us, fighting 2 prove that peace is a true man's happiness if he/she fights, and adorn one's self in not the attitude of corruption, but of the blood that must be shed for and on our behalf. The revolutionary terrorist, martyr; insist on bettering us, not the world that has been closed off from what's real. Even though we know that our life's blood may not affect the masses as a whole, we refuse 2 worry about a name going down in history, which diffuses the true impact. This causes doubt, nervousness, and separation from the cause. To understand such logic, just may be the only weapon needed at that time, and no matter what time, it is always necessary 2 be brave and put everything on the line.

This way of life isn't easy, it doesn't come with perks, we are not rebuilding. The terrorist has come to destroy the common, and the people's commonality. This is no longer about peace, or justice and jobs. We aren't coming together we are integrating 2 set ourselves apart, not from the cause but from those altering the mentality which makes people conformist. If you believe that society and this kountry called Amerikkka, will not be torn down than you are crazy, and you are easily misled by our foes, and their imposters. Please believe that there is but so much that I, can write about to you in this book, but in many ways this book is an introduction 2 futuristic events, that cuts society out of the picture, but adds the terrorist formation in which we stand.

It is neither written 2 inspire anyone to violence in a capacity that cheats the people and the revolution. To write a book that blatantly tells people 2 commit acts of deliberate criminality, is not worth it. This book has been designed for the terrorist revolutionary to kill psychologically, as well as physically there's a big difference. Murder the falsehood, the weak orientated, and the system that brought the people 2 this disfigurement. We are not a group of people who are conspiring to commit criminal acts, that is what the establishment uses as propaganda, for our belief, undermines capitalist, and politicians who do war crimes against its kountry's population.

May the keen eyed understand these wordz that I have typed 4 us.

This world is against us,
but it is not at war with us.

The world is against us,
but it is not at war with us.

Do you not understand?

This world wants the people 2
see things their way, and not
our own way…….

Here I'm talking about the
powers that be.

That's the commercial all-seeing
eye, not the Almighty's eye.

They want to be in the dominant
role of everything, and watching
2 control everyone.

It sees you and us destroyed!

It shows us running for our lives.
And it has implanted this philosophy
in the world's mind.

It the system, has planted
tracking devices in and on us,
2 prevent us from hiding from them.
This is why we can no longer be like
the old guard of revolutionist, and
militant revolutionaries.

We are under attack until we come
under compliance 2 seeing things one way.

> "Read the symbols and look at the signs!
> The bricks which are masonic customary dictum, is placed and built up around them 2 fortify them, and it's been built to keep the people altogether out. It's the wall, and at the top are those who sees things going their way, which is the all-seeing eye, that satellite, that sees everything we as a people do, in the public's eye, as well as in the private sector of our homes."

A real martyr dies R.E.A.L., and a metaphorical death. It is our creativity, and originality that remains the virus 2 their computer wisdom. For the establishment knows that the terrorist revolutionary's death sets their plans back some ten to one hundred years, yet that will be no time 2 celebrate. That will be the time for the terrorist, to grow more fiercer, because the next time the system reboots it'self, it will strike out at the people with more vicious and fatal blows, which will destroy a great number of the people and our accomplishments. Their vengeance will be relentless, and you and I, may never recover or get another opportunity 2 see that next portion of the war, but thats just it; think about your children who will.

It will be them who will have the chance 2 face the political machine which will be another forceful dogma, that will tell them 2 forfeit their armz and stance. It may be your great-great spoiled brat grandchildren that are or will become the co-conspirators, trying to deceive you and I, or the others who follow behind in our footsteps.

> "For their world is against the people, for it is their world that doesn't want revitalizers of rebellion."

Do you not comprehend?
The world that G-d, has created for the people, he wants the people to defend it, even if we lose our life and the natural resources which was given to <u>us</u>, 2 aid our health and well-being as working men and women. For the world which G-d, had envisioned initially for mankind is within <u>us</u>! We have the power 2 utilize the common things of this earth 2 combat the technology our enemies use against the people to rule over them. The field is our world, and we are the true inheritors, of it, and no one can take that inheritance away from <u>us</u>, except <u>us</u>! This is not a warning or a war cry; this is a war that has become inevitable. In the Al-Qur'an, Surat 47, Ayat 4, states: "Therefore when you meet the unbelievers in fight, smite at their necks, at length. When you have thoroughly subdued them, bind the captives firmly; Therefore, is the time 4 either generosity or ransom, until the war lays down it's burdens."

> "Thus are you commanded, but if it had been Allah's will, he could have certainly exacted retribution for them himself; but he lets you fight, in order 2 test you, some with others. But those who are slain in the way of Allah, he will never let their deeds be lost.
> Soon will he guide them and improve their condition, and will admit them to the garden which he has made known 2 them.

O, you who believe!

If you will help the cause of Allah, he will help you, and plant your feet firmly, but those who reject Allah, 4 them is destruction, and always will Allah, bring their deeds to naught.
This is because they hate the revelation of Allah, so he has made their deeds fruitless.

Do they not travel through the earth, and see what the end of those before them who do evil? "

CHAPTER 12

PENETRATING

Understanding places and people to target, should always be 1st and foremost 2 a revolutionary terrorist. Most guerrilla groups, and menial terrorist, target places like Embassies, Military Barracks, Bridges, Schools etc., but those aren't places that endanger the enemy. Those particular places are pointless.

Those places that were named take up too much time to plan out and hit, besides it's crawling with all kinds of soldiers, agents, and local officers. The terrorist revolutionist, wants has to be his/her needs as well. We should be hitting places that can quickly be attacked, and where there is definitely no or not a lot of friction attached to it. For the motto of our cells is "In And Out!"
The terrorist revolutionist, has 2 overstand that this has to be our will as well as our need. Places that hold the world's attention, distracting the establishment from counter attacks, that can't prevent our terrorizing of their cities, kountry, and states.

When terrorizing, there can be big explosions, 2 plain and random **fire-arm-assaults**, which cuts off traffic, while the enemy are, in traffic. This goes for the city's entryways, to the state's intersecting points...which is all to prohibit the authorities from just waltzing in and stopping our cell's invasions. For no terrorist wants the authorities, 2 extinguish their terrorist attack. Take the protest regarding the new president Donald Trump, these protestors literally stopped the traffic. But imagine if those people were in fact terrorist, and they had been armed with bombs, versus Molotov cocktails, and other forms of artillery. The ratio damage along with the impact would have devastated those stuck and trapped out there in the streets. The devastation would've been too much for the president and those who are a part of the Amerikkklan elite. If the trained revolutionist, went head on against the National Guard, Armed Militias, Seal Team Six, etc., the terrorist must pre-pare 2 say fuck everything and commence to doing what it is the terrorist does which is combat, but not loosely. Plotting a terrorist attack on the law, is Capital Punishment, so there is a need 2 learn what it means to go to war. There is no turning back, once you are in the thick of it all. Everywhere that you can think of the terrorist must ambush, and take the breath away from those who seal this constitution, with force and arms. For there is no kountry of oppression without force and arms. When targeting, you don't look at the space per se, or those you are trying to make your move on. A human is a human regardless of the badge or political seat. What the terrorist revolutionist must understand is that what we are assessing, is the big picture, which is the impact that this attack will have on this nation, or whatever that you are attempting to terrorize. The concentration lies in the **psychological impact**, 4 it is first and foremost 2 the revolution, its revolutionary terrorist, and this machination which gives them their methods of morale.

The detriment, is always the transferring of power in the war. It is the essence of effecting the greatest outcome in warfare. Remember, that terrorizm is mental, so the meditation should revolve around this concept. Wear down, the kountry, state, or city, and it's established elite as well as citizen if need be, mentally, and the strength of that target will fatally collapse.

Analyze this scenario with me; for congress, has two specific groups which makes up it's political body. The House of Representatives, and the Senate, which I'm sure some of you already know this. But did you know that if you found out where each member resided and where their children and grandchildren went to school and came up with a plan to not kidnap, but kill damn near the entire congress, at the same time, what a dilemma and shock wave that would run through this kountry, and these other world powers.
There should be nothing that is too hard 4 the terrorist revolutionary, or should I say the **terrorist nation**! The elite won't just start fearing

the tactical thinking of the revolutionist, they will go into temporary panic mode, then regroup in order 2 exterminate every cell in their kountry. The terrorist revolutionary, must know that their government won't be going into hiding, hell no; thats not their style if they are a real established Gov't. For this USA, will not go out without a fight. They will come together to rectify the problem in which their nation is having. Calling on all armed forces, militia groups, etc., but this is where the war and the warfare, puts them on top, or the terrorist.

The terrorist revolutionary can't fear this, for we must stay the course by all meanz necessary. Right after we hit congress, than it's on to the media, the judges, high and low, while we set the kourts aflame. Next it's the prosecutors, and lawyers, paid 2 these lying public defenders. There is no need to murder a person like the president, for in this era, assassinating him is useless, he's small potatoes and he's only one man. We want the commander-in-chief, to sit wherever he is and watch this disaster, as he prays that his troops, and special agents find the culprits, who is personally responsible 4 his kountry falling prey to the oppressed and so-called inferiors. It will be the president's hope that this kountry will be strong enough to get this situation under control or he will lose heart in this psychological war where the inferiors have come to destroy these so-called superiors.
This is the correct way 2 penetrate, since the establishment began using the term urban guerrilla, to describe the inferiors, of guerrilla warfare, like the Black Panther Party. This is not what the terrorist revolutionist represents, for we are not described We are the new definition of **Real Retaliation**! We are not trying to break down a larger army, with small engagements. Wolf Warfare attacks in ways that are not small in combat, it's vast, and the masses are more affected by the sporadic and impulsive waves of relentlessness, simply because they are not head on attacks, but psychological attacks. Yet when head on, it still isn't in small engagements, it is in an all-out attack, as the martyr concept requires.

The Tsurnev brothers, or the Boston Bombers, targeted a marathon race, which of course caused a rukus, but the impact wasn't strong enough to hold the public's eye nor the attention of the government, as we've seen. These terrorist domestic, were captured instantly and thrown away in the more recent media topics like Covid-19, and the peaceful protest around the world for the death of George Floyd. Yes, the unexpected explosion caused a scare 2 a degree, but this kountry was never totally traumatized.

Traumatizing comes with uniqueness.
It comes with methods of triggers, and pressures, that's placed in certain areas, of the mind and nervous system, which causes exhaustion of the mind, body, and spirit/will, until these effects begin to shut down the human Physical capacity completely.

This weapon of force can't be let up, for it was designed esp., for the revolutionist, for it is our only concern 2 concentrate all our efforts so that the direction of the war drives it's way and we take the reins to annihilate this celebrated system.
In other words we ride the wave in the direction that the war alone tends 2 turn in, for better or for worst, wars are still un-predictable, but we are not trying to predict the outcome of win or lose, the only outcome to a revolutionary terrorist is destruction, and the psychological devastation that we must apply on those who fight against us.

In North Vietnam, the Vietcong, used a strategy that forced the U.S., soldiers, 2 play their game, and that tactic worked. The consistent bombing, and constant proving that the Northern Communist's children, women included, would give up everything they had which included their lives, 4 to be exploited by these so-called superpowers, was not going to happen, 4 they would rather die than 2 konform. Therefore, they orchestrated a strategy that wildly threw themselves into the Amerikkkin troops. For the kind of war that they were offering, it was never seen before, or encountered and it made it hard 4 U.S., troops, to counter the attacks. By this unheard of unseen, formality, and formation, the shit mentally killed those Amerikkkins that had to battle against such unorthodoxy.

They utilized their kountry as a mask, and wore it's terrain like skin all 2 carry out the oneness of the jungle and their war methods. Amerikkka, didn't understand how to actually train their troops 4 this kind of situation, for once in the jungle the jungle came alive like it was under some sort of sorcery.

You couldn't tell the difference from the civilians, and their cadres, and when you can't separate the two, you do as the U.S., troops, did...you panic, and start slaughtering every soul that they saw or thought they saw moving including their own men.

The Vietcong, created at every stage of the war confusion, 4 these resistors retaliated with such enigma, and camouflage, that the Amerikkkin soldiers, paid dearly with their minds. The psychological state took shape once in the jungles and upon Amerikkka's soil when the troops made it back home. There became more addicts dependent on illegal narcotics, 2 prescription drugs, and alcohol, than any other soldier that either volunteered or was drafted to go to war in history. World War II, may have had 60 million deaths, in it's war but the effect of Adolf Hitler, was not to the point where the people's minds, were fatally impacted. In Germany, they were introduced to the Nazis, and also the charisma of Hitler, yet the psychological aspect was never seen before when it came 2 the penetration of the northern portion of Vietnam, and their Communistic war.

It has been documented that the soldiers who were returning back to the shores of Amerikkka, were coming back to the states suicidal. Over the course of time due 2 the mental deficiencies of the war, the U.S., troops began to suffer from nightmares, and making sudden outburst, to reacting paranoid to sudden sounds. Such emotional strains and agony that therapy couldn't even aid these combatants. There was true psychological damage which caused these troops to use heavier dosages of narcotics, and even with them trying to suppress their conditions through this they could never function the same after the war, these troops of Amerikkka, never healed from their attackers.

Their behavior became volatile, and this abusive behavior was transferred over to their spouses, children, families, etc., and as a result, marriages split because no one could control the fits, and rages that they suffered from on a daily basis, the Vietcong, trained themselves until they were the psychology, and the effects that makes terrorism such a beautiful thing, 4 it's not an act of terrorism, it's a war of terror!

Besides this, the biological warfare that took place was too good to be true. The chemicals used in the jungles of Vietnam, combined with the suicidal attitudes of the Vietcong, created a situation that the Amerikkkin soldier, couldn't come back from.

This was a peculiar and specific way designed to engage the adversary. The hot heat played a vital role, along with the Napalm, the mosquitoes, etc., all mixed with the air, the troops sweat, and the water which was breaking down the U.S., troops with every step they took. Once in the troops bloodstreams, the many hallucinations in the heads of these men took them over the hill, it was a death trap. One must keep in mind that it does not matter how many people dies in a war. All that matters is how much damage can be done psychologically.

Al-Qadea, Isis, etc., haven't grasped the whole ideal of terrorist warfare, or Guerrilla warfare for that matter. Technology barely unlocks fear, only men in their extremes, and G-d, can produce such nerve shaking, and nerve shattering strategies.
Pimps, 2., Willie Lynch, the Amerikkkin slave breaker, used an semi-uses this method of psychological warfare. But the damage of a female, is in her inability to keep her self-worth. At times, voluntarily, yet most

instances she is put into a mental control tactic out of love and desperation. But the actual slave was physically forced into the role of both slave and animal, yet in some circumstances even less than.
The slave both male and female were visited by vicious, and savage raids by the whites of any status. The slave was subjected 2 kidnappings, rapes, legal and illegal transports, all 2 be indoctrinated by words that would eventually educate them to not be themselves, but that of another which was a far more less degree. The constant beatings, separations, starvations, and un-expected murders of the slave and their kind, 2 the consistent defilement of their characters, warped their psyche. Becoming their NIGGER, and BOY, is the way that Amerikkka, initiated the slave into his national and international role as PET, their pet, under CRACKERISM. And this was all that was necessary, that the slave became the labor system, and inferior 2 that system because the psychological warfare that created them in and by that labor system. Their names were no longer theirs 2 have, 4 they were now surnamed by this new imagery. This form of psychological warfare was meant to breed the slave broken, and have them fetching, whatever the master wanted them to fetch, and answering their master's every whelm. For now and 4 ever, the NIGGER, was the pet of his masters, and that identity of PET, gave Chem their rights of passage through indefinite servitude. These niggers would see this psychology/education as the right that was given 2 them from a man, 2 further their servitude of those 2 lazy to work for themselves.

These modern day wars of the middle east, aren't, and weren't, as harsh on the minds of the Amerikkkin troops, in noway shape or form, for it really doesn't compare. But in Vietnam, these Amerikkkin troops, became savages due 2 the Vietcong's tactics, and battle doctrine. The Vietnam War, changed the U.S., troops; and those who have survived the conditions and symptoms of that war, still to this day prove what psychology can do 2 control both-the-enemy-and-the-servant.
In the Willie Lynch Letters, the damage psychologically still shows how it effects black people as a race. It's horrible nature continues to

hold fertile ground in the black lives that many believe still matters as it once did. This should allow you that are reading this book 2 witness 4 yourselves just how powerful this ideology is; "**Cause The People 2 Konform, And the War, Has Already Been Won!**"

The **enemy** must not have an attitude of pride when we are striking fear in their kountry, but we as terrorist revolutionaries, should be guided by a moral path always, for this prevents us, from not becoming them, that immoral spirit of arrogant will, and decay.

In order 4 one to get a real footing in any kountry, the terrorist revolutionary, has 2 target the right things and the right people. Persue all that think that they have defeated justice, and have capitalized off the lives and deaths of the people.

Napoleon, to general William Tecumseh Sherman? used certain war strategies of trick, to pull off their victories...but the terrorist revolutionist, have no tricks 2 pull off, just pure will and determination. Those leaders such as Napoleon, selected elephants, and longer poled staffs, to overcome the armies of more fiercer opposition. Even the 300 Spartans, used collectivism, and fierceness 2 win wars, but the fierceness of their warriors were not enough, it caused rage in their enemies hearts, not the normal fear that they expected from other nations as they scared them rather than put complete fear in them who am I speaking of when I, say them...the Persians. They the warriors of Sparta, only initiated brief fear, the terrorist revolutionary, don't want to instill brief fear, in the hearts of our adversaries.

The revolutionist, wants to put complete fear in our enemies, heads, hearts, and wherever else we can put it.

Golliath the Philistine, tried this with the Israelites, under the rule of King Shaul/Saul, but it only got the Philistines, but so far with that scare tactic shit. Because as we see, there was a youth who G-d, rose up to not just become a warrior, but also the new king of Eretz Yisrael. A shepherd boy, came to fight with a man of war, with a sling shot, and not a warrior's sword. This youth took the heart from this gigantic man-of-war, and with his enemies' sword, chopped his head off. The youth, by the name of David, didn't do a lot of talking but came to show the people that with a little faith in the creator, the right time, and the right elements, any war can be tamed by the most weakest group of people or person willing to give their all.

The revolutionary terrorist knows that it is his/their fate, 2 strip the power out the hands of this so called alleged impenetrable institution. Our cells are grass rooted which means that we are nothing more but peasants, and farmers, not warriors. Poor people, who must not use terror as a temporary relief. No cell is democratic in this structure and foundation. The principia, lies in this structure only this is the base, which are the guidelines to overthrowing our oppressors and their oppression.

Sept., 11, 2001, or 911, as they call it yes the people think about it, because many lost family etc., but the actual effects of it are long gone. It's over, it happened, we built from it, and the common lingo is that it took some time, but we've moved on.

But had the so-called terrorist of that time, reinforced their assaults, Amerikkka, would still be under attack and in mourning to this day. And the apolitical Amerikkklans, whose lives and memory of their friends, family, etc., they think that this kountry protected...would be on the brink of collapse if not already devastated, 4 they would still be at the mercy of the terrorist. Yet as long as the alleged citizen chooses to intervene, and interfere, then the strategy has not done its job correctly, and terrorizm, has not penetrated. When elite groups such as the Illuminati, wants 2 cause disturbances in people's lives, and it's kountry, they create panic, status is threatened, food shortages, economic collapse, etc. These people use the tactics of terrorizm. But these people want to rule, and that's the difference between terrorist revolutionaries, and secret elite groups/societies.

Elite groups need the masses to bow 2 their wills, 4 they want 2 be served, and want us, 2 be the ones that are serving them. The terrorist revolutionary, train it's cells 2 kill with no regard 4 power, or money, and never to make anyone who is and have been oppressed, made to feel inferior. To the terrorist, there is no value in owning un-necessary things. We see the kountry and it's populous for what they are....places 4 humanity 2 be able to dwell in. For we know that the people if given the opportunity 2 be able to demonstrate life without being in fear of being victimized, then they can act and be humane for now they can find peace, so that they can live in harmony and be civilized.

To control people is an act against true revolution, and revolutionary etiquette. Yet both sides have seen the struggle, and the wars of trial, and error. Personally, I, don't fight to finish revolution…I, war, to continue the training 4 our survival. There is no success in training, and then dying 4 other people's demented causes, and ideologies. For there is no celebration, for what do the terrorist revolutionary, gain behind celebrating? We are not trying to be our adversary's competitor, for war is not competitive, neither is it a competitive sport. For there is no sense of real purpose, nor strength, behind celebrating. For war is death, 2 bring forth life. Cells who want to go about terrorist attacks, but don't quite know who, or what 2 target… attack these colleges who recruit those who will one day benefit from the political poles 2 undermine the people. Target the professors, and deans, for they 2 need to realize also that they are just as guilty as those who are out in the ghettos, and elsewhere selling drugs, pulling the triggers on guns, and exploiting women, which is sexism, and this we all well know promotes various types of criminal activity.

The revolutionist, must go at this situation like no other resistance movement has went at the establishment before. No **Negotiations Whatsoever**!

Those who think that they are too smart for their own good, and too secured, must become feint-hearted. These elite professors must find that their education is not going to elevate those who are in their classrooms. The revolutionist, has 2 make them see the error of their ways. Kidnap them and make them sit down in front of their phones, and 'pads, t.v.'s etc., and cause them 2 watch them as they see the deaths of those who learned from their stupidity. Let them look at the horrendous catastrophe, that has come to plague their communities, and places of employment. The terrorist revolutionist must cause them 2 fear riding in a cab, or and Uber, the bus, carpool, train, hell make them fear taking their own vehicles out for a daily cruise up the mountain.

We must have them in soo much fear that they know that there is no place for them 2 hide, move, or run. Cause them not 2 see or hear a threat, but the actual devastation through and from our actions. We are not claiming that we are the cause of the chaos, again that's not terrorist thinking. There is no such belief in injuring, there will be no insurance policies to collect from these agencies. For many have ripped off the public, and they 2 shall reap what they sowed. Target these daycare centers, for abusing your children while you were slaving hard at work, to these senior citizen homes, and caretakers. Let nothing and no one slide.

Don't poison the water ways, unless they lead to a specific target of an important person's residence. Do not target the Brooklyn bridge, if your cell decides to raid clinics, and hospitals, don't take away from the poor, only if that clinic, or hospital was legendary for denying people entrance, and overcharging emergency fees....do your research before you cause an issue that we feel is insubordination. And if you so happen 2 raid these facilities, make sure that there's a doctor in the cell or a nurse, someone who is in the medical field so that they cannot just assist you when there's trouble but also the people that we know need insulin, and other drugs to be able to live and function...for the terrorist revolutionary save lives, we don't just take them.

We'll use all that they give to these crooked people and the kountry meaning their monetary. We'll live off the land for we have been promised from the creator that we will not suffer as these evil doers. We will buy and use as we need and it seems fit, and if by chance we are in such turbulent circumstances that these securers of the land won't let us, buy, then we are to take their shit. Whatever goods we need, and they got and refuse to give it up than just like a robbery, we are going 2 take that shit off of their hands by Any Meanz Necessary!

This is how we penetrate; you don't ask you just simply take, from those who have been stealing, and robbing, and extorting, the people. I, understand the heartache and demands that they place on our children, and health, when we don't deserve it. WE HAVE WORKED OUR ASSES OFF FOR THIS SYSTEM, AND WE HAVE HAD OUR LIVES, LAND AND IDENITY STOLEN FROM US FOR THEIR BENEFIT OF FINANCIAL GAIN AND OPPRESSIVE POWER!

You set everybody house on fire along with their businesses. You create the terror from all sides. You don't give the enemy a chance to breathe. You burry them in confusion, and you end their will 2 survive. And you never give the enemy a way to pinpoint your next move.
You step in their arena, and utterly destroy everything that they stand for, and hold dear to them no matter how precious. But there is no raping of any female or man, we are not savages, we are terrorist revolutionaries, and we love females...whether grown, and mature or little toddlers, to you crazy teenagers. We appreciate women unless they are of a homosexual genetic pool, than they can be simply killed! There are no habitual manners, or traditional customs, of hanging banners. The terrorist revolutionary again wears no emblems, etc., nor do we have million man marches/women marches. When one truly compares the times and the people in them who say, while others do, we can see that there is no say in the matter any longer. Wanting to be

heard got people murdered, and wanting to be seen, got people slandered. So once you've completely thought about this task, and work that is at hand, than you alone can decide and not be converted by the Art Of Persuasion, for once you become a revolutionary terrorist, there is no turning back.

No Terrorist Revolutionary-Retreats!
And No Terrorist Revolutionary-Surrenders!

When they open up their doors, hearts, and homes to us, make sure that it is you the revolutionist who locks the door behind you. **Souljah Salute!**

Those who are not combat ready, or orientated in the field of psychological warfare, should not be placed there, 4 there are other positions of importance. A terrorist revolutionary is only as good as his or her penetration. The terrorist can't just be anybody...the terrorist revolutionary, is anyone. The schoolteacher, school counselor, janitor, chef, sports coach, banker, receptionist, flight attendant, bus driver, scuba instructor, librarian, nurse, homeless person etc., the terrorist, can be anybody, who is nobody rather than somebody!

Terrorist revolutionaries need 2 always keep in mind that when it comes 2 attacking, we must spread out while doing so, and not spread ourselves thin. The terrorist revolutionary initiate all kinds of races, and people of different backgrounds so that having access to whatever deems it'self-necessary will be obtainable without causing an alarm. That's another difference between guerrilla warfare, and Wolf Warfare. Che Guevara, wrote in his Guerrilla Warfare Maximums that:

> "Guerrilla Warfare, is a strategy used to annihilate the adversary little by little until the Guerrilla Band, grows big enough. Growing to the size of a conventional traditional armed force. "

Yet the fault that lies in that is this:

> "Why start and create this rebel mantality, that is completely different than what was ever assembled in warfare, along with style, than once grown become the emulation of what you and your army have initially fought for, and supposedly is still fighting against? "

Wolf Warfare, continues to operate as individuals, for it is by this individuality that our cells keep and function as our own identity in warfare. For this is our very own unique form of creativity and abstract mobility. Wolf Warfare, is against everything conservative, and conventional. For this is a science and not an Art Of War!

It is our origin so to speak the man-child mantality, in a new era of armed diabolical resistance. Wolf Warfare is not a phase, like in Guerrilla Warfare. This is our embodiment, which cancels out all illogical group thinking, for a terrorist mantality, goes by one man's theory, idea, and ideal. This is the manifesto, that gives the people that rareness that they need 2 operate in this modern-day era of warfare. Yet this is only simplified and suitable 4 the terrorist revolutionary, because we don't lay out plans of action; we think on our feet.
Wolf Warfare, outflanks the adversary and penetrates not only places to terrorize, but the destruction of the minds of those that are a combination of the enemy, 2 the people who are not on the field of intimate battle.

Again, Wolf Warfare, was not designed 2 take over lands, etc., but to overthrow and dethrone imposters as well as oppressors, who have captured the resources along with the people who by nature.:. are the victors not the continuous victims. When one can divide the opposition which on a bigger scale is considered breaking the ranks of the opposition, than one can claim victory without really having to.

Che further states:

> "In Guerrilla Warfare, guerrilla bands or the soldiers within their bands, are generals of himself, and dies not in front of his soldiers or in every battle, but he is ready 2 die not 2 defend an ideal, but 2 convert it into a reality."

Yet to the revolutionary terrorist, Wolf Warfare, is a cadre's reality already. The Wolf, is not ready 2 die 4 an ideal, for we are the prototype ideal already. Born and bred 2 resist, 4 this is what makes our world and everything about it so significant. 2 be Nobel, and horrifically Honorable, as well as Holy is a sure death that will always be our reality, for this is life...but not the war which keeps the scientist all for it'self, because it is its warfare. For the terrorist revolutionary comes pre-assembled in its form and although we may need 2 compartmentalize our levels of genius, it is the warfare it'self, which creates the character of the collective and individual. This evolutionary process never finds it'self-immobile. We are born and bred 4 war, which has made the individual not a general, but an ultimate warrior. For the term general is nothing more than a souljah, and as we all know a souljah becomes a souljah, from learning war. For it is our master, rather past or present, therefore as a student we understand that life is granted 2 those who help create or formulate it, not modifying life 2 try 2 sustain it 4 that is a victim's state of mind.

To modify war only produces oppressors, and a system that man alone made in order to assemble and make slaves. In other words, it becomes headed by weak authorities assembling together weak-, and small-minded people 2 establish institutions of control, but not the kind that values it's masses, but manipulates it by force, and penalty.
The Generic Guerrilla War, seems interested solely in replacing well not replacing but replicating poverty, which doesn't necessarily make it capitalistic, or imperialistic, although monetary and other political combinations give it it's face, when it wants 2 destroy moral principles,

which has always been true social injustice, and demonstrative rebellion, not peace, or freedom, which a lot of militant groups or organizations say that they want.

Let us, now again take a look at Cuba, or new Cuba, versus old Cuba, which overthrew Batista. Embargoed, before the death of Fidel Castro, due to his liberation style and beliefs of rule which differed from other kountries and their methods. Yet it offered political asylum 2 certain freedom fighters or soldiers of liberation who understood individual idea, versus collective democratic detriment not devised by the people but created by the establishment, and their secret elite groups, or families who only comprehension of nation and kingdom is to enslave and kill the masses of people who don't want 2 believe in it's koverment's dream, or other theories when being brain washed to.

In 2017, under Ruel Castro's rule or oversight, the biological brother of the deceased Fidel Castro, wants 2 bargain or bargin, with the United States who is a sworn enemy 2 Cuba, to have the embargoes that Amerikkka, set in place years ago removed. This will slowly but surely allow the liberation armies under political asylum 2 become captured and become detainees of the tyrannical oppression of those who scream liberty, peace, and equality, we better know them as Amerikkka. But because of cadreship, they were never captured, by bounty, or any other hunter/tracker... yet now there's no doubt in my mind that these resistors of the past will be subjected 2 subtle apprehension. Fidel, although his kountry faced hardship due 2 his non-konformist stance which by this stance caused economic deprivation of his kountry Cuba. His kountry may have suffered greatly, his loyalty, and resistance showed the cadres that staying separated if one chooses to understand, they would never groan or feel defeated seeing how the system of corruption kept them destitute because they didn't want 2 play ball and wanting 2 stay free from its ideology, and "**Commercialized World Trade**."

Ruel, sees this kountry meaning his kountry Cuba, in shambles, but believes that his kountry and autocratic imperialistic corporation kountries like Amerikkka, can share a mutual benefit that can have a better outcome for the people of Cuba, through "**Socialism!**"
True there are benefits 2 rebirthing or breathing life back into a dead kountry, meaning a economical deprived kountry, yet the hisstory between the two kountries should prove that things have not changed. For Amerikkka, is still a Bay Of Pigs!

The term means not a part of the larger more popular whole. It is the outsider, the poor, and underprivileged, undeveloped klass. This is the klass that doesn't appeal to those who are greedy, and notably snobbish, and thoughtless. 2 make it more clear 4 you 2 understand, the wealthy/The Bourgeois. Ruel, was a part of the Communist philosophy, or at least a student of its agenda which is Socialist Thought, or socialist thinking...but as we search deeper into the definition of the term Third World, we begin 2 see the undermining of the people within an oppressed kountry.

Merriam Webster's Collegiate Dictionary 10th Ed. defines 3rd World, as a group of nations esp., in Afrikkka, and Asia, that's not aligned with either Communist or non-Communist blocs. Can you comprehend what I'm saying?
Can you now see the tricks that are used on the populous? Fidel Castro was a student of Socialism, but he was a stronger Communist. Cuba, was not a Latin kountry that was in complete ruins before the arrival of Fidel. Cuba, actually had one of the lowest mortality-rates, and it ranked 2nd in numbers of doctor's, per 1,000 people....3rd in Dentist per 1,000 people, first in the numbers of cars per person. Third in percentage of literacy and 1st, in percentage of education. All of this was before the Communist Takeover of Fidel Castro. For once he came into power with this dogma, the kountry started 2 deteriorate, and as it fell, it fell into great ruins.

The Castro brothers, are both backed by no other kountries except the good-old-U.S.-of-A. It was Amerikkka, that aided in Fidel's rise to power, and it was an Amerikkklan interest that stopped arms 2 who was also a puppet of theirs Batista, which caused his overthrow because Amerikkka no longer viewed him as **their man**. Why? Because the kountry itself was a paradise, and the people there was prosperous. Prosperity, Freedom, Life, along with high moral standards, is not what these koverments want in a people, and 4 the people. They want us, becoming thieves, rapist, and killing our own bloodlines, they want all these things 2 kill us, the people! They not only know that economic stagnation kills our unity, and trust of ourselves, they want us, 2 be totally dependent on them the establishment. And the best way 4 us, 2 play into their hands is by their dogma of divide and conquer.

Can you imagine them looking at us, thriving in and on the land, with healthy families, like them versus the people just being flat out peasants, and farmers? These people use capital, 2 kill the capitalist, right after they accomplish what the real true currency holders wanted out of the situation in which they alone are building up, but reduce us, the people and use us, the now divided and conquered.

They don't want the people thriving in their religion, so they recreate a false religion which seems as the true religion of the people's ancestors, but it's all just a mirage, and a fine similarity. They don't want the people thinking about hope and faith, that disrupts the establishment's system. Those are the attributes that destroy the image in which they have created as the G-d, of the people. Yet lets not go too far in this for we must understand that one brother comes along with a conditioning program, and keep this program active until the people see no other way or know no other way but work, and slave, than the next brother comes along as if it is doing the people a favor and tries 2 boost the economy, but again it's never for the people only the establishment. We the people are like Batista, being supplanted. As we assess this observation, really scrutinizing, this war waged by the guerrilla armies of Fidel Castro, to his little brother Ruel's rule; we see that all our back breaking work is futile. They use this Iconic Idealizm, considered warfare 2 condition the people 2 do more work, with less freedoms, which is nothing more in essence than slavery. The great Guerrilla, Che, failed 2 comprehend this. He went blindly into a war which was far from his way of seeing and thinking. For the army that he was involved in shaping, he was turning them into slaves of their masters/capturers without allowing it to penetrate his eyes, why do I say this? Because Che, made crazy statements such as this:

> "Guerrilla Warfare, is suppose 2 bring forth a new society, 2 break the old molds of the outdated, and to achieve the social justice in which guerrillas fight for."

No absolutely not, it just gave that illusion. That was the propaganda, 4 Guerrilla Warfare, like he said was only a tactic being used to transform the peasant army into a imperial army, or my favorite another oppressive government, and nothing more.

A terrorist revolutionary, rather domestic, or international, have not the luxury of staying stationary with a base of operations. A leader should not be dispatching orders, neither should they know the location of it's body. A leader of a cell, should first listen to what is being said, and study more before it ends up in turmoil and his cadres get crushed for being misled into battle. A terrorist revolutionary should be lightly equipped, only armed with the tools that keep the day 2-day operations moving ahead. A laptop, is one of the essentials in the terrorist revolutionary's arsenal. For let these words penetrate in your minds until they become one with your actions, that the war it'self is the landscape, the target it'self is only a piece of the understanding and it is such a small piece. What is of great importance is the thinking revolutionist, 4 we are the omnipotent general. Che, had his heart in the right place when it came to him trying to empower the people, but his mental capacity was not of brilliance, but a slave being told what to do and when to do it.

A terrorist revolutionist must be their own head, eyes, and ears. Interference can't be ran to stall, and various techniques should only be utilized when working 2 achieve a certain goal. Too many lines of communication get crossed, and it lays at the doors of our enemies, information that will eventually crush whomever cell who isn't operating accordingly. Information for we should all know leads 2 us, being infiltrated. The terrorist revolutionary, involved in Wolf Warfare, must learn how 2 read between the lines. The cause, in which one is born, or have chosen 2 be associated with, should educate it's cell members upon these guidelines.

Ninety-seven different positions keeps law enforcement agents far more busier than four grievous terror attacks. If the said attacks are not sporadic, then pinpointing a cell or it's attack will always be 4 them a certainty. But since there is no leadership/head, nor signatures, imprints, etc., we are and will be 4ever in our adversary's heads, and ears!
They should 4ever be listening out 4 weaponz being loaded and cocked, as well as fired without rest. And our enemies should never stop seeing their loved ones blown 2 bits. When will this take place? As soon as you people stop being fearful!

For we do not want them 2 stop seeing and witnessing these violent attacks, and this should be our main and only focus. It should repeat it'self over and over and over again, *BOOM_BOOM_BOOM_BOOM*!
4 this is the way that terrorist penetrate, it is our mantra, battle doctrine, Gospels, and it is the true meaning of **Terrorist Warfare**!

CHAPTER 13

STRONG UNIONZ

The world has been split apart for a decision to be made, and by that shift, a gift was given 2 those who possessed nothing in life besides a true spirit and a honorable belief.

This is who and 2 what we **owe**, the pleasure to bond. We found the examples that G-d, has left for **us**, 2 be challengers of one another and his eternal will. Our rings are not ritualistic, our rings beget the circle of **Immortal Life**. A circle that not only surrounds our finger, and wrist, but it's a completion that deepens how we understand, trust, and that will that protects the devoted constantly around the clock 2 uphold the very people that are in its midst, sharing the **common** action of a said union.

2day, we see and hear the vows of so many, but the personal vow is **between a man and a woman, and G-d**, as well as the cell who witnessed the exchange of bravery belonging 2 the war as a whole which brought **us**, all together.

Who can separate this Holy union?

This is matrimony at the **highest** level of performance. To love and 2 cherish the G-d, that we put our faith in and the cause that gave **us**, hope when others gave up and abandoned it. Our hand is one, in one palm, and our fingers are just individual digits placed together 2 one day slip through time, no that's not good enough, it is to hold in place our circle, for it has needed 2 be placed in our hands 2 secure this time we have on this earth, and in this fight 2gether.

Our fingers are not marked with tattoos, that are designed 2 throw off and away a fleshly loyalty, and companionship. The medal and ribbon, signifies the outcome of a perfect union.

The dedication is beyond a **heart**, it is the equality of spirit and human balance. We have married into the blessing and belief of monotheism, monogamy, and eternal membership.....the three **models of manifestation**, that makes the whole creation of love bearable to keep **us**, firm and united till death do **us** part. This is what makes **us**, whole and a tactical methodology as a revolutionist. Under the **Arc of cadres and rifles**, standing side by side, is the structure and discipline, that belongs hand in hand. This can never be thrown away or cast aside because time is the only thing that is still semi-tangible. It's tangible so that we can grow within its power as a sign 4 **us** 2 see the truth of our unity, **saluting what is now responsible for souljah hood around the world**.

We alone symbolize what it means to be one; respecting the code of conduct proving who we are and what we **stand for**, in sickness and in health, until we ascend into the greater realms of life. We are unwilling 2 be fictitious beauty, for real beauty is those who have wills 2 remember, remain, and resist those very things that causes all relationships to perish.

Only G-d, can administer 4 **us**, this calling for **us**, 2 be War-Ministers. For it was he and he alone who has ordained and anointed **us**, to be **War Brides**, and revolutionary terrorist. We ask Ha'ish, 4 his mercy, grace, and favor for it is only through him that we receive these things as he calls 2 attention all who he sees as fit 2 obtain his glory and blessings. Love is a thing that we must endure together! Poverty, is something that people who consider themselves rich, label others out of frustration of their own design and lives, but 4 richer or for poorer, under this **Arc Of Extended Rifles**, we vow 2 appreciate whatever is given of **Terrorist Warfare**.

We have been brought together because we were assigned a destiny in this world. A destiny that awaits **us**, and fulfills men and women's desires and passions. **Life Is War**, and we have been invited 2 keep the war strong no matter the opposition against **us**.

For it is Ha'ish, who teaches those he has separated from the opinions and defected privileges of the world, therefore we represent his laws and not man's concepts which make up kountries, societies, and human religion. There are to be **seven rifle shots**, after the bride and groom kiss 2 further their bond of sacredness, and committed duty 2 this revolutionary cause and marriage union. Our marriage is not of a celebratory fabrication...it is a peace and harmony of two souls choosing 2 become one another's companion on the battle field.

Those who are not given the service of worldly appearance shall not enjoy extravagance, for expense takes away from the natural bond. When one is truly bonded, they are meant 2 be born for the **sub-ground**, for their allegiance is to the higher power, not involvement in worldly influences, that breaks down the union of the people and the power of its organization. This was the actual way initially intended from the creator and from those who serve the cause. For a decision had to be made in order 2 create a **surfaced cell**, which could function above ground. **Twenty-One** candles, shall be lit. **Seven placed in a circle**, where the couple stand 2 recite their vows.
The other **fourteen**, shall be placed alongside each revolutionary terrorist holding their rifle in a house arc, type formation, facing each other.

(7), to the left, and (7), to the right. The revolutionary rosary better known 2 us, as **Ri-chi-yah**, shall be adorned upon the neck of he who bares the responsibility of husbandman, once taken (2), more rifle shots are to be fired, bearing witness that the scales of balance have allotted him fullness in the eyes of G-d.

One cup of hard liquor mixed with a baby spoon of gun powder shall be shared between the couple…this will be because of the hard road that shall accompany the two, and the intoxicating effect will be symbolic due 2 the **Holy Spirit Of G-d**, 4 this and love, both will always be found enticing between the 2, as alcohol does to those who are under its influence.
Photos may only be taken with masks on, and it will solely depend on the parties who are being married for **memorable** times, as the years pass tough, as well as easy....but remember that being a terrorist revolutionary, you must be mindful of the photographs that you take of yourselves. There are no selfies, etc. We must protect our identities at all times, for the smallest things holds evidence against you, and can have you in their **kangaroo kourtz**. So, stay behind your **anonymous lifestyle**!

The war bride, as with the revolutionary milikan structure, will be used with the ceremonious veil, which covers the female terrorist head and face. This veil must be either charcoal gray, or black.
Charcoal gray is for being in harmony with oneself. It means surrendering, for she has decided **2 surrender** her **independence**, and

her independent **role as**, a individual, not that she is being placed in a submissive role like a slave. Her submissiveness only signifies and reflects what she alone has chosen 2 become. She has submitted 2 being and staying a **War Bride**!

Accepting counsel from her husband and vice versa, to her staying dedicated 2 her G-d, if she follows this way of resistance. She has become a helper and glorifier of the terrorist war. 4 this she does not lose her independence, she only shares it with her husband, cell, and herself, making it a life's decision to come into her own without persuasion. Black, is the color she will wear if she decides to bare this oath, 4 it is the color of those who have waived their right 2 normalcy. This color if she swears by this vow, will mean that she shall remain **caused**!

This waiver means that even if her husband should fall in battle, she will never be able 2 marry again, this includes her entire sexual identity. For her there will be no flirting, or having a male friend or sexual partner, male or female. This is very vital for the female terrorist 2 learn and understand. Flings, and attractive encounters are 4bidden, and punishable by death. She shall remain a warrior until her demise.
Three, times should she be asked if she is sure that she wants 2 accept and perform this duty, 4 this color is total devotion, 4 it is the highest female honor as a female terrorist. If she in anyway violates this honor, she will receive a harsh torturous death.

All women who become married along this color will be specifically sent by Ha'ish, not just any kind of female can take on this type of oath, so this color is 2 remain off limits until those who are called 2 carry out this obligation. **Shahid**, will be her last name no matter what, because she is a female warrior 4 her G-d, before her husband, and before her cell.

All males in the cell under Ha'ish's advisement, regardless of what they are 2 be given the name **Shahid**. The veils for the war bride, must cover their entire head, and face....only their eyes will show, nothing else. Yet this is solely for this day only. There are no engagements, 4 each terrorist must first know their counterpart, before an actual union can be **consecrated**.
The man is not the face of the war neither is he the face of the marriage.

He is only a partner, he shares his identity with his wife at all times, even in his moments of **entangled weakness**, 4 he is 2 dress as follows: In **black fatigues**. No gun belt, no hat, neither any form of head covering. This will be the only time such a thing should ensue.

Three passages, should be said:

1. From the New Testament
2. From the Al-Qu'ran, and the other,

from their own words rather to the bride, their cell, or of some significant author who illustrated what the revolution is all about and should be all about.
The passage from the New Testament, should come out of the book of **Mathew, chapter 27, verses 15-26**, and a passage from out of the Al-Qu'ran **Surah/Surat 47, Ayat 4.**

You have had revolutionaries in the past who believed in **communal sex**, groups like the Black Panther Party, FMLN-Compass, and the Weather Underground. In our cells, our laws reflect a pattern almost similar 2 the KNU, or Kawthooleis, of Burma. Their system like ours, in regards 2 being married are 2 be married to **one husband or one wife**. No sexual promiscuousness, or orgy styled group **fuckin** this is forbidden by G-d, and **us**, and the **parties** involve will be terminated if caught. Although some religions authorize up to **three wives**, and as many as **four**, this is an organization of terrorist, not preachers of churches, imams of mosques etc., or anything 2 that extent.

The day 2 day obligations of a terrorist becomes over extreme therefore to cut down unlawful children or procreation, envy, disease, etc., this is **Law**, and is not 2 be taken lightly, 4 a person losing a limb, behind this shows that a cell has the authority to right their wrongs **by any means necessary**.

Punishments will be severe if not taken seriously, since revolutions are based on different conditions, and formalities, this, that I'm stating is a logical stance and or position 2 take due to financial shortages and non-stationary issues.

This is also to keep those that want 2 wed dutiful, 2 the war, rather than just being ' **fruitful and multiplying**.' Our kids are bred so that a people's empowerment can come from such a struggle which defines our identity, religion, and or race.
Therefore,
2 breed to fast and especially in the midst of war, will only kill the war before it ever gets 2 fully function. This, will cause **immobilization**. And we wish not to be sitting ducks, or easier targets than others have been already. It is best I think 4 everyone to wed and breed wisely.

With constant bombing, harsh air borne contaminates, highly gaseous toxic chemicals used **2**-make explosives, lack of warm comfortable shelter; the terrorist and that mindset, is constantly on the move and we can't afford 2 place toddlers, and infants in situations such as these, for again we don't prescribe to killing the innocent, our mentality isn't just destroy, its destroy on the grounds of those hindering our lives to enhance theirs, 4 the **sub-ground doesn't practice oppression and ridiculous genocide**.

There are numerous health concerns from shortages of medical sedatives, and supplies. Hygiene scenarios, to other necessities such as nutritious food. This is not a true environ, for a baby, or **pregnant** female, who wishes 2 see their child born liberated, versus in this ungodly world.
On the other hand, I too must remember that I am writing 2 and 4 those who are on top of the surface, not just 2 and for those underground. On this note: the above ground terrorist, your bond of marriage shall not be in the same form as those underground.

You must however treat your wedding ceremony as if it is normal. Pictures can be taken if you want, and you can have a wedding cake, and a music playlist to dance to if it so pleases you. Your wedding can have all the bells and whistles. Rather small or large, public or private, it can be lavishly laid out if you choose.
This goes for bridal showers, bachelor party, etc., you can go all out...but, and this is where things get a bit technical, it is a absolute direct order that you invite at least (3), of your terrorist cell

members. They are 2 be invited to be observant, and to complete the ritual of the **Union**. The cadre member of your choice does not necessarily have 2 be of your assembly. To them, your invitation must read: **"Please Be My Caterer, Bestman, Brides Maid, or Matron Of Honor."**
The best man, must always be a photographer, so that the cell members photos are taken, but not on a spot on manner. This can also mean that **the** cell member who so happens 2 be the picture woman or man, can act as if he is snapping shots, but in all actuality it's all for show.

If a bachelor party is a part of the pre-marital event, the best man must give the bridegroom the **21 Masonik Ring**, before the marriage bond takes place preferably while the exotic dancers are being used 2 distract the other invited guest's attention. This particular ring is to be placed behind the wedding band, and it should have the engraving of the **movement's birth-10.28.02, issue # 324, and Lifer # meaning the serial number of the founding service member which is 10.27.79**, the date **rifle-revelations, came down 2 the terrorist revolutionists**.

In a Playful manner as the best of pals would do and act, esp., when they are allegedly drunken fools, the revolutionary cup shall be drank before the eyes of the best man, after the best man personally gives him the cup. This is called the **Terrorist Revolutionary drink of being bonded**. The groom should not be drunk when this is given 2 him to drink. He should be sober, only seeming 2 be intoxicated, because he needs to be clear headed 2 be able to perform this portion of the ceremony, it needs to be taken seriously, cautiously, and graciously, because this custom validates his bond to the cause, his cell members, war bride, and G-d. All our lives are placed in his hands he is responsible for any injury 2 his partner in marriage, **and us**, his fellow terrorist revolutionaries. This drink is a mixture of hard liquor, but (**2**), tablespoons of gun powder is 2 be added rather than one which was initially intended 4 the **sub-ground**.

The reason for this is because your roles are not as intense. The best man should have you say in an indirect way so that those who are attending outside of the cell can't understand the code:

"This Vow Of Liferz, Shall Never Taste Death 4 In Independence The Circle Closes Tighter."

Three pats on the back or shoulder (left side), should commence and then followed up by a quick embrace **and** the removal of the cup, while the best man says: **Okay Okay I see you've had a little to much 2 drink**.

The matron of honor, has the same obligation, except the matron of honor has to pick the wedding dress, and the color must be white. This symbolizes the bride's surrendering 2 her God, husband, and position as a **War Bride**. The war bride, should take into account that it is not just these parties that she surrenders 2, but also to herself. Yet unlike the **sub-ground** war bride, the above ground female terrorist must have a black leather thin single strap wrapped around her left wrist, the wrapped strap should wrap around her wrist (7), times.

This shows her outward resistance, and distaste 4 society and the world in which she lives. Her left wrist symbolizes one arm still trapped in slavery, which is the system she fights against, and her breaking semi-free, of that system and bondage. Once this procedure is fulfilled the duty of the war bride is now considered active.

CHAPTER 14

CACHES

These rights are reserved for the **Martyr**. There are no labels as you have already been informed, of Cptn., Lt., Sgt, Colonel, etc. With **Martyrz**, we are all the same. These titles take away from the character of the cadre. Our job is 2 perform a special duty and this duty reflects the entire cell, which to us all that matters is that **We Stay Non Konformist**, due to this gov't., forcibly trying to supplant the overall essence of the people.

There is no justice or liberty in a freedom that we already own. You and I have already decided to enter into a pact, to take on all forms of **oppression**, so that we can wipe our slates clean of kontradictory behavior. Righteousness is the only **truth**, that can teach the revolutionary terrorist what life is…death and its temporary touch. As the cell gathers to pay respect 2 our dead, each member shall wield his or her **Armz**, parallel with the rifle resting on the left shoulder.

All black shall be the attire worn by the assembly. The dead should be clad in charcoal gray, and black. The only thing gray on the deceased should be the Ministry Sash, that he or she wears around the waist, along with the Tez'rah, upon his head.

All terrorists must be fully dressed from head 2 toe in their field dress. His **War Bride**, if married should be dressed in all black, even her veil...should be like the one that she was married in…seeing nothing but her eyes.
The **Veil**, should not be sheer...this goes 4 both the surfaced (**above ground**), female terrorist, and the **Sub ground**, female revolutionist.

The ribbon or bracelet that wrapped around her left wrist the day that

she was married shall be taken off and placed across her husband's chest as a sign of her faithfulness. A white ribbon or string shall be granted 2 her if she wishes to one day remarry, but this ribbon shall be worn until the day that she dies, because she would have completed two terms of a full marriage.
But,
if she refuses 2 re-wed, then she will not be expected to attend her late husband's funeral. She is only to send her marriage ribbon through a carrier who is also a cell member 2 place the ribbon at the deceased feet. Then an all-**black** ribbon shall replace her initial one...because it is to grant her wish of becoming **Caused**, which is her new role to embrace...because this would mean **full active war hood**.

If it so happens 2 be the female warrior who has died in action, she is to be adorned in **white**, with her face veiled in a sheer white covering. Her ribbon or bracelet should be removed from her left wrist; but **only by her husband**, and a black ribbon shall be tied in its place...4 she has been **Martyred** and **caused**, by active duty.
Her husband shall take the removed ribbon or bracelet and wrap it around her right finger. Her weapon of war should be buried with her in the way of stashing caches. Her weapons of war should be properly oiled, bagged and stored, alongside eight fully loaded cartridges in case there ever happens to be a shortage on artillery, or ambush, this is necessary supplies. And this will be the only time that the grave can be opened so that cell members can gain access to the weapons that have been buried with her remains. Following immediately afterwards, her grave site must be rededicated but this time in a field of peace, a place where there is no blood shed or war.

This parcel of land is to be **Deemed Holy**, it should be completely secure and sacred for this female terrorist revolutionary fought for the creator and her people, or just 4 the people themselves.

As with the men, no matter the length of service....as long as it was honorable, he 2 shall be buried with a, service weapon, by the decision of the cell. The reason for this is because the revolutionist has to be buried a certain way. Even in death the revolutionary terrorist can still be active in duty, but it is up to the members of his cell.

He can be buried with his weapon of war, but his grave can never be touched or opened like the female terrorist, or he can be used as a weapon of war himself.

What this means is that a male terrorist revolutionary even in death can be used as a booby trap. His casket and body can be rigged up in certain sections of the said territories that he is buried in. The grave of the male terrorist can be used for combat purposes, incase an enemy tries to desecrate the grave, or the adversary tries to take out the contents within them.

Even in such cases where the enemy is encroaching the land that the deceased is buried in, the grave sight can be used to keep back the enemy, which brings me 2 the next level of his burial arrangements.

The male terrorist revolutionary can also be used as a stash spot or caches for money of all forms, jewels, gold, silver, etc., but once that cell member's body if not used as a bomb 4 combat purposes, or a cache, than no one can utilize his grave, yet once it's been utilized once already it can no longer be touched and must immediately be rededicated **2 Ha'ish**, placed in a pure field never in one of war and blood.

The revolutionist, because we have become this it is our kulture and custom 2 always be **Armed**, in death as well as in war for we must always uphold the terrorist revolutionary's motto of **DEATH BEFORE DISARMOR**.

If the revolutionary terrorist male or female dies of sickness, or giving birth by way of some form of complication than, they are not to be buried as the other **Martyrz**.

They are 2 be totally left alone, never is their kaskets 2 be opened or re-opened. Nor shall their grave site be boobytrapped, neither is anyone allowed to stash anything around or within their kaskets. These cadres are always deemed **caused**, no exceptions. Neither should there be burials of these terrorist with a rifle, only a semi-automatic, handgun.

These terrorists should have an accumulation of (9) shots fired on their behalf. Three cell members should be standing with their rifles angled at a 45-degree arch.
The second (3) souljahs should kneel under the 1st (3) waiting 2 fire straight forward after the first cadre finishes firing their (3) shots. The last (3) revolutionary terrorist should end the ceremony with the **souljah salute**, by firing one single shot individually.

The meaning 2 all this is:

-The first shot is the respect shot, honoring the duty the cadre has performed or tried 2 perform.

-The second shot is 4 all present 2 understand the war which is not always with a weapon but with fighting the daily complications of survival.

-Third is the final shot this is the shot that we give 2 glorify Ha'ish the lord and G-d of all creation.

This brings us under the understanding of terrorist uniformity, which is our military dress/uniform. It is not solely about unity our essence is the mentality that properly not commercially clothe us.

If a cadre so happens to catch the ill fate of dying and his/her body is in pieces versus being intact, from explosives, or otherwise, and cannot

be identified except by some small limb, than these cadres should be buried in total silence.
These are the terrorist revolutionaries that meet the requirement of bond fire funeral rites. This means that there is no gun fire, whatsoever. Because whatever is the cadre's remains, they are apart still of the whole cell body yet they died as complete individuals. And although they cannot be totally identified in most cases, they shall always be remembered by the eternal flame. They should be annually visited and paid respect 2, respecting the way that they died, because behind their deaths symbolizes the depth of **our war, sacrifice, love, and devotion**.

To us, these members will always be looked at as the beloved of us terrorist. The **fires**, of these members shall be of natural resources....no matter what.
No other fuels, shall be used...and when I say natural resource, this means **wood**, **coal**, or **oil which must be taken from the ground only**! These and only these shall be the only igniter!
These remains are not 2 be cremated!!!!
They shall be buried with cardinal points. For those of you who don't know what cardinal points are they are the initials of (**N**), (**S**), (**E**), and (**W**), which marks the head of the grave or the mythic demise of the man on the stick, as if the arms were extended out.
If your cadre can be identified, then the ribbon, or sash, 2 whatever it is remaining clothing etc., these items can be, cremated in and by the burning of the bond fire. This cremated style and the thereafter ashes, should be placed inside a .223, shell casing, anointed in olive oil and the entire cell's blood, by pricking each member's finger (**trigger**), 2 extract a small portion of blood, and one from a freshly squeezed olive. Next the ritual prayerz should be said so that **Richiyah's**, can be given 2 the cell in order 4 all who are involved in the cell can look upon it to gain encouragement.

These are caused members!

Those who have been allotted their freedom, shall be placed in a sacred cabinet or anointed alter. For those who choose to represent the higher calling of the revolutionary terrorist, need 2 keep in mind that a **Martyr**, has his greatest testimony in the eyes and heart of the creator, not just the small perception of the people. A beautiful kasket is not acceptable. There shall be no elaborate coffins, for a terrorist. An **urn**, is acceptable, but a plain pine box is to be utilized for all cell members no exceptions! The earth and or dirt holds us all equal without separation. The only thing that separates the way that each of us are buried are coordinates 4 boobytraps, and all that has been laid out 4 you throughout this book.

If the body of a surfaced cell terrorist has fallen due to whatever reason, natural causes etc., 2 have a correct or proper funeral ceremony, the underground must come to evacuate the body of the said cell member...regardless the cost **it must be done**.

These funeral rights are reserved 4 revolutionary terrorists, and since there are separate conditions for burying for the surfaced as well as underground terrorist, the funerals themselves must be conducted by both parties.

There are absolutely no society orientated funerals, it shall only be conducted by terrorist, although one can be merciful and wait until the family of the terrorist have their viewing and necessary mourning...that is their right, but a terrorist is not a civilian by way of **society's** standard, therefore the cell member's family can contest all they want, but it is **soley** up 2 your cadres and if this is decided: "**HEED NO PLEAS**."

The body of your cadre must be in your hands, it is to be obtained by you and your/his party, **stolen if need be**! We have a duty 2 place all the blessings and attributes upon our own.

"**The cause holds the highest value in this war of warz.**"

No terrorist revolutionary should feel empty or abandoned. No kountry makes a man or a woman, nor does it kontrol its human possibility. For the core of humanity is his or her diligence towards righteousness. **We Govern We, meaning the people, not leadershipism, or personality** politiks **this is not a belief in moral re-armament, and this supersedes kultural resistance.**

CHAPTER 15

PAYING OUR RESPECT

Almighty Ha'ish,
I present 2 you my first fruits, and everything that I cherish from my soul, well-being, time, children if any, and every weapon that I have been afforded.
Ha'ish,
help me with love, faith, patience, and wisdom. Bless those who you bring 2 us to encourage, inspire, train, and educate.

Let us never think that we don't need you 4 guidance. Help us 2 always see the good in all things so that we may correct ourselves when necessary. Though we fight, bless those who die in your cause for it is your will. Satan, has his place in the world like we all do, and he like us all, have a job to do and a role 2 play in this war. May your people always remember that Satan's job is to show us the **mirror**, so that we can constantly work on one another's behavior so that we won't continue to fall into the sins that has cost previous generations their lives.

To you Ha'ish, alone do we come to, when happy and saddened, but never confused, although we may be uncertain at times. It is you G-d, who we are faithful 2, and you are the only deity that we praise and give thanks. **Holy,** are the weapons that you have given us to go 2 war with. Revolution is our religion, and spirituality. Please 4give us for the blood that has 2 be shed 2 resist our enemies kingdoms as well as their unlawful ways.

When it is time 4 us 2 fast, give us the strength to be able 2 do so.

When it's time for spouses to be placed 2gether, I pray that you supply us with balance, and able partners who are able to withstand on going pressures, and issues that plague marriages to split, and become dysfunctional.

Give us partnerships that will help 2 strengthen your cause with understanding, not just with any kind of male or female counterpart, because that would only fracture the beliefs that you have put inside our hearts when it comes 2 love, true emotions, and dedication to our bond as well as your cause.

Don't let us **wed** worldly partners, only those spared and separated for the war in which you have called on us to fight.

Allow us both the opportunity 2 sharpen each other's skills, 2 constantly endure your will. Teach us how to accept flaws of our own and others, so that we can bare the relationships that you have caused us to value as we try with patience, firmness, and devotion 2 complete companionship in this way of life that you alone have prescribed for us, which includes the collective whole, protecting them as well as ourselves. May your **Rifle Revelations**, provide each cell not just with a ritual, or belief but with a essence rather than customs and traditions that come under reform instead of being a people of **Non Konformity**, living out a infinite liberty.

Let your wordz be translated 2 all cadres, willing to die bravely in the thick of battle, not concentrating on **Martyrdom**, but upholding your commands. Never do we want 2 ever feel as though we or you have failed us in action. Open our hearts and minds 4 strategic methods, to conquer the lands that your beloved faithful, will always inherit. We ask that you keep in our memory those **b4** us who performed their duties righteously.

Those who had no descendants, or empires, before you alone set them into existence. May your **militant eternal nation**, understand that we are not solely a religious community, we are a spiritual empowerment, governed by you and you only in accordance with revolutionary terrorist principles. We do not inspire 2 lead. We are separated 2 fight in your name 2 bring about justice to the orphan, righteousness we bring to the widow, healing 2 the sick, and religion to the poor in spirit, both male and female parties and groups that you favor.

All prophets have accepted you over time not knowing where they would end up, or what would become of them and their families. They tried to trust you with all their heart, soul, and body, which many damn near collapsed due 2 anxiety, nervous break downs, etc., because **your will**, was that hard 2 bare in the flesh. Yet they carried on the sacrifice by giving themselves more and more. They carried on carrying around various armz, 2 protect them from harm, but most of all 2 keep them on the right path which guides men to a place of no return. Many met their demise colliding with different nations to guard your word from corruption.

In all aspects of respect, we prostrate without regard for blessing or what others consider karma. We prostrate armed, with a faith that can't be denied, 4 we give ourselves completely over to you 4 your judgement, never bowing down 2 anything, including any man or woman on earth. Believing in no cremation or consuming any foods/drinks that you have not approved for us. If heaven or paradise be your will 4 us than let us go in full stride and die honorably 2 enter our places of security, in which you deemed fit. Our daily piece of bread is enuff. Your name we volunteer 2 glorify with nothing more but 2 honor each other, your lands, and all that you've created and sent down 2 guide mankind.

CHAPTER 16

HIGH PRAIZES

Almighty Ha'ish,
we are gathered 2gether 2 bring honor to your Holy name and have come to present 2 you our most finest and beloved contributors to your cause.
With respect, we ask that you glorify our Martyrz, and give 2 them respectable names in your book of life, which describes our acts, as well as actions so that both heaven and hell, will see what it took 2 be solid Souljah's in this war that you have drafted us, in.

Let us, not weep in silence, nor sadness. May we see one another as each other's strength, in a world that's weak and growing weaker. In return we ask that you continue 2 allow us, 2 lean on your **Rifle Revelations**, with more diligence than ever b-4.

Ha'ish, the father of mankind, we come 2 you in like mindedness, and with one voice, we confess that we are not burying friendz, spouses, or family. We are simply birthing them into existence, so that they may give life 2 your **Terrorist Nation**, by supporting the people that have signed up 2 achieve the mission that you alone have set before your believers.

If the war never ends 4 us may it assist others in aiding in their peace of mind. And if it quickly ends for some, may it pre-pare others 2 hear, and sincerely look upon such a war that causes them 2 run boldly 2 pick up the rifle with G-d...speed, 2 join the ranks of our revolutionary terrorist, without giving it a second thought. Placing themselves within the walls of this **Holy War**, that those before us, have laid at our feet 2 coherently understand the example of what revolution truly is.

G-d give our enemies into our hands. Prove 2 them what real retribution is through your **Native Terrorist**, while at the same time giving your people eyes 2 see your swift and powerful hand as you fight alongside your believers, causing us, 2 be able 2 dodge and maneuver around our adversaries, and their strategies, 2 their pointless tactics.

Ha'ish, we present 2 you and before you not just casualties or fallen cadres. We have come 2 prostrate in front of your Nobel, and glorious throne, 2 submit a people of Non-Konformity. These warriorz shall be with your grace and mercy 4ever **Immortalized**, because you have given them the spirit of love, and resistance, not just souls and breath, but eternal flames, 2 be able 2 uphold the good, when evil tries 2 steal and take advantage of our destiny, and decision to serve only you.

Ha'ish accept please our Martyrz. Call forth your heavenly host, in order for them 2 be able to witness these believers, and **Cadres In Armz**. When your angels hear the shots of war from our rifles, let them praise you, because you have given them full overstanding of our **Honorary Salutations**. May they all prostrate, at the same time we prostrate not as individuals but as your sacred kingdom, 4 we as a whole make up your glory. Regardless of who they may be, for you have taught us, that it makes no difference who any man, woman, child, or angel may be, good or evil. For as a collective whole we are what makes up **Monotheism**.

May they all pay respects to your eternal nation. For it is your holiness Ha'ish, that has chosen men and women, to be your oneness and uniformity. Bless our gifts without our egos breaking down your war ministry. Enrich us and empower the great and small alike. Cause the believer not 2 hate our enemies, but 2 respect them because even they are your creation. Help your cells 2 be able 2 encourage more people when things begin to get a bit much, yet even then let it be your will 2 embrace your war, and eternal law, forever and ever everywhere in a terrorist revolutionary's heart AMEEEEEEN!

ABOUT THE AUTHOR

The author is currently a prisoner held captive by the state of Maryland and wishes his identity to remain anonymous so that his oppressors can't retaliate against him brutally, or claim that this book in which you are now in possession of is the said property of the state of Maryland, rather than the blood, scars, sweat, and pain 2 Milikian thoughts of the author Danyil Hettainz.

Made in the USA
Middletown, DE
07 January 2023

21634864R00166